Guide to Qualified Retirement Plans:

A Plain Language Primer

Guide to Qualified Retirement Plans:

A Plain Language Primer

by Stephen Abramson

INTERNATIONAL FOUNDATION OF EMPLOYEE BENEFIT PLANS

The opinions expressed in this book are those of the author.
The International Foundation of Employee Benefit Plans disclaims
responsibility for views expressed and statements made in books
published by the International Foundation.

Edited by Sheila Nero

Copies of this book may be obtained from:
  Publications Department
  International Foundation of Employee Benefit Plans
  18700 West Bluemound Road
  P.O. Box 69
  Brookfield, WI 53008-0069
  (262) 786-6710, ext. 8240

Payment must accompany order.

Call (888) 334-3327, option 4, for price information or see
www.ifebp.org/bookstore.

Published in 2005 by the International Foundation of Employee Benefit Plans, Inc.
©2005 International Foundation of Employee Benefit Plans, Inc.
All rights reserved.
Library of Congress Control Number: 2004109745
ISBN 0-89154-591-3
Printed in the United States of America

1M-9.04

Dedication

I would like to dedicate this book to my family:
my wife Phyllis, my son Michael and his wife Deborah,
my daughter Lisa and her husband Brian,
and my grandchildren Alex, Ethan, Jack, Rachel and Jordyn.

Table of Contents

About the Author

Stephen Abramson is president and co-founder of APS
Pension & Financial Services, established in 1977. APS is
a midsized actuarial firm that specializes in pension and
pension-related services. For over 26 years, APS has been
providing closely held businesses with financial services—
including pension design and administration, business
succession planning and wealth preservation planning.
In addition to his business management background,
Mr. Abramson is a certified pension consultant (CPC)
who has taught professional-level education programs for

the American Society of Pension Actuaries; been interviewed several times on
"Dollars and Sense," a financial talk show on cable television; lectured to various
professional groups, including the Nassau Bar Association and the C.W. Post Tax
Institute; and conducted continuing education seminars for certified public accountants for the past 26 years. He has written *Financial Professional's Guide to Qualified
Retirement Plans* and co-written *Plan Smart, Retire Rich.* He is the lead author of *Retirement Financial Management for Clients At or Near Retirement.* Mr. Abramson is
also a chartered financial consultant (ChFC) and chartered life underwriter (CLU).
He earned his degree in finance and business management from Cornell University.

Introduction

CASE SCENARIO

You're the benefits manager at the National Construction Company, Inc., a privately held, family-owned business employing 2,500. You've just been advised by the CFO that the purchase of Local Construction Company, Inc. by National has been signed, sealed and delivered. This is the first you've learned of this transaction.

Local employs 50 nonunion employees and offers a safe harbor 401(k) plan (see Chapter 5) using a third-party administrator's prototype plan document (see Chapter 2). Almost two years later, during an internal audit of National's retirement plan(s) and subsidiaries, it is discovered that Local Construction Company's plan document requires coverage of all companies in the controlled group of companies (see Chapter 10). Because National Construction Company and Local Construction Company, Inc. are a parent-subsidiary controlled group, the employees of both companies must be covered beginning in the plan year starting January 1, 2003.

Absent any negotiated settlement with the Internal Revenue Service (IRS) (see Chapter 14), National Construction Company would be responsible for a 3% safe harbor contribution for their employees plus investment earnings based on the performance of the assets in Local's plan for the plan year. In addition, National Construction Company's plan document may require it to cover the employees of Local Construction Company, Inc. in its plan.

To avoid this nightmare, financial professionals and benefit administrators should be aware of the basic issues to be addressed during a merger of two companies or the acquisition of one by another (see Chapter 10).

CASE SCENARIO

You've just received the day's mail. Prominent on top of the pile is a letter from the IRS. Concerned, you open it to find that your retirement plan has been selected for audit. You call your financial advisor/stockbroker who assisted you in setting up your plan.

You: Jack, I just got a letter from the Internal Revenue Service. They want to audit my company retirement plan. What should I do?

Jack: I wouldn't worry. Most of these audits are pretty simple. Remember the plan was prepared by our company (e.g., brokerage firm). I'm sure they know what they're doing.

You: Well, who should handle the audit for me? My accountant doesn't know that much about pension audits and my benefits administrator is on vacation.

Jack: Just let the agent come to the office and give him the papers he asks for. You should have everything he needs in your office.

You: OK. I'll let you know what happens.

THREE WEEKS LATER

You, noticeably upset, call Jack.

You: Jack, IRS disqualified my plan! They said it wasn't complying with IRS and Department of Labor regulations. My deductions for the last two years were disallowed. I owe back taxes, interest and penalties that will probably be more than I contributed to the plan. How could this happen? You assured me that the plan was OK. You're responsible for this.

Jack: I just handle the investments. I'm not a pension expert. I depended on my company to provide the plan.

You: I dealt with you, not your company. I expect you to take care of this. If you don't, I'll sue you and your company!

Although this scenario is extreme, it is not uncommon. Many of the qualified plans established by medium-sized companies (under 500 employees) are set up by financial advisors who are not well versed in the complexities of the qualified pension plan rules and regulations. If the company is too small to have a benefits administrator familiar with the complexities of qualified plans, defects could result during the operation of the plan, causing adverse results as above.

As readers will learn in this book, establishing and operating a qualified retirement plan involves much more than filling in the blanks on one of these financial institution's plan documents. Before completing these "simple" prototype documents, readers must understand what they are doing and why:

- Which option should you choose for entry date? What does *entry date* mean? (See Chapter 2, Effective Date of Participation/Entry Date)
- Which *vesting schedule* can you use? (See Chapter 2, Vesting)
- Should the *plan year* be the same as the company's tax year? (See Chapter 2 and Chapter 3)
- Should the plan be a *profit-sharing plan* or a *pension plan?* (See Chapter 1)
- Should the company adopt one plan to satisfy its needs or two plans? (See Chapter 11)
- What are the issues to be considered in the ongoing administration of the plan? (See Chapter 13).

These types of questions go on and on. The answers can easily be found in the pages of this book. Although it is not the intention of this book to make readers a pension expert, it is the intention to be sure no one becomes a statistic on the IRS' audit database.

The best way to understand that what *seems* simple is not, is to consider these examples:

- Most prototype plan documents offer several choices for vesting. The most common are 100% immediate vesting and a seven-year graded vesting schedule that provides 20% vesting in year three, increasing by 20% per year, until 100% vesting is reached in year seven. Also, most plan documents offer different choices for eligibility. The most common is one year of service and two years of service. Since the stated purpose of many qualified retirement plans is to retain employees, it would seem logical to choose two years of service for eligibility and seven-year graded vesting to encourage the employees to stay. Unfortunately, those choices do not comply with IRS regulations. If more than one year of service is required for eligibility, you must then provide 100% immediate vesting. This is a seemingly simple issue that could cause the plan to be disqualified on audit.

- Although there is a three-year statute of limitations which would imply that generally only three years of deductions could be disallowed on audit, that is only true if the plan filed a Schedule P, the trustee's statement, with the Form 5500 each year. Again, a seemingly simple issue.

- The concept of entry dates is widely misunderstood. Let's consider a typical situation in which a company adopts a profit-sharing plan. The owner and his accountant are told by the financial advisor that set up the plan that eligibility is two years and the employee must be at least 21 years old. Jane, the receptionist, was hired November 15, 2001. As of the end of 2002, Jack and his accountant determine that Jane does not have the required two years of service and therefore do not make a contribution for her. As of the end of the year 2003, Jane has satisfied the two-year requirement and Jack and his accountant advise her that she will be receiving a contribution in the year 2004 now that she has satisfied the two-year requirement. Early in 2005, the IRS audits Jack's plan for 2003 on a random audit program. When they check eligibility they determine that Jane should have been included in the plan in the year 2003 since the definition of *entry date* is "the first day of the plan year in which the eligibility requirements are satisfied." Since Jane is well past age 21 and satisfied the two-year requirement on November 15, 2003 she should have become a participant as of January 1, 2003 (the first day of the plan year *in which* she satisfied the requirements) and received a contribution for 2003. At the least Jack will have to make up the contribution with all past investment earnings based on the plan's past experience and at the worst, although unlikely, the plan could be disqualified.

The purpose of this book is to provide an overview that in most cases will avoid the types of problems described above and familiarize readers with the basics of qualified retirement plans. Most pension literature is written for the pension specialist at a very high technical level or for the financial professional at a somewhat lower technical level. It is my intention to communicate these concepts in terms that are clear, understandable and that can assist in avoiding costly plan defects. We will cover the practical and most prevalent aspects of qualified retirement plans, those that are most likely to be encountered. All numerical examples used to illustrate a concept will be based on a limited number of participants for simplicity but applies to larger plans as well.

In the following chapters, we will cover how to choose the "best" plan depending on employer goals and priorities (see Chapter 1). Once a plan type is decided, we will follow the process of establishing that plan and the rules that guide the process (Chapter 2). Now that the plan is established, what are the rules we have to play by? How do we comply with those rules and monitor that compliance? If we inadvertently overlook one of those rules, how do we correct our error with the least amount of pain, financially or otherwise (Chapter 14)?

Since there are marked differences in the rules depending on the type of plan adopted, we will cover the nature of each type of plan that would normally be considered, including the advantages and disadvantages of that plan type, the benefit and/or contribution limitations and the potential pitfalls (see Chapters 3 through 7).

Last, since nothing is forever, we will discuss terminating a plan (see Chapter 15). Depending on the type of plan, termination rules will vary. In some cases, a simple company resolution and filing of a final Form 5500 with the IRS is sufficient. For other plans, a filing with at least two federal agencies—the Pension Benefit Guaranty Corporation (for defined benefit plans only) and the IRS—may be necessary.

So now the tone is set. Readers may want to follow this book from cover to cover or use it as a reference book when an issue arises. In either case, it will help readers stay out of trouble and ensure that the qualified plan adopted accomplishes its purpose: to provide a comfortable retirement for the plans' participants with minimum burden.

How to Choose a Retirement Plan

Chapter 1

With all the choices available, deciding on the right plan for your business is, to say the least, a challenge. Profit sharing, age-weighted profit sharing, new comparability profit sharing, traditional 401(k), SIMPLE 401(k), SIMPLE IRA, safe harbor 401(k), defined benefit (DB), cash balance, money purchase, target benefit, employee stock ownership plan (ESOP)? The list gets longer each year. Should you consider two plans or one plan to accomplish your goals? What features should be included in the plan? Who should help with these decisions: your insurance professional, your investment broker, banker or a specialty pension consulting firm?

As Congress passes more and more legislation affecting qualified plans, this decision becomes more complex. Consider that when 401(k) plans became popular in the 1980s there was only one type, the traditional 401(k) plan. We now have four choices. Where to start?

CHOOSING THE "RIGHT" PLAN

To determine which qualified plan best suits a business, two fundamental issues should be considered: (1) the purpose of the plan, i.e., who is it to benefit and (2) the company's budget to fund the plan. Is the plan to be adopted truly intended to be an employee benefit plan, to be used primarily to attract and retain employees? Or is the plan intended to benefit a select group of employees? The larger the company, the more likely it is that the purpose of the plan is to provide an employee benefit. The answer to these questions can be at either extreme or at any point between the two extremes.

Once these questions are answered, the next issue is the consistency of deposits. If the company is well established and has a fairly level or growing cash flow, then the plan can be designed with fixed deposits (i.e., required funding each year). However, if the cash flow is erratic, then the flexibility of deposits is a key design feature. Generally, pension plan contributions are mandatory and profit-sharing plan contributions are discretionary, although fixed or mandatory contributions can be adjusted via plan amendment.

Pension plans include DB plans (see Chapter 6), cash balance plans (see Chapter 6), target benefit plans (see Chapter 4) and money purchase plans (see Chapter 4). All other plans, including 401(k) plans, are some form of profit-sharing plan and therefore discretionary (see Chapter 4). Many qualified retirement plan rules do, however, have exceptions. For example, even though safe harbor 401(k) and SIMPLE 401(k) or SIMPLE IRA plans are, or were, derived from profit-sharing type plans, employer contributions are required before such a plan can qualify for safe harbor or SIMPLE status. 401(k) plans are covered in more detail in Chapter 5.

Looking at the two extremes, we can match up plan types, which fall into one of the two categories described above: true employee benefit plans and plans for selected employees.

TRUE EMPLOYEE BENEFIT PLANS

These plans treat all employees, including the owners and key employees, the same and do not attempt to weight the plan benefits in favor of any group of employees. Their primary purpose is to attract employees in a competitive labor market and retain those employees for the long term. True employee benefit plans include:

1. *Traditional 401(k) plans* allow nondiscriminatory employee pretax deferrals from salary and discretionary nondiscriminatory employer profit-sharing contributions and/or matching contributions. The sum of all deductible employer contributions cannot be more than 25% of the compensation of the plan participants and no more than $41,000 for any one participant (for 2004). For this purpose, compensation for any one participant is limited to $205,000 (in the year 2004) as adjusted in the future by cost-of-living factors. A participant is an employee who has satisfied the plan's eligibility requirements.

2. *Profit-sharing plans* allow discretionary nondiscriminatory employer contributions up to 25% of the compensation of plan participants, with the same compensation limit as in item 1. The sum of all deductible employer contributions cannot be more than 25% of the compensation of the plan participants and no more than $41,000 for any one participant (for 2004).

3. *Money purchase pension plans* require mandatory employer contributions as a percentage of the employee's compensation, as provided in the plan, with a maximum individual contribution of the lesser of 100% of compensation (same compensation limit as item 1) or $41,000 in 2004 (see Chapter 3). The sum of all deductible employer contributions cannot be more than 25% of the compensation of the plan participants.

4. *Target benefit pension plans* require mandatory employer contributions based on age and compensation, with a maximum individual contribution of the lesser of 100% of compensation (same compensation limit as item 1) or $41,000 in 2004. The sum of all deductible employer contributions cannot be more than 25% of the compensation of the plan participants (same compensation limit as item 1) or $41,000 if less (for 2004).

5. *DB pension plans* (in larger companies, government entities, public schools) require employer contributions necessary to provide a promised retirement benefit, usually expressed as a percentage of compensation, in the form of

monthly retirement income beginning at a specific retirement age (e.g., 65). There is no limit to the contribution, only to the benefits provided. Benefits are currently (in the year 2004) limited to the lesser of 100% of the high consecutive three-year average compensation or $165,000 (see Chapter 6).

The limit on deductible employer contributions is not the same as the limit for an individual participant, generally referred to as the *annual additions limit*. The individual limit (annual additions) includes employer contributions, employee contributions and forfeitures (see Chapter 2) that are reallocated to active plan participants. This limit is the lesser of 100% of compensation or $41,000 unless the participant has or will reach their 50th birthday in the year in question in which case the limit is increased by the 401(k) catch-up contribution (see Chapter 5) of $3,000 (for 2004) if the employee is participating in a 401(k) plan.

PLANS FOR SELECTED EMPLOYEES

These plans are designed with the assumption that you the business owner and/or key employees are usually older and more highly compensated. The benefits of such plans are weighed in favor of the owner and key employees or in some cases a group of employees, e.g., a specific department of the company. The remaining employees receive those benefits necessary to satisfy the nondiscrimination rules (see Chapter 9). In some plan designs, the other employees are excluded from the plan and may or may not be covered by a different plan (see Chapter 11). Plans providing this type of benefit include the following:

1. *Safe harbor 401(k) plans* allow employee pretax deferrals from salary and discretionary nondiscriminatory employer profit-sharing contributions. Limited mandatory contributions by the employer guarantee satisfaction of nondiscrimination rules for the employee deferrals (see Chapter 5). The sum of all deductible employer contributions cannot be more than 25% of the compensation of the plan participants and no more than $41,000 for any one participant (for 2004). For this purpose, compensation for any one participant is limited to $205,000 (in the year 2004) as adjusted in the future by cost-of-living factors.

2. *Age-weighted profit-sharing plans* allow discretionary employer contributions up to 25% of the compensation of plan participants based on the employee's age and compensation (see Chapters 4 and 9), same compensation limit and employer contribution limit as item 1.

3. *New comparability profit-sharing plans* allow discretionary employer contributions of up to 25% of the compensation of plan participants based on the employee's age, job group or other business-related group (e.g., geographical location of jobsite) (see Chapter 4), same compensation limit and employer contribution limit as item 1.

4. *DB plans* for a select group of employees require those contributions necessary to provide a promised retirement benefit in the form of monthly retirement income. There is no limit to the contribution, only to the benefits provided, which are currently (in the year 2004) limited to the lesser of 100% of the high consecutive three-year average compensation or $165,000 (see Chapter 6).

5. *Two-plan combinations* allow two different plans of the types listed here to benefit different groups of employees so the result is most beneficial for the select group or groups of employees chosen to participate in each plan (see Chapter 11).

PROVIDING TRUE EMPLOYEE BENEFITS

Generally, defined contribution (DC) plans that are used to provide true employee benefits allocate contributions or benefits based on compensation. For example, a traditional profit-sharing plan will allocate the company's contribution based on each participant's compensation as a percentage of the compensation of all participants in the plan, as illustrated in Table I.

Table I

CONTRIBUTION ALLOCATION:
TRADITIONAL PROFIT-SHARING PLAN

	Salary	Percent of Total Salary	Contribution	Percent of Total Contribution
Owner	$100,000	50.00%	$15,000	50.00%
Employee 1	45,000	22.50	6,750	22.50
Employee 2	35,000	17.50	5,250	17.50
Employee 3	20,000	10.00	3,000	10.00
	$200,000	100.00%	$30,000	100.00%

Contribution for owner: ($100,000/$200,000) × $30,000 = $15,000

The exception to this rule is a plan that includes *Social Security integration* and the "new comparability profit-sharing plans" referred to previously. Social Security integration allows the plan sponsor to take into consideration the benefits provided by Social Security in determining the benefits being provided by the qualified plan adopted by the employer. Because the use of Social Security constitutes "reverse discrimination" (i.e., Social Security provides lower benefits as a percentage of compensation to higher wage earners, usually owners and key employees), the qualified plan can be used to equalize that disparity.

The same company illustrated in Table I could adopt a profit-sharing plan integrated with Social Security with the following results (see Table II).

Table II

CONTRIBUTION ALLOCATION:
PROFIT-SHARING PLAN INTEGRATED WITH SOCIAL SECURITY

	Salary	Percent of Total Salary	Contribution	Percent of Total Contribution
Owner	$100,000	50.00%	$15,344.85	51.15%
Employee 1	45,000	22.50	6,594.82	21.98
Employee 2	35,000	17.50	5,129.30	17.10
Employee 3	20,000	10.00	2,931.03	9.77
	$200,000	100.00%	$30,000.00	100.00%

In this plan, the contribution is allocated in a two-step process. The first-level contribution is 5.7% of compensation in excess of $87,900 (the year 2004 Social Security wage base). The remaining contribution after the first-level allocation is based on each participant's compensation as a percentage of total compensation as shown in Table I. Plans using Social Security integration are discussed in more detail in Chapter 4.

Contribution for owner:

$(\$100,000 - \$87,900) \times 5.7\%$ = $689.70 (1st-level contribution)

Remaining contribution = $29,310.30 ($30,000.00 − $689.70)

$(\$100,000/\$200,000) \times \$29,310.30$ = $14,655.15 (2nd-level contribution)

Total contribution for owner = $689.70 + $14,655.15 = $15,344.85

Since the owner is the only employee with compensation in excess of $87,900, he is the only employee who participates in the Level 1 contribution.

The employer's contribution in a 401(k) plan (generally, the employer matching contribution) is usually based on each employee's contribution and compensation (e.g., 50% of the employee's contribution (salary deferral), limited to a maximum employer contribution for any one employee of 2% of that employee's compensation (i.e., the match is the lesser of 50% of the employee's deferral or 2% of his or her compensation)).

Table III

CONTRIBUTION ALLOCATION:
401(k) PLAN

	Salary	Employee Deferral	Deferral Percent	Employer Match	Match Percent
Owner	$100,000	$8,000	8.00%	$2,000	2.00%
Employee 1	45,000	4,500	10.00	900	2.00
Employee 2	35,000	2,500	7.14	700	2.00
Employee 3	20,000	600	3.00	300	1.50
	$200,000	$15,600		$3,900	

Employees 1, 2 and the owner in Table III are limited by the 2% of compensation maximum match, while Employee 3 is limited by the 50% of deferral. Employee 3 would have to defer at least 4% of compensation, or $800, to get the maximum match of 2% of compensation.

A money purchase pension plan specifically defines the percentage contribution to be made for every eligible employee (e.g., 25%) in the plan document. A 25% of compensation money purchase plan would look like Table IV.

Table IV

CONTRIBUTION ALLOCATION:
MONEY PURCHASE PENSION PLAN

	Salary	Percent of Total Salary	Contribution	Percent of Total Contribution
Owner	$100,000	50.00%	$25,000	50.00%
Employee 1	45,000	22.50	11,250	22.50
Employee 2	35,000	17.50	8,750	17.50
Employee 3	20,000	10.00	5,000	10.00
	$200,000	100.00%	$50,000	100.00%

The money purchase plan also may be designed with Social Security integration so the contribution for the higher paid owners and key employees is more heavily weighted, as it is in the profit-sharing illustration in Table II.

Some DC plans that focus on employee benefits also take the age of the participant into consideration. In this case, the employer is taking the position that because older employees have less time to accumulate retirement benefits, a larger contribution must be made for them each year. This is true of the age-weighted profit-sharing plan and the target benefit plan. Contribution allocations to these plans are illustrated below and are discussed in more detail in Chapter 4.

DB plans are also true retirement plans. A DB plan promises retirement income benefits—for example, a retirement benefit of 50% of an employee's average compensation payable for life beginning at retirement age as defined in the plan (e.g., age 65). The DB plan takes age, service and compensation into consideration.

The most common application of the DB plan is for unions, municipalities, organizations within municipalities (public schools) and midsized private or larger public companies. In the last ten to 15 years, small to midsized companies generally stopped using DB plans because of their complexity and high cost of funding and administration, however, smaller companies are beginning to use DB plans again. DB plans are discussed in Chapter 6.

PLANS FAVORING A SELECT GROUP OF EMPLOYEES

At the other end of the spectrum are plans designed for a select group of employees. Most of these plans base contributions on the age and compensation level of the participant, and include the following:

1. Age-weighted profit-sharing plans (beneficial to the older and more highly compensated owners and key employees allowing for discretionary contributions, see Table V)

Table V

**CONTRIBUTION ALLOCATION:
AGE-WEIGHTED PROFIT-SHARING PLAN**

	Salary	Percent of Total Salary	Age	Employer Contribution	Percent of Total
Owner	$100,000	50.00%	55	$25,000	77.9%
Employee 1	45,000	22.50	44	5,078	15.8
Employee 2	35,000	17.50	25	1,050	3.3
Employee 3	20,000	10.00	32	947	3.0
	$200,000	100.00%		$32,075	100.0%

Comparing this to Table IV, you can see there is a significant difference in the allocation of the contribution.

---

2. New comparability or cross-tested profit-sharing plans (which allow for discretionary contributions beneficial to the older and more highly compensated owners and key employees)

Table VI

CONTRIBUTION ALLOCATION: CROSS-TESTED PROFIT-SHARING PLAN

	Salary	Percent of Total Salary	Age	Employer Contribution	Percent of Total
Owner	$100,000	50.00%	55	$25,000	83.3%
Employee 1	45,000	22.50	44	2,250	7.5
Employee 2	35,000	17.50	25	1,750	5.8
Employee 3	20,000	10.00	32	1,000	3.3
	$200,000	100.00%		$30,000	100.0%

Comparing Table VI to Table IV, you can see there is a significant difference in the allocation of the contribution.

3. DB plans when used in addition to a DC plan (which allow for much larger contributions than a DC plan for older owners and key employees with less time to accumulate retirement benefits). The plan in Table VII provides a benefit of 100% of compensation payable monthly, beginning at age 65, for life. DB plans are discussed in more detail in Chapter 6.

Table VII

CONTRIBUTION ALLOCATION: DEFINED BENEFIT PLAN

	Salary	Age	Monthly Benefit	Employer Contribution	Percent of Total
Owner	$100,000	55	$8,333.33	$81,006	84.95%
Employee 1	45,000	44	3,750.00	10,845	11.37
Employee 2	35,000	25	2,916.67	1,765	1.85
Employee 3	20,000	32	1,666.67	1,741	1.83
	$200,000			$95,356	100.00%

4. Two-plan combinations that allow each plan to be designed for a specific group of employees (e.g., rank and file vs. owners and key employees). These plans allow the employer to use a variety of plan design options to provide higher benefits for the owners and key employees of the company sponsoring the plan.

Sometimes it takes a combination of two plans to accomplish the company's goals. It is not uncommon for companies to adopt plan combinations such as:

1. A DB plan (see Chapter 6) and a traditional 401(k) plan (see Chapter 5), where the DB plan provides significant benefits for the owners, key employees, and limited rank-and-file employees and the 401(k) plan provides benefits for the remaining employees

2. A safe harbor 401(k) plan (see Chapter 5) and a new comparability profit-sharing plan (see Chapter 4), allowing the owners and key employees to defer the maximum allowable amount, yet satisfy the nondiscrimination rules and maximize their DC allocation (the lesser of 100% of compensation or $41,000 in year 2004) in the new comparability profit-sharing plan, which is weighted for older higher paid employees

3. A DB plan (see Chapter 6) and a class-allocation profit-sharing plan (see Chapter 4) to provide substantial benefits or contributions for both older and younger owners and key employees as efficiently as possible.

These combinations are beneficial because they allow the benefits to favor the owners and key employees of the company sponsoring the plan while still providing some benefits to the remaining employees. These are by no means the only plan combinations that are available. As with any plan design, each company is different and all factors must be considered in choosing the "right" plan or plans.

One of the most common two-plan combinations, the 10% money purchase plan together with a profit-sharing plan, has been eliminated with the increase in the deduction limit on profit-sharing plans to 25%. Prior to 2002, with a 15% limit on profit-sharing plans, a combination 10% money purchase plan and profit-sharing plan allowed the employer to vary contributions depending on the profitability of the business. That contribution could range from 10%, the mandatory money purchase contribution, to 25% when the profit-sharing plan was funded in highly profitable years. Beginning in 2002, the same result can be accomplished with a profit-sharing plan, with the added benefit that the entire contribution could be discretionary. With this in mind, there is no longer a need for money purchase plans or target benefit plans.

All of the various plan types and combinations, their limitations and applications are analyzed in detail in later chapters.

EFFECTIVE PLAN DESIGN

Once the goal of the plan is determined, the key to effective plan design is complete and accurate data. This includes the obvious: employee information (including date of birth, date of hire, annual compensation and job description); company tax year-end; owners of the company; and officers of the company. It also includes the not-so-obvious:

1. Are any employees related to other employees, particularly if either is an officer (used to determine top-heavy status, see Chapter 9) or owner of the

company (used in nondiscrimination testing, see Chapter 9)? This is important in determining whether a plan satisfies the nondiscrimination rules, which generally state that a plan may not discriminate in favor of highly compensated employees.

2. Are any other companies owned by all or some of the same owners of the company for whom the plan is being designed (the plan sponsor)? This is also important in determining whether a plan satisfies the nondiscrimination rules, because all companies considered to be a controlled group are considered one company for purposes of the pension nondiscrimination rules (see Chapter 10).

3. Is the company a Subchapter S corporation, a C corporation, partnership, or organized in some other form? The form the plan sponsor takes will determine compensation for the owners. In a Subchapter S corporation, profits that are taxed to the shareholders are not considered compensation for purposes of pension benefits or contributions.

4. Did the company have a plan in the past? In some cases, benefits in a previous plan must be taken into consideration to determine the limit on benefits in a new plan. In addition, the plan number (see Chapter 2) must be sequential for a plan sponsor with the same federal ID number. A sponsor adopting a new plan some time after terminating an old plan would be adopting plan number 002. Using the wrong plan number on the Form 5500 (see Chapter 13) could cause confusion and time-consuming inquiries from the Internal Revenue Service (IRS).

5. Are any of the employees, including the owners, members of a union? Some plans automatically exclude union employees, while others offer that feature as an option. If the owners are inadvertently excluded because they too are members of the union, the purpose of the plan has been defeated.

All of these issues and many others have a significant impact on the type of plan that can be adopted, the design of the plan, limits on the benefits or contributions that can be provided and, most importantly, whether the plan will satisfy all the requirements necessary to maintain its status as a tax-qualified plan. Following are some examples of problems that can occur without proper information.

Example 1. A medical office is a candidate for a DB plan that would provide significant benefits for the owners and key employees. If it were not known that the owners of the medical office also own a testing laboratory with 50 employees, that same DB plan could bankrupt them because of the need for additional contributions on behalf of the laboratory employees.

Example 2. It might not have been known that one of the employees is the daughter of the owner because she is listed under her married name. In such a case, the plan could have been disqualified, because the daughter would have been incorrectly treated as a nonhighly compensated employee when testing for nondiscrimination causing the plan to pass the nondiscrimination testing when it would have failed if she were correctly treated as a highly compensated employee.

Example 3. If compensation is reported without knowing that the entity is a sole proprietorship or partnership, the contribution for the owner(s) would be over the maximum allowed and may cause the plan to be disqualified. If the company is a corporation, the compensation would be reported on Form W-2. This is also true of a Subchapter S corporation. Shareholder's compensation does not include the Subchapter S profits, which are considered dividends. If the company is a sole proprietorship, the compensation would be reported on Schedule C and, if a partnership, on a form K-1. The maximum deduction for W-2 compensation of $100,000 in a money purchase plan is $25,000, while the maximum deduction for net Schedule C compensation of $100,000 (after adjustment for self-employment tax) is $20,000 (see Chapter 3).

Example 4. In some contracting companies, the owners are union members in order to take advantage of some of the union benefits (e.g., health insurance). Although they may not consider themselves to be union members, for pension purposes they could be and would be excluded from participation if the plan excluded union employees.

Example 5. Without knowing that a company had a previous plan that was terminated, the new plan would be numbered 001. When the IRS received the annual filing (Form 5500), its records would show that plan 001 was terminated. The IRS might then challenge the termination, trigger an audit of the termination or initiate some other time-consuming inquiry to clarify the discrepancy.

These are only some of the potential problems that can be encountered without complete and accurate data. It is the responsibility of the financial advisor who assists in establishing the plan to ask the right questions, not the responsibility of the adopting company to know what is needed.

The most common compliance issue in IRS audits is coverage. Use of the coverage rules allows different plans to be adopted for different groups of employees (see Chapter 9). Are all the employees who have satisfied the eligibility requirements (age and service) actually being covered by the plan? The second most common compliance issue is nondiscrimination. The basic tenet is that a qualified plan may not discriminate in favor of the highly compensated employees (HCEs). This one statement has generated hundreds of pages of regulations over the past several years.

A *highly compensated employee* is any employee who is either a 5% owner at any time during the current or prior plan year or who received compensation in the prior year in excess of $95,000 (in 2004) as indexed, from the employer. Because the determination of whether an employee is highly compensated is based on prior-year compensation, the $95,000 limit for 2004 would actually be used to determine whether an employee is highly compensated in 2005, i.e., based on prior-year compensation in 2004 of $95,000. To determine whether an employee is highly compensated in 2004, prior-year compensation in 2003 would have to be considered, at which time the limit was $90,000.

In all cases, the determination of whether a plan is discriminatory is based on a comparison of benefits or contributions between the HCEs and the *nonhighly compensated employees* (NHCEs). A nonhighly compensated employee is any employee who is not a highly compensated employee by definition.

In determining who are owners of the sponsoring company, there is a concept known as attribution (i.e., ownership by some family members is attributed to other family members as if those other family members are owners). See Chapter 10 for a full discussion of attribution and entities under common control. Without knowing the family relationships in the company, it is impossible to determine who is an HCE and satisfy all the nondiscrimination rules.

Following is an example of what can happen when critical information is not made known to the advisor:

> **Example 6.** A CPA has a client who has had a retirement plan for the last five years. He is a dentist and set up the plan with XYZ financial institution. The CPA discovers that the client also owns 20% of a dental lab with his son who owns the remaining 80%, and that the dental lab has no pension.
>
> The result could be either that, on audit, the plan would be disqualified because the employees of the lab are not included, causing the plan to be discriminatory in favor of the HCEs. All prior deductions not covered by the statute of limitations would be disallowed and the client would owe back taxes, interest and penalties. In addition, benefits may become immediately taxable. Alternatively, the plan could also be taken to one of the IRS voluntary compliance programs (see Chapter 14) to correct the defect. If so, there would be a sanction that might range from a zero payment to a payment of $70,000, depending on the size of the plan and the severity of the defect. In addition, the company would have to make up all contributions that should have been made for the excluded employees going back to the date they should have been included in the plan, i.e., the statute of limitations does not limit the number of years to be corrected. They would also have to make up the investment gains for those employees according to the actual prior investment experience of the plan.

PLAN-SPECIFIC AND ANCILLARY ISSUES

In some cases, there are additional considerations that are unique to the plan. For example, consider an ESOP. This is a profit-sharing plan designed to invest solely in the stock of the company that sponsors the plan. Although an ESOP is a profit-sharing plan and is subject to all the rules and regulations of profit-sharing plans, it is also subject to an additional set of rules and regulations specific to ESOPs (see Chapter 4). In a closely held private company, the primary purpose of adopting an ESOP is to create a market for the company's nonpublicly traded stock when the owners want to dispose of their stock or diversify their holdings at or close to retirement. In larger companies, an ESOP creates widespread ownership among the employees giving them a financial interest in the profitability of the company.

Last are the ancillary plan design options. Should eligibility be one year, two years or some other more appropriate definition (e.g., all employees employed on the effective date of the plan are eligible immediately and all future employees are eligible after one year of service). One-year eligibility is typical, because that choice allows the plan to use a vesting schedule that is graded over seven years. A seven-year graded vesting schedule begins in the third year at 20% and increases by 20% each additional year until the participant is 100% vested in year seven.

If it is likely that employees will remain employed for two or more years, the graded vesting schedule is usually the best choice, because nonvested benefits are forfeited and (depending on the type of plan and the plan provisions) used either to increase the benefits of the remaining participants or to reduce the employer's future contributions. If two years of service are required for participation in the plan, the vesting must be 100% immediate upon entry to the plan. If the plan requires more than one year of service for eligibility, including partial years (e.g., 1½ years), the plan must provide for 100% immediate vesting upon satisfaction of the eligibility requirements. If employee turnover usually occurs in under two years, the two-year eligibility may be an effective option, because most employees will never become eligible. In some cases, the sponsor of the plan would like to include all employees employed as of the effective date of the plan but require some service for future employees. A new company that currently only employs the owner(s) and has been in existence for less than one year, but is growing, would be able to establish and fund a plan just for the owners for the first year or two, until newly hired employees satisfy the eligibility requirements.

What is the appropriate choice for entry date (i.e., the date on which an employee is eligible to participate in the plan after satisfying the eligibility requirements)? Should retirement age be 55, 62 or 65, and what is the impact of that choice? Generally, the funding is affected by retirement age only if the plan contribution is in part based on the age of the employee (e.g., DB plans, target benefit plans). Should the plan offer loans and/or hardship distributions and accept the additional administrative work required? The list goes on. These choices and many others are discussed in detail in Chapter 2.

PLAN DESIGN CHECKLIST

Although choosing the appropriate qualified plan can be difficult, a logical process can be followed to make the right decision for a specific company. In fact, in each case it is possible to arrive at more than one suitable choice of plan. The following checklist can assist you in determining the company's needs.

1. Current annual budget for contribution $_____

2. Is the cash flow consistent or erratic?   _____
   - ☐ Fixed deposit   ☐ Flexible deposit

3. ☐ Employee benefit   ☐ Select group of employees
   Are benefits to be provided for all employees equally or to be weighted for the owners and key employees?

4. If the answer to item 3 is "employee benefit," consider using the following:
   - ☐ Traditional 401(k) plan
   - ☐ Profit-sharing plan
   - ☐ Money purchase pension plan
   - ☐ Target benefit pension plan
   - ☐ DB pension plan (in larger companies)

5. If the answer to item 3 is "select group," are the owners and key employees of the company older than the rank-and-file employees?
   - ☐ Yes   ☐ No

6. If the answer to item 5 is "yes," consider:
   - ☐ Age-weighted profit-sharing plan
   - ☐ New comparability profit-sharing plan
   - ☐ Safe harbor 401(k)
   - ☐ DB plan

7. If the answer to item 5 is "no," consider:
   - ☐ Safe harbor 401(k) plan
   - ☐ Two-plan combinations

8. Are there any special issues to consider? For example:
   - ☐ Disposition of stock in nonpublicly traded company
   - ☐ Estate planning issues
   - ☐ Business succession planning issues
   - ☐ Multiple companies controlled by the same owners
   - ☐ Family-owned business

Once the preceding questions have been answered, be sure to secure accurate data, as described earlier in this chapter. The right plan does not work if it is disqualified because of incomplete or erroneous information.

Establishing the Plan and Plan Design Features

Establishing a qualified retirement plan is an exacting process. The primary reasons companies make the effort required to adopt qualified plans are the tax benefits. As a tax shelter, a qualified retirement plan has many favorable features. All contributions made by the employer are tax-deductible and not taxable to the employee (Internal Revenue Code (IRC) Sections 404, 403, 402). In 401(k) plans, contributions made by employees are pretax (contributions are subject to Social Security taxes), earnings on investments are tax-deferred (IRC Sections 401, 501) and distributions from the plan may be subject to favorable tax treatment (IRC Section 402(d)). In addition to the tax benefits, qualified plans tend to attract employees in a competitive labor market, have vesting provisions that tend to reduce employee turnover, increase employee incentive to be more productive in profit-sharing plans and assist employees in accumulating funds for retirement. To take advantage of all these benefits, a qualified retirement plan must satisfy the following requirements:

1. The plan and trust must be a definite written program that sets forth all the provisions necessary for qualification.
2. The plan must be communicated to employees in writing.
3. The plan must be permanent. Although there is no statutory definition for what period of time constitutes *permanent,* in the absence of mitigating circumstances, three years would usually be considered permanent if there is a valid business reason for terminating the plan after the three-year period.
4. The plan must be for the exclusive benefit of employees and their beneficiaries. Benefits may not be provided to any individual who is not an employee of the company sponsoring the plan, e.g., an independent contractor.
5. Contributions or benefits provided must not discriminate in favor of the highly compensated employees. A *highly compensated employee* is defined as a 5% or more direct or indirect owner of the company in the current year or prior year and any employee who earned more than $90,000 (in 2003 to determine 2004 highly compensated) in the prior year (see Chapter 9).

6. The plan must satisfy the minimum vesting rules (see below).
7. The plan must satisfy minimum participation and coverage requirements (see below).
8. Plan assets cannot be diverted or used for any purpose other than providing benefits to employees. Excess assets in a terminated defined benefit (DB) plan may, however, revert to the employer, subject to excise tax and income tax (see Chapter 15).
9. The plan may not provide contributions or benefits in excess of statutory limitations (see Chapter 3).
10. The plan must provide for required distributions (see Chapter 8).
11. The plan must provide that, in the event of partial or total termination, the employees' right to accrued benefits will become 100% vested (see Chapter 15). In a defined contribution (DC) plan, the employee's account balance represents his or her accrued benefit. In a DB plan, the portion of the employee's projected monthly retirement benefit that has been earned to date based on total years of service or years of participation in the plan represents his or her accrued benefit (see Chapter 6).
12. The plan must provide that benefits may not be assigned or alienated except for plan loans as provided for in IRS regulations.
13. The plan must provide that only the first $205,000 (for 2004, as adjusted) of an employee's compensation may be taken into account to determine contributions or benefits.
14. The plan must benefit the lesser of 50 employees or 40% or more of the employees who otherwise satisfy the statutory eligibility rules (age and service, see below and see Chapter 9). This applies to DB plans only.

These requirements, and other plan-specific requirements, must be satisfied in order to maintain the qualified status of the retirement plan. In the event of non-compliance, the plan may be disqualified by IRS.

PLAN DOCUMENT TYPES: DEFINITIONS

A qualified plan must be in writing. Establishing an investment account in the name of the plan is not sufficient to substantiate the adoption of a qualified plan. The timely execution of the plan document (prior to the end of the tax year of the plan sponsor) and the company resolution adopting the plan is what establishes the plan. Following are some of the methods for committing a plan to writing, as well as definitions of some key related terms.

1. *Master plan.* A plan made available by a sponsor for adoption by employers and for which a single funding medium (e.g., a trust or custodial account) is established, as part of the plan, for the joint use of all adopting employers. A master plan consists of a basic plan document, an adoption agreement and a trust or custodial account document. This type of document is commonly used for associations that offer retirement plans for their members (e.g., the American Institute of Certified Public Accountants, the American Bar Association).
2. *Prototype plan.* A plan made available by a sponsor for adoption by employers and under which a separate funding medium is established for each

adopting employer. A prototype plan consists of a basic plan document, an adoption agreement and a trust or custodial account document. These documents may be individually prepared or included in one document. The adoption agreement is usually in the format of "fill in the blanks," allowing for some customization of plan provisions, e.g., eligibility. A prototype plan may be sponsored by a pension consulting firm, an accounting firm, a brokerage office, a bank or any other financial organization that satisfies the definition of sponsor.

3. *Volume submitter plan.* A plan that is submitted under the procedures described in Section 9 of Revenue Procedure 2000-6. These procedures govern filing requests for volume submitter advisory letters (similar to a letter of determination) and requests for determination letters with respect to an employer's adoption of a plan that is substantially similar, but not identical, to an approved volume submitter plan. A volume submitter plan is generally developed by a company that specializes in providing pension documents to consulting firms, but generally does not offer the document to the end user. When the advisory letter is received by the company that developed the document, it is then made available to the consulting firms (the sponsors), to be used by a consulting firm's clients and submitted on their behalf by the consulting firm to IRS, for a determination letter. The volume submitter program allows IRS to expedite the issuance of determination letters for individually designed plans that are not "custom plan documents," because most of the language in the volume submitter document has been preapproved. *Custom plan documents* are original documents written with provisions that cannot be included in any of the document types above due to the unique nature of the plan provisions. These documents should be submitted to IRS for a favorable letter of determination providing reliance on the language in the plan.

Generally, the master and prototype plan documents are the least flexible in plan design. The volume submitter plan tends to be more flexible because it is similar to a custom plan document (i.e., one that is drafted with custom language specifically for the employer sponsor of the plan). Depending on the type of document (e.g., prototype, master plan, volume submitter or custom plan) and the type of organization sponsoring the plan (not the employer adopting the plan) (e.g., insurance company, brokerage office, pension consulting firm, law firm, bank), there may be a fee for preparing the plan document. This may range from a few hundred dollars up to several thousand dollars for larger employers that require a custom plan document. Typically, for the small to midsized employer, fees in the range of $750 to $2,500 are common. Some financial institutions provide the documents free, but may not provide assistance in completing the adoption agreement. If their representatives (insurance brokers, stock brokers, bankers) are knowledgeable, they may be able to assist.

PLAN DOCUMENT TYPES: ANALYSIS

The most popular plan documents are the master and prototype plans. These are preapproved plan documents that have been developed by large industry-specific organizations and financial organizations. The master plan is one that is usually developed by national organizations in which participating employers use an adoption agreement to join (the American Bar Association Plan is a master plan). Contributions from all participating employers are deposited into a single funding vehicle (e.g., a master trust). The regional prototype plan is usually sponsored by financial organizations (e.g., a pension consulting firm or law firm, an insurance company or brokerage firm). The organization sponsoring the master or prototype plan submits the plan to IRS for review and will receive an opinion letter from IRS when approved. The regional prototype plan allows each adopting employer to choose its own funding vehicle. There are usually two parts to the master or prototype plans: (1) the trust document or basic plan document and (2) the adoption agreement. The trust document embodies all of the required language and definitions to establish the plan as a tax-qualified plan, while the adoption agreement allows the client (the adopting employer) to choose from among several options in a fill-in-the-blank format for such features as eligibility, vesting and retirement age. Some prototype documents merge the two parts into one document.

Regional prototypes are the most common in the small to medium-size business and come in two popular forms, standardized and nonstandardized. The standardized form offers more restrictive options to the plan sponsor for such things as eligibility (see below), allocation of contributions and definition of compensation (see below). Employers cannot adopt a standardized plan if they maintain another plan at the same time unless it is a paired plan, as discussed later in this chapter.

A typical nonstandardized plan document offers several options not available in standardized plans. For example, the client can exclude certain employees by job class or some other business-related group such as a company subsidiary, hourly, salaried or commission-only employees; specific job groups like managers, associates or salespeople, in addition to the statutory exclusions requiring a minimum age and minimum service. As long as the plan satisfies the coverage test (see below), it is still considered to be a qualified plan. In addition, the nonstandardized plan can define compensation to exclude certain types of income like bonuses or overtime.

The last major difference between the two types of regional prototype plans deals with the allocation of contributions. The nonstandardized plan may require that an employee complete a year of service in order to share in the employer's contribution. For a terminated employee, the plan may require employment on the last day of the plan year and/or the completion of a year of service (a 12-month period during which the employee completes at least 1,000 hours of service) in order to share in the employer's contribution.

Although it is not mandatory to submit a plan to IRS for a determination letter and IRS does not encourage it, employers using custom plan documents will submit their plans to be sure they comply with all IRS rules and regulations. If, upon review, IRS finds a defect, the plan sponsor (the employer) is given an opportunity to correct the defect without adversely affecting the qualified status of the plan. If the plan is not submitted to IRS for review and the defect is found on audit, the plan can be disqualified.

Even though the plan has been preapproved as to its form and the design options available, the more liberal plan design options provide a greater opportunity to create a plan that is not in compliance with the nondiscrimination rules and regulations. Following is an example.

	Base Salary	Commissions	Overtime	Bonus
Owner	$205,000	None	None	None
Employee 1	40,000	$25,000	None	None
Employee 2	30,000	None	$8,000	$2,000

In a nonstandardized prototype profit-sharing plan that defines compensation to exclude commissions, overtime and bonus, the allocation of a 15% contribution would be as follows:

	Considered Compensation	Total Deposit	Deposit as Percent of Total Compensation	
Owner	$205,000	$30,750	15.0%	($30,750 ÷ $205,000)
Employee 1	40,000	6,000	9.2	($ 6,000 ÷ $ 65,000)
Employee 2	30,000	4,500	11.3	($ 4,500 ÷ $ 40,000)

The result in this case would constitute discrimination in operation, even though the nonstandardized plan document may allow for these choices in defining compensation. To avoid this, a nonstandardized prototype plan is submitted to IRS with supporting documentation to illustrate that the choices made in the adoption agreement are not discriminatory in operation. In the case illustrated, the submission package would include a schedule showing the percentage of each participant's compensation that was being considered in allocating contributions:

	Considered Compensation	Total Compensation	Percent Compensation Considered
Owner	$205,000	$205,000	100.0%
Employee 1	40,000	65,000	61.5
Employee 2	30,000	40,000	75.0

Clearly, this does not treat all participants equally. IRS guideline requires that the difference between the percentage of compensation considered for nonhighly compensated employees (NHCEs) and highly compensated employees (HCEs) must be *de minimis*. This is a facts-and-circumstances determination. The preceding example does not fall within this guideline.

When a plan is submitted to IRS for review, all interested parties must be given a notice indicating that an application was made for a determination letter, providing them with the opportunity to comment to IRS on that application. Failure to provide the notice prohibits the employer from appealing an adverse determination letter from IRS.

If a standardized plan document is adopted, the company that uses that plan document (the employer) need not submit it to IRS for approval, but may rely on the opinion letter secured by the financial institution that offers the prototype plan document. Any changes to the available options in the adoption agreement invalidate its status as a standardized prototype, which means the client may not rely on the approval letter, but would have to submit the plan to IRS for approval as if it were a custom plan document.

Also unique to prototype plans is a principle known as paired plans. This allows two standardized plan documents (e.g., a profit-sharing plan and a money purchase pension plan), sponsored by the same financial institution, to be adopted by the employer without submitting the plans to IRS. If the plans are not paired, the documents must be submitted for reliance to illustrate that the limit on contributions to multiple plans has not been exceeded (see Chapter 3) and to determine which plan will satisfy the top-heavy minimum contribution and benefit requirements (see Chapter 9). This is accomplished through reciprocal language, included in the paired prototype documents, that deals with those issues.

In many cases, a prototype document is not valid unless an authorized representative of the financial institution that sponsors the plan document signs the adoption agreement. In addition, it is the responsibility of the sponsoring organization to update the plan as new legislation changes the pension rules and regulations. From time to time, the financial institution will send its adopting employers updated documents to sign as a result of these changes. It is not uncommon for such a document package to be set aside by the adopting employer, who does not understand its importance and then finds on audit that the plan is disqualified because it was not updated to comply with various new rules. This happens more often when the financial institution does not maintain a pension compliance department.

The last two document types, volume submitter plans and custom-designed plans, are similar in that they are full-text documents (i.e., no blanks to be filled in). Like prototype plans, volume submitter plans are preapproved, but they allow for minor changes in the basic language. The custom plan creates all of its language from scratch to accommodate special needs of the company using that document. If the changes to a volume submitter plan are too extensive, then it is considered to be a custom-designed plan and cannot rely on its original approval letter. Generally, volume submitter plans offer more flexibility in their design options than any of the prototype plans.

To encourage the establishment of qualified plans by small employers, the Economic Growth and Tax Relief Reconciliation Act of 2001 (EGTRRA) eliminated user fees for certain qualifying employers when submitting their plans for determination letters. This exception to the user fee requirement generally applies for the plan's first five years. Specifically, the user fee exception does not apply to any request made after the later of (1) the fifth plan year of the plan's existence or (2) the end of any remedial amendment period (discussed later in this chapter) for a plan, beginning within the first five plan years. Even though the five-year waiver for user fees is effective after 2001, the plan would not have to be adopted after 2001 to qualify for the waiver, as long as the plan has not been in existence for more than five years when a determination letter request is made.

There is a two-part test to determine whether an employer is eligible for waiver of the user fee:

1. The employer cannot have had more than 100 employees for the preceding year who received at least $5,000 in compensation from the employer.

---

2. The employer must have had at least one employee who participates in the plan who is not a highly compensated employee.

In addition to the plan document, the sponsoring employer must provide all eligible employees and beneficiaries with a summary plan description (SPD). This is a condensed version of the plan document written in layman's terms. The SPD must be updated every five years to reflect changes that have been made during that period. If no changes have been made, then the SPD must be updated every ten years. In the practical operation of a qualified plan, it is more likely that a change will be made during that five-year period, as a result of either a change in the plan design initiated by the employer or the need for a plan amendment in order to comply with new legislation. During the five-year period, any material modification must be disclosed to participants and beneficiaries in the form of a summary description of material modifications (SMM). Unlike the SPD, the SMM describes only the specific change that was made, usually by plan amendment, and its effect on benefits. All of these administrative functions are usually done by the organization that sponsors the plan if a prototype or volume submitter plan was used or by the law firm if a custom-designed document was used.

BASIC PLAN DESIGN FEATURES

Allocations to Active and Terminated Employees

Other than standardized prototype plans, the allocation of contributions in a DC plan, i.e., profit-sharing, money purchase or target benefit plan, can be withheld from employees based on the number of hours worked by an active employee (if less than 1,000) and/or whether an employee is employed on the last day of the plan year. Use of this option would require an annual statutory nondiscrimination test of the result (see Chapter 9).

Compensation

This is the basis for contributions or benefits in all qualified plans. The plan can define the 12-month period to be used in measuring compensation and, depending on the type of document, can define what is included in compensation, e.g., overtime is to be excluded. Compensation for employees of corporations is based on their W-2 compensation. In a Sub-Chapter S corporation, the profits (taxed to the stockholders on a form K-1) do not count as compensation for those stockholders for pension purposes. This income is considered dividends, not earned income. For a sole proprietor, compensation is the net Schedule C income adjusted for Social Security taxes and, for partnerships, the K-1 income for each partner is also adjusted for Social Security taxes.

Conditions for Distributions Upon Termination

When an employee participating in a qualified plan terminates employment, his or her benefits must be paid out. Although a plan may delay these payments until retirement age, that is usually not practical since the employer would have to locate the employee at that time, possibly many years later. Generally, the employee is

---

paid out based on hours worked in the year of termination. In most cases, if the employee has worked less than 500 hours in that year payment is made in the following year. If the employee has worked more than 500 hours in the year of termination, the distribution is delayed one additional year. Regulations do allow for distributions to be delayed for up to five years after termination of employment but is usually not practical in the small to midsize company since the employee would have to be located at that later date.

Conditions of Eligibility

This refers to the statutory requirements of eligibility, including age and service. An age requirement cannot exceed 21 years of age and service cannot exceed two years (one year in a 401(k) plan). The service requirement also allows for full-time employment defined as at least 1,000 hours during the year (including all paid time, e.g., vacation time). If a plan requires more than one year of service for eligibility, vesting (discussed below) must be 100% immediate. An employee who is a member of a union in which pension benefits are the subject of good faith bargaining may also be excluded regardless of age and service.

Coverage Rules

Coverage is somewhat related to eligibility. The general rule allows a plan to exclude up to 30% of otherwise eligible (statutory eligibility for age and service) nonhighly compensated employees (see definition of highly compensated employees at the beginning of this chapter; all others are considered nonhighly compensated). The exclusions may be based on any business criteria, e.g., job description, geographical location. This provision is used in small plans to minimize the cost for rank and file employees or in larger companies to provide different benefits for different groups of employees (see Chapter 9).

Directed Investment Accounts

This is an optional provision that would allow each participant in the plan to manage and direct his or her own investments (in DC plans only). This is common in 401(k) plans. Including this option does not relieve the plan sponsor (the employer) from fiduciary responsibility regarding the plan investments.

Effective Date of Participation and Entry Date

While the eligibility requirements determine the year in which an employee becomes a participant, the entry date determines that date within the year that the employee becomes a participant. There are many choices for this design option although the most common is establishing two entry dates, e.g., January 1 and July 1, assuming a calendar year plan. An employee would become a participant and therefore eligible for benefits or contributions on the entry date immediately following satisfaction of the eligibility requirements. If, for example, an employee who had already reached his or her 21st birthday was hired March 10, 2004, his or her entry date would be July 1, 2005, the entry date following one year of service (March 10, 2005). If the employee was hired August 14, 2004, his or her entry date would be January 1, 2006, the entry date following one year of service (August 14, 2005). Other options for entry dates are the first day of the year in which the eligibility requirements are satisfied; the first day of the plan year in which eligibility requirements are satisfied if hired during the first six months of the year or the first day of the next plan year if hired during the last six months of the year; and the first day of the plan year if eligibility is six months and age 20½.

Forfeitures

Forfeitures represent the nonvested portion of an employee's benefits. If an employee terminates employment before becoming 100% vested, the remaining benefits may be used to increase the benefits of the remaining participants (in a DC plan only) or to reduce the employer's contribution in following years (required in a DB plan).

Form of Distributions

This provision determines how benefits will be distributed at termination of employment for any reason including retirement. The choices may include a lump sum, periodic payment or life contingent payments, i.e., annuity payments based on the life of the participant and/or the participant's spouse. The most common in small to midsized plans is lump-sum payments. Pension plans, i.e., DB, target benefit and money purchase, require that the distribution be made in the form of a 50% joint and survivor annuity to a married participant unless the nonparticipant spouse waives that requirement.

Hardship Distributions

This is an optional design feature in plans that are profit sharing in nature including 401(k). Hardship distributions are limited by statute for specific purposes, e.g., unreimbursed medical expenses, and are subject to income taxation when made. In addition, if the employee is younger than 59½, an additional 10% excise tax is due. If the plan allows for participant loans, that source of funds must be exhausted before a hardship distribution may be made (see Chapter 8).

Life Insurance

Another optional benefit in qualified retirement plans—life insurance—may be provided for plan participants. Depending on the type of plan, DC or DB, the amount of insurance is limited since the primary purpose of the plan is to provide retirement benefits. Generally in a DC plan, the premium is limited for whole life insurance to less than 50% of cumulative contributions and forfeitures, while with all other forms of life insurance the premiums are limited to 25% or less of cumulative contributions and forfeitures. In a DB plan, insurance is generally limited to a death benefit from the insurance of no more than 100 times the monthly retirement benefit, although there is another method (Revenue Ruling 74-307) that would allow for higher death benefits if necessary. Premiums paid for life insurance are considered part of the plan contribution and are deductible except for a small portion of the premium that regulations consider currently taxable. Since the death benefit is considered a current benefit, i.e., providing an immediate benefit, rather than a deferred benefit, i.e., payable at retirement, the value of that "current economic benefit" is taxed. The amount to be taxed may be based on an IRS table, the PS-58 table or the insurance company's term rates.

For example, if the employee was aged 35 and the insurance amount was $200,000 the PS-58 cost per $1,000 of insurance would be $3.21. For the year in which the insurance was purchased, assuming no cash value in that year, the participant would realize income of $3.21 for each $1,000 of insurance or $642. Suppose that in year two, the insurance policy has $2,000 in cash value. In that year, the participant would realize income as follows:

(Face amount of insurance − cash value) /1,000 = ($200,000 − $2,000) / 1,000 = 198

198 × PS-58 of $3.41 (the participant is now 36) = Taxable income of $675.18

Loans to Participants

The availability of loans is another optional benefit and may be included if the employer chooses (see Chapter 8). A participant's benefits are used to secure the loan generally limiting the maximum loan to the lesser of 50% of vested benefits or $50,000. The loan must be repaid over no more than five years with interest at a reasonable rate. If the loan is used to purchase a primary residence, the loan may be for a period in excess of five years although this is not a practical option since the employee may terminate employment before the loan is fully repaid. In addition, the plan may issue a loan of no more than $10,000 even if the participant's account balance is not sufficient security if additional security is provided. This is not a practical option.

Plan Administrator

The general belief is that the third-party administrator, i.e., the pension consulting firm that provides the administrative services, is the administrator. This is incorrect. For purposes of the Employee Retirement Income Security Act of 1974 (ERISA), the plan administrator is the employer that sponsors the plan unless the employer formally designates another party to serve as plan administrator, e.g., a committee made up of employees and management. The plan administrator is responsible for several administrative functions, most of which are carried out by the third-party administrator hired by the ERISA plan administrator.

Plan Number

Each plan adopted by an employer is assigned a sequential plan number. If, for example, an employer adopted a profit-sharing plan years ago, terminated that plan and at a later date adopted a new 401(k) plan, the new plan would be plan number 002. Incorrectly numbering plans will cause confusion when IRS reviews the Form 5500 and lost time when attempting to correct the error.

Plan Year

The plan year can be any 12-month period. Usually the plan year is chosen to coincide with the employer's tax year, but that is not required. In some cases, there are financial planning opportunities available to the employer when the plan year and the tax year of the employer are different, e.g., the timing of a required contribution in a pension plan can be delayed until the employer knows the availability of cash to fund the plan (DB, money purchase, target benefit, cash balance). Funding regulations require that a contribution to a pension plan be made no later than 8½ months after the end of the plan year. If both the plan year and tax year end December 31, the contribution would be due by September 15 of the next year. If the plan year ended after the tax year, for example March 31, an additional three months would be available to fund the plan.

Retirement Age

In smaller companies, the choice of retirement age impacts vesting, since a participant must be 100% vested at retirement age regardless of service. It impacts the amount of the contribution in plans that base contributions on age (DB, target benefit, age-weighted profit-sharing plan). In larger companies, the choice of retirement age may be a function of company policy in addition to the impact on vesting.

Vesting

The vesting schedule determines the portion of a participant's benefit that is nonforfeitable in the event of termination of employment, either voluntarily or involuntarily. The most common vesting schedules are 100% immediate after two years, graded vesting beginning in year three at 20% and increasing each year by an additional 20% until 100% vested in year seven, and graded vesting beginning in year two at 20% and increasing each year by 20% until 100% vested in year six (required for top-heavy plans, see Chapter 9).

ADOPTING A QUALIFIED PLAN

The last step in the process is the adopting resolution. The employer must execute a resolution adopting the plan, and the plan document must be executed within the tax year for which the employer wishes to take the tax deduction. This is also true of plan amendments, which must be executed by the end of the tax year and plan year to which they apply. If a plan amendment has the effect of reducing contributions or benefits, there is another issue: When does an employee have a right to receive the original unreduced benefits? Generally, in a pension plan the employee has a right to the benefit or contribution once he or she works 1,000 hours. An amendment reducing benefits or contributions must be adopted prior to that date; otherwise, the employee is entitled to the higher benefits or contributions for that year. In a profit-sharing plan, the employee is considered to have a right to share in the contribution if he or she is an eligible employee as defined under the eligibility requirements of the plan, i.e., the age and service requirements, unless the plan requires employment on the last day of the plan year or a year of service during the plan year before an employee can share in the contribution.

If the employer's qualified plan is audited, an IRS agent will certainly ask for a copy of the plan document and all amendments. All too often, the agent sees prototype documents that have never been signed. All or most of the blanks may be filled in, but the adoption agreement was never executed by an officer of the employer adopting the plan. This employer does not have a qualified plan. Also, it is advisable to keep a copy of the opinion letter or determination letter, depending on whether the plan is a prototype, volume submitter or custom document.

Many rules for qualified plans have exceptions. One of those exceptions is the remedial amendment period. Several times over the past 15-plus years, Congress has passed legislation that changes the rules that regulate qualified plans. Once the legislation is passed, it is the responsibility of IRS to publish its interpretation of those changes and offer guidance necessary to update the various plan documents to comply with the changes. While IRS is developing this language, existing plans are required to comply in operation (i.e., follow the new rules), but they may wait until IRS issues the language before they actually update the plan documents. A perfect example of the exception was the Tax Reform Act of 1986 (TRA 86). Congress mandated that IRS provide the necessary guidance by February 1988 and that employers adopt the necessary amendments by the end of the 1989 plan year. Until then, plan sponsors had to comply with the new rules but could not amend their plan until the guidance was issued. The actual guidance from IRS was issued in 1994. In practice, many employers were operating their plans to comply with the new rules but not consistent with their plan documents. In the absence of the remedial amendment period extension, this would have caused plan disqualification.

The eight years between the time Congress passed TRA 86 and the time IRS issued guidance created two complications. Prior to TRA 86, there was a limit on compensation that could be considered in determining benefits or contributions of $200,000 if the plan was top-heavy (see Chapter 9). This was changed by TRA 86 to $200,000 for all qualified plans. Suppose an employer adopted a money purchase pension plan that required a contribution of 10% of compensation. Because the plan document was not rewritten until several years after the change in the law, there was a conflict in determining a participant's contribution if his or her compensation was over $200,000 and the plan was not top-heavy. The document provided that the 10% should be applied to total compensation, but the law limited the 10% to $200,000. In operation, the law had to be followed. Could the participant sue the employer for the higher contribution? To avoid these types of issues, the employer would have to adopt an interim amendment covering conflicting rules like this.

The second problem arose if the employer chose to terminate its plan prior to the issuance of IRS guidance necessary to update the plan. Revenue Procedures 97-41 and 98-14 reiterated IRS Notice 87-57 to the effect that, if a plan is terminated before the expiration of the remedial amendment period, it must be amended to comply with the changes that have an effective date prior to the date of termination. If the plan is submitted to IRS for review and approval upon plan termination (see Chapter 15 for a discussion of plan terminations), in many cases IRS will provide sample language to amend the plan. Although submission to IRS upon termination of a qualified plan is voluntary, in this case it almost becomes mandatory because there is no other source for acceptable language to amend the plan to comply with these changes. This situation exists again today with the so-called GUST amendments. IRS extended the remedial amendment period for these changes to the end of the 12th month beginning after the date the approval letter is issued to the prototype or volume submitter sponsor (the financial organization or institution offering the prototype or master plan document). This extended remedial amendment period is only available if the prototype or volume submitter sponsor submitted its specimen plan by December 31, 2000. For employers that have adopted these prototype or volume submitter plans, the list of sponsors that submitted their plans on a timely basis can be found on IRS Web site at irs.gov/ep. In Revenue Procedure 2002-73 the deadline was extended further to the later of the above deadline or September 30, 2003.

In the recent changes under GUST, there are several options available to the employer to comply with some of these new laws (e.g., how highly compensated employees will be defined, how 401(k) plans will be tested for nondiscrimination and how minimum distributions will be administered for less-than-5% owners who continue to work past age 70½). Because of the various options available to satisfy the rules, it is very important that the employer keep detailed records as to how the plan was operated so that when it is amended, the amended plan complies with the prior operation of the plan. These types of document issues, which are very complex and beyond the scope of this book, should be discussed with the client's document provider.

(GUST refers to the following: the Uruguay Round Agreements Act (GATT), the Uniformed Services Employment and Reemployment Rights Act (USERRA), the Small Business Job Protection Act of 1996 (SBJPA), the Taxpayer Relief Act of 1997, the Internal Revenue Service Restructuring and Reform Act of 1998 and the Community Renewal Tax Relief Act of 2000.)

In the midst of the restatement process for GUST, the Economic Growth and Tax Relief Reconciliation Act of 2001 (EGTRRA) was passed with additional substantive changes to many of the pension rules. Although many of the changes become effective for plan years beginning on or after January 1, 2002, IRS has established a separate remedial amendment period ending on the last day of the first plan year that begins on or after January 1, 2005. This extension creates problems similar to those discussed for the GUST restatement, i.e., the plan document is different than the operation of the plan. An example of this dilemma is a change that now allows the use of employer matching contributions to satisfy the top-heavy rules (see Chapter 9). Prior to EGTRRA, if a DC plan (profit sharing, 401(k), money purchase pension, target benefit pension) was top-heavy, a minimum 3% contribution had to be made for each non-key employee. Matching contributions can now be used to satisfy that requirement, so the additional 3% that would otherwise be made may not be made. This is considered a cutback in benefits that would not be in compliance with the anticutback rules in IRC Section 411(d)(6). In order to prevent noncompliance, the plan would have to be amended to allow matching contributions to be used to satisfy top-heavy rules before any non-key employee could be entitled to a top-heavy contribution, i.e., before the last day of the 2002 plan year when the top-heavy contribution would have been required, rather than the extended remedial amendment period defined previously.

Once the decision has been made as to the type of document to use when adopting the plan, the next step is choosing the specific plan type. Chapter 3 will provide an overview of the various plan types, the benefit and contribution limits and the timing requirements for contributions.

Summary of Plan Types, Limitations and Deductions

Chapter 3

The most widely accepted benefit of a qualified retirement plan is the deductibility of the plan sponsor's and, in some plans, the participants' contributions. The rules governing deductibility, funding requirements and benefit limitations are specific to the type of plan. This chapter addresses those rules specifically as they apply to defined contribution (DC) plans and general rules for defined benefit (DB) plans. Chapter 6 will cover funding and other specific plan issues in more detail as they relate to DB plans.

TIMING OF CONTRIBUTIONS

The basic rules of tax deductibility dictate that the plan contribution must be made by the due date of the plan sponsor's (the employer's) tax return, including extensions. Consider the following example:

Tax year ends	12/31/2003
Due date of tax return	3/15/2004
Extended due date of tax return	9/15/2004

In this case, the contribution would be considered timely if deposited on or before September 15, 2004 even if the tax return is filed before the contribution is made if the employer is on the accrual method. If the employer is on the cash basis, the contribution must be made by the date the tax return is filed. This assumes that the employer has a valid extension to file the return and designates that the contribution was made with respect to the prior year. In one case, the employer mailed the contribution to the trustee of the plan. Because the postmark on the envelope was before the extended due date of the tax return, the Internal Revenue Service (IRS) ruled that the contribution was timely. Although these rules apply for deductibility, they do not apply for minimum funding standards.

Minimum funding standards define the minimum contribution required to satisfy benefits provided for in DB plans (see Chapter 6) or contributions to a money purchase or target benefit plan (see Chapter 4). If the minimum funding standards are not satisfied, IRS may levy a 10% excise tax. If the deficiency is not corrected, an additional excise tax of 100% may be levied.

All pension plans—money purchase, target benefit and DB plans—are subject to minimum funding standards. To satisfy the minimum funding standards in these plans, the contribution must be made by 8½ months after the end of the plan year. Chapter 2 discusses the determination of the plan year and concluded that the most common choice was to establish a plan year to be the same 12-month period as the employer's tax year. Here is another situation that supports that choice:

Employer's tax year ends	12/31/2003
Tax return due date	3/15/2004
Extended tax return due date	9/15/2004
Pension plan year ends	6/30/2003
Minimum funding standards due date	3/15/2004

Even though, for deduction purposes, the contribution can be made as late as September 15, 2004, the employer must fund the plan no later than March 15, 2004 to satisfy the minimum funding standards. If the minimum funding standards are not satisfied by the due date, a 10% excise tax is imposed. If the deficiency is not corrected by the earlier of the date of mailing of a notice of deficiency by IRS or the date on which the 10% tax is assessed, an additional excise tax of 100% may be imposed on the employer.

For a DC plan (money purchase plan or target benefit plan) the minimum funding standard is the contribution percentage defined in the plan, e.g., 10% of compensation, or, in the case of a target benefit plan, the contribution necessary to fund the theoretical benefit (see Chapter 4).

On another note, a tax court case substantiated that contributions made with respect to compensation earned after the end of the employer's tax year are not deductible in that prior tax year. This issue is of particular importance in 401(k) plans, where the plan year ends December 31 but the employer's tax year ends on a month other than December 31, e.g., September 30. If the employer makes a matching contribution for the plan year ending December 31, 2004, the portion attributable to employee compensation earned after September 30, 2004 would not be deductible until the tax year ending September 30, 2005 as illustrated below (assuming the deferral and salary occur evenly over the year):

Employee salary	$40,000	Employee deferral	$4,000
Fourth quarter salary	$10,000	Fourth quarter deferral	$ 500
Matching contribution	$ 2,000		

In the above example, the matching contribution for the fourth quarter, $500, would not be deductible for the employer's tax year ending September 30, 2004 but would have to be carried over the following tax year. This would be an ongoing adjustment every year. The deduction for the matching contribution would be the total of the last quarter of the prior plan year and the first three quarters of the current plan year for each tax year.

PROFIT-SHARING PLAN LIMITATIONS

The limit on deductions to a profit-sharing plan is 25% of compensation. Two questions have to be asked and answered to calculate this limit: Over what period is compensation measured? Whose compensation should be included? The answer to the first question is based on the employer's tax year. The 25% limit is applied to compensation earned during the employer's tax year ending with or within the plan year. The effect of different periods being used for the employer's tax year and the plan year is as follows:

Employer's tax year-end	12/31/2004
Compensation for 12 months ending 12/31/04	$300,000
Plan year-end	6/30/2005
Compensation for 12 months ending 6/30/05	$400,000

For the plan year ending June 30, 2005, the maximum deduction would be $75,000, i.e., 25% of the employer's tax year (December 31, 2004) compensation ending within the plan year (June 30, 2005) or $300,000. If a contribution is made in error based on the plan year compensation of $400,000, there would be a nondeductible contribution of $25,000 ([$400,000 × 25%] − [$300,000 × 25%]). This nondeductible contribution would be subject to a 10% excise tax but could be carried over and deducted in the next tax year. This assumes that the contributions made *during* the 2004 tax year plus any prior nondeductible contributions are in excess of the maximum deduction of $75,000.

Although the Employee Retirement Income Security Act of 1974 (ERISA) requires that plan contributions may not inure to the benefit of the employer, a contribution to a DB plan made as a result of a mistake of fact may be returned to the employer. If a contribution is conditioned upon the deductibility of the contribution under Internal Revenue Code Section 404, then to the extent the deduction is disallowed, the contribution may be returned to the employer within one year after the disallowance of the deduction. For ease of processing, IRS has established a rule allowing for the return of *de minimis* contributions of up to $25,000 without an IRS ruling if the plan specifically provides in the plan document that contributions, to the extent not deductible, may be returned to the employer.

The next question is: whose compensation is to be included? Treasury regulations say, in determining whose compensation to include, ". . . the limitation shall be based on the compensation otherwise paid or accrued by the employer during such taxable year of the employer to the employees who, in such taxable year of the employer, are beneficiaries of the trust funds accumulated under the plan." This implies that the compensation for all participants who share in the contribution or have an existing account balance in the plan (trust funds accumulated under the plan) is considered in determining the total compensation on which the 25% limit is based; however, additional research proves this conclusion wrong. Revenue Ruling 65-295 deals with a profit-sharing plan that required the employee to be employed on the last day of the plan year to be eligible to share in the employer's contribution. IRS position in this revenue ruling is that the terminated employee's compensation is not included in the total plan compensation for purposes of determining the 25% deduction limit. The revenue ruling refers to Treasury Regulations Section 1.404(a)-9(g), which shows an example of the calculation of the 15% limit (pre-2002 limit). There is a footnote on the line listing compensation that reads, "Compensation otherwise paid or accrued during the year to the employees who are beneficiaries of trust funds accumulated under the plan in the year." The plan in question does not accumulate funds in the year (contributions) for employees terminated during the year and therefore compensation attributable to those employees is not included in the 15% limit in the example. This guideline on the calculation of the limit on deductions is mandatory under Treasury Regulations Section 1.404(a)-9(g) in all profit-sharing plans. Furthermore, the 25% limit is still based on total compensation even if it is defined, for purposes of allocating contributions, to be less than total compensation (see Chapter 2).

A profit-sharing plan contribution may also be made and deducted on behalf of permanently and totally disabled employees. A contribution may be made in the case of a participant in any DC plan who is permanently and totally disabled (as defined in IRC Section 22(e)(3)) and who is not a highly compensated employee (HCE). The term *participant's compensation* means the compensation the participant would have received for the year if the participant had been paid at the rate of compensation paid immediately before becoming permanently and totally disabled. Amounts contributed must be nonforfeitable when made.

Although the contribution to a profit-sharing plan is discretionary, some plans may require that the plan sponsor (the employer) has a profit before making a contribution. In some cases employees may not receive a contribution when a profit-sharing plan is adopted by two or more affiliated employers (see Chapter 10) and one of the employers has a loss. The remaining employer may, if profitable, make the contribution and deduct it on behalf of the affiliated employer having no profits.

In addition to the preceding limitations, an individual's compensation is further limited to $205,000 in 2004 for purposes of determining contributions and benefits in all qualified plans. The limit is adjusted for cost-of-living increases in increments of no less than $5,000, i.e., a numerical increase of $4,999 has no effect and a numerical increase of $9,999 increases the limit by only $5,000.

401(k) PLAN LIMITATIONS

Although we refer to "401(k) plans" there is no provision in the Internal Revenue Code for a "401(k) plan." In fact a 401(k) plan is a salary deferral option included in a profit-sharing plan. Over the last several years due to the popularity of 401(k)-type plans the list of variations has expanded considerably. In addition to the traditional 401(k) plan we also have the SIMPLE 401(k), the SIMPLE IRA and the Safe Harbor 401(k). The limitations in a 401(k) plan are really a combination of profit-sharing limitations and salary deferral limitations. The maximum allowable salary deferral for 2004 is the lesser of 100% of compensation or $13,000. If the employee reaches his or her 50th birthday during the year, an additional "catch-up" deferral is available limited to $3,000 for 2004. These limits do not apply to the SIMPLE plans. The comparable limits for SIMPLE plans for 2004 are $9,000 and $1,500. As a practical matter, an employee may not defer 100% of their compensation. If compensation is $16,000 in a traditional 401(k) plan, a deferral of $16,000 would not leave any funds available to withhold for Social Security taxes.

These limitations all apply to the employee. In addition to the specific limitations for the 401(k) deferrals, there is a further limit for the employee called the *annual additions limit*. For the year 2004, that limit is the lesser of 100% of compensation, limited to $205,000 for 2004, or $41,000. The catch-up contribution is in addition to this limit, i.e., the limit for a participant aged 50 or older would be $44,000. Included in that limit are employee contributions, both before-tax and after-tax contributions, employer contributions and forfeitures (see Chapter 2). Again the practical limit would have to take into consideration other deductions from compensation such as payroll taxes, health insurance premiums, etc.

From the employer's view, the deduction limit is 25% of participants' compensation limited to $205,000 for any one participant. The salary deferral including the catch-up contribution does not count toward this limit. As an example, in a one-employee company, if the employee's compensation was $50,000, that employee could defer $16,000 (assuming he or she had or will reach his or her 50th birthday during the year), and the employer could still make a matching contribution and profit-sharing contribution of up to $12,500, 25% of compensation. This change became effective in 2002 as a result of the Economic Growth and Tax Relief Reconciliation Act of 2001 (EGTRRA). In a small company, the question of adding a spouse to payroll is now a valid planning device. In many small companies, the owner's spouse may assist in the office or in other tasks without pay. In the past, the cost to add a spouse to payroll was always too high due to payroll taxes vs. the benefits received from a retirement plan, usually some form of profit-sharing plan.

Owner's salary, age 51	$100,000
Spouse's salary, age 50	$ 22,500

Prior to 2002:

Owner's contribution	$15,000
Spouse's contribution	$ 3,375
Spouse's Social Security Tax (Employer and Employee)	$ 3,600 (approximately)

In Year 2004:

Owner's contribution	$44,000	($28,000 profit sharing, $16,000 deferral)
Spouse's contribution	$18,625	($ 2,625 profit sharing, $16,000 deferral)
Spouse's Social Security Tax (Employer and Employee)		$ 3,600 (approximately)

The various types of 401(k) plans will be discussed in more detail in Chapter 5.

MONEY PURCHASE PLAN LIMITATIONS

The deduction limit for money purchase plans and target benefit plans (see Chapter 4) is the amount necessary to meet minimum funding standards. This would be the amount required by the plan document to be contributed on behalf of each participant. For example, if a money purchase plan provides for a contribution of 10% of compensation, the sum of each participant's contribution (10% times compensation) would be the minimum funding standard. In addition, the amount that can be *allocated* to each participant is limited to the annual additions limitation as discussed above for profit-sharing plans, i.e., the lesser of 100% of compensation or $41,000 in 2004, including employer contributions, employee contributions and forfeitures. The deduction limit is 25% of compensation as discussed above, i.e., the same as for profit-sharing plans.

The funding for a target benefit plan is based on theoretical future retirement benefits, not a percentage of compensation (target benefit plans are discussed in detail in Chapter 4). The deduction rules that apply to target benefit plans apply to all pension plans, including money purchase plans and DB plans, i.e., the deduction is equal to the contribution necessary to satisfy the minimum funding standard.

The deduction for a pension plan (money purchase, target benefit and DB plan), unlike the deduction for profit-sharing plans, is not attached to only one tax year. The funding for a pension plan may be deducted in accordance with any one of three methods:

1. Deduct the contribution in the tax year in which the plan year begins
2. Deduct the contribution in the tax year in which the plan year ends
3. Deduct a pro rata portion of the contribution in each tax year that the plan year overlaps.

Example: The three pension plan deduction methods are illustrated below. Suppose the following is true for Company A:

Tax year	1/1/04 to 12/31/04
Plan year	5/1/03 to 4/30/04
Plan contribution	$75,000
Plan year	5/1/04 to 4/30/05
Plan contribution	$100,000

Under method 1, Company A would take a $100,000 deduction in its tax year ending December 31, 2004. Under method 2, Company A would take a deduction of $100,000 in its tax year ending December 31, 2005. Method 3 would have the company take the following deductions for the December 31, 2004 tax year:

4/30/04 contribution × [4 months (1/04 to 4/04) / 12 months (5/03 to 4/04)]

$75,000 × (4/12) = $25,000

PLUS

4/30/05 contribution × [8 months (5/04 to 12/04) / 12 months (5/04 to 4/05)]

$100,000 × (8/12) = $66,667.67

Total deduction for Company A for the tax year ending 12/31/04 $91,667.67

As a practical matter, both the prior year's contribution and the current year's contribution must be known before the deduction can be determined via method 3, which may not be possible, depending on the relationship between the tax year and the plan year. For example, if the plan year ends November 30, 2004, it could be too late to calculate the contribution in time for the employer's deadline of September 15, 2004 for the filing of the 2003 tax return. In a DB plan, however, the contribution may be calculated as of the last day of the plan year or the first day of the plan year. For the tax year ended September 15, 2004 the contribution for the plan year ended November 30, 2004 can be determined as of December 1, 2003 allowing for a pro-rated deduction.

DB PLAN LIMITATIONS

Since DB plans refer to "retirement benefits," the limits are also defined in terms of benefits. For the year 2004, the maximum benefit that may be paid at retirement is the lesser of $165,000 annually or 100% of high consecutive three-year average compensation, beginning at retirement age and payable for life. To be eligible for the maximum dollar benefit, i.e., $165,000 annually, the employee must have worked at least ten years for the employer. This benefit may not be paid earlier than age 62 without reducing the maximum benefit for the longer payment period and may be adjusted upward for retirement past age 65 to recognize the shorter payment period.

Once the benefit is determined, based on various assumptions including mortality, rates of return on investments, turnover (in larger companies) and several other assumptions, a contribution is calculated that will be sufficient with investment earnings to pay each employee the promised monthly benefit. A more expanded discussion of DB plans can be found in Chapter 6.

LIMITATIONS ON MULTIPLE PLANS

For an employer maintaining both a DC and a DB plan covering some or all of the same employees, there is an additional rule limiting deductions for the combined plans. That limit is the greater of 25% of the total compensation (limited to $205,000 per employee for 2004) of all participants, or the contribution necessary to satisfy the minimum funding standard for the DB plan. Nondeductible contributions during the tax year are subject to a 10% excise tax, although those contributions may be carried over and deducted in a subsequent year.

As a practical matter, this limitation has to be considered when the employer adopts a DB plan and a 401(k) plan. Although the employee deferrals do not count against the 25% limit, any matching contribution or mandatory contribution necessary to satisfy the requirements of a safe harbor 401(k) plan may not be deductible.

Example:

Total participant compensation 2003	$800,000
DB contribution 2003	$175,000
Matching contribution 2003	$ 25,000
Total participant compensation 2004	$840,000
DB contribution 2004	$210,000
Matching contribution 2004	$ 30,000

In the year 2003, the sum of the DB contribution and the employer matching contribution is within the 25% deduction limit. In 2004, however, the sum of the DB contribution and the employer matching contribution is $30,000 in excess of the 25% limit. That excess contribution would be subject to a 10% excise tax.

When two DC plans are adopted by the same employer, e.g., a profit-sharing and a money purchase pension plan, the maximum deduction is the same as the limits for either plan, i.e., 25% of plan compensation, as described above. The maximum allocation to any participant is the lesser of 100% of the total compensation (limited to $205,000 per employee for 2004) or $41,000 (for 2004).

FLEXIBILITY OF CONTRIBUTIONS

One of the issues that concerns smaller companies sponsoring qualified retirement plans is the flexibility of contributions. Suppose the plan sponsor has a bad year. Is the contribution still required? The contribution to a profit-sharing plan is discretionary unless the profit-sharing plan includes a 401(k) provision that requires a contribution, e.g., a 3% contribution in a safe harbor 401(k) plan. Pension plans have mandatory contributions, the minimum funding requirement. Does that mean that once a pension plan is adopted, the sponsor is forever committed? No, there are several alternatives available to alter the funding requirements for a pension plan.

Generally, once benefits are earned they cannot be taken away, but future benefits can be reduced by reducing the rate of contribution in a money purchase or target benefit plan or reducing future benefit accruals (benefits earned) in a DB plan. Depending on the language in the plan document, benefits may be earned at different times during the plan year. For example, if a DC plan requires employment on the last day of the plan year, an employee does not earn the right to a benefit or contribution until the last day of the plan year during which that employee was still employed by the sponsor of the plan. If the plan requires a *year of service,* generally defined as a plan year during which the employee has completed 1,000 hours of service, the employee does not earn the right to additional contributions until completing a year of service. Based on these provisions, the plan could be amended before the time the employees earned the right to a benefit or contribution, i.e., before completing a year of service or before the last day of the plan year. If the plan document does not impose either of these requirements, the plan should be amended before the plan year in which the amendment is effective.

Any action that reduces future benefit accruals under a pension plan must be communicated to all participants at least 15 days before the effective date of the amendment—for example, if the contribution to a money purchase plan is reduced from 15% to 10%, or if the benefit formula in a DB plan is reduced from 50% of high three-year average compensation to 40% of high three-year average compensation. This is done with an ERISA Section 204(h) notice, which must be provided enough in advance to allow the plan sponsor to amend its plan before the employees have earned the right to additional accruals of benefits or contributions based on the preamendment provisions. The notice must explain the amendment and its effective date. This may seem redundant, but the notice is designed to clarify the effect of the amendment, i.e., that it reduces benefit accruals, and the effective date of that reduction, in more basic language.

A second choice in a DC pension plan would be for the owners of the company to irrevocably waive their contributions for the year. Usually, in small companies, the contribution for the owners represents the majority of the total plan costs. This would allow the company to reduce their contribution substantially for that year.

A last alternative is to apply to IRS for a waiver of minimum funding standards. This application must be filed no later than 2½ months after the close of the plan year for which the waiver is requested and no earlier than 180 days before the end of that plan year. Although this may be a tedious and costly process, it is less costly than potential penalties for failing to satisfy minimum funding standards. The general rule allows for waiver of minimum funding standards if the plan sponsor cannot make the contribution without temporary substantial business hardship and if meeting the funding standards would harm the interests of the plan participants. While evaluating the application, IRS will consider several issues, including:

1. Is the employer operating at a loss?
2. Is the employer's industry experiencing a serious downtrend?
3. Are overall sales in the industry in a downtrend?
4. Will the plan be continued if the waiver is granted?

Although these are not necessarily all the issues IRS will review, the main concern is whether the business hardship is temporary. If so, the waiver will likely be granted.

If all else fails, the plan sponsor always has the right to terminate the plan. This option is discussed in Chapter 15.

Defined Contribution Plans

Chapter 4

Defined contribution (DC) plans include profit-sharing plans, money purchase plans, target benefit plans and simplified employee pension plans (SEPs). Although SEPs are not considered qualified retirement plans but are actually a type of IRA, they will be discussed because of their popularity in very small companies. As part of the discussion of profit-sharing plans, the various methods of allocating contributions will be illustrated and compared including cross-tested, Social Security integration (permitted disparity) and traditional allocation methods. With the passage of the Economic Growth and Tax Relief Reconciliation Act of 2001 (EGTRRA) and liberalization of the limits for profit-sharing plans, there is no longer a need for money purchase plans. A discussion of how to most efficiently dispose of this type of plan will also be addressed. Target benefit plans, an age-based money purchase plan, also fall into the category of DC plans.

WHAT IS A PROFIT-SHARING PLAN?

A *profit-sharing plan* is defined as:
A plan established and maintained by an employer to provide for the participation in his profits by his employees or their beneficiaries. The plan must provide a definite predetermined formula for allocating the contributions made to the plan among the participants and for distributing the funds accumulated under the plan after a fixed number of years, the attainment of a stated age or upon the prior occurrence of some event such as layoff, illness, disability, retirement, death or severance of employment.

The term *plan* implies a permanent as distinguished from a temporary program, although the employer may reserve the right to change or terminate the plan and to discontinue contributions. The abandonment of the plan for any reason other than business necessity within a few years after it has taken effect will be evidence that the plan from its inception was not meant to be permanent and therefore was not a bona fide program for the exclusive benefit of employees in general. To be a profit-sharing plan, there must be recurring and substantial contributions for the employees. Although *substantial* has not been quantified in regulations, the minimum top-heavy contribution of 3% is a generally accepted guideline (see Chapter 9).

The original concept and basis for profit-sharing plans was for employees to share in profits, but that was changed by the Technical and Miscellaneous Revenue Act of 1988 (TAMRA). TAMRA eliminates the need for contributions to be based on profits and allows for the adoption of profit-sharing plans by tax-exempt organizations. As a result of that change, a "profit-sharing" plan is really a discretionary DC plan.

A *DC plan* is a qualified retirement plan in which *contributions* are defined in the plan document as a percentage of compensation, or contributions are deemed discretionary on the part of the plan sponsor and the method of allocating the contributions to the plan participants, when made, is defined in the plan document. Retirement benefits are based on each participant's account balance at retirement so DC plans are sometimes called individual account plans.

In addition to the typical profit-sharing plans, there are variations of profit-sharing plans that have unique characteristics. A *thrift plan* is the predecessor to the 401(k) plan. In a thrift plan, the employees were able to make after-tax voluntary contributions that would be matched by the employer. These after-tax contributions are now subject to the same nondiscrimination requirements that 401(k) plans must satisfy for after-tax employee contributions, i.e., the actual contribution percentage (ACP) test (see Chapter 5). In addition to the matching contributions, the employer was able to make discretionary profit-sharing contributions. A *stock bonus plan* is also a profit-sharing plan but makes distributions in the form of employer stock, although the employee has the right to request and receive a distribution in the form of cash. A profit-sharing plan may also be an employee stock ownership plan (ESOP) in which the funds are invested primarily in the employer's stock.

The determination of permanency in a profit-sharing plan is a facts-and-circumstances issue. If the plan has a fixed formula, i.e., the contributions are dependent on profits, the fact that no contributions are made in years with no profits generally does not adversely affect the qualified status of the plan as it relates to the permanency requirement. A business that fails to make contributions to a profit-sharing plan for five years because of net operating losses during those five years, resulting in the corporation's having no current or accumulated earnings or profits at the end of any of those five years, has not permanently discontinued payments. This is so only if the plan requires the corporation to resume contributions as soon as it has profits.

A fixed formula could read as follows: "A contribution will be made of 10% of profits in excess of $50,000." The formula and the method of allocation to each participant have to be set forth in the plan. With the change in the nature of profit-sharing plans to discretionary DC plans, the issue may change to a more limited interpretation of *permanent*. Permanency and recurring and substantial contributions are closely related.

Distributions from profit-sharing plans must be made at a specific future date or occurrence of a specific event. Generally profit-sharing plans provide for distributions at retirement age as specified in the plan, death, disability and separation from service whether voluntarily or involuntarily. If the plan document allows, distributions may be made to participants still employed from vested funds accumulated in the plan for at least two years and may also allow for distribution of all vested funds in a participant's account after five years of participation.

In an interesting case, three employees left a company before normal retirement age to work for a direct competitor. The trustees of the company's profit-sharing plan were not obligated to make accelerated, lump-sum distributions of vested account balances to the employees simply because the trustees had made accelerated payments of vested amounts in plan accounts to departing employees in the past. The trustees denied lump-sum payments to the three employees under a policy of not granting accelerated distributions to employees who went to work for competitors in cases where the amount of vested benefits exceeded $10,000. This policy represented a justified effort to preserve the plan assets because an exodus of key employees would reduce the growth and financial strength of the plan. By implementing this policy, the trustees sent a message to employees that they would not be rewarded with accelerated distributions if they decided to leave to work for a competitor.

As discussed in Chapter 3, the deduction limit for profit-sharing plans is 25% of eligible compensation for the tax year ending with or within the plan year. Because a profit-sharing plan, like all other DC plans, is an individual account plan, the assets have to be valued periodically to determine each participant's accrued benefit, i.e., the value of his or her individual account balance. This valuation is required to be done at least annually. In most cases, this is a simple matter unless the plan holds assets that are not easily valued, e.g., real estate, limited partnership shares or collectibles. These assets should be valued by an outside appraiser and appropriate documents in support of the appraisal should be kept on file with the plan documents.

Because each employee's benefit is directly linked to the value of plan assets, the security of the assets and the timing of the asset valuation are of prime concern. In response to a publicized case involving the theft of plan assets, the Department of Labor (DOL) issued proposed regulations that would make small plans (those with fewer than 100 participants) subject to the Employee Retirement Income Security Act of 1974 Section 103(a)(3)(A), which requires the engagement of an independent accountant to prepare an audit of the plan's assets. This could add significant additional costs to administer the plan. Under final regulations issued by DOL, the audit can be avoided if the plan satisfies all the following conditions each year:

1. (a) At least 95% of the assets of the plan constitute *qualifying plan assets* (defined later) or (b) any person who handles assets of the plan that do not constitute qualifying plan assets is bonded under ERISA Section 412, with the amount of the bond being not less than the value of the nonqualifying assets.

2. The summary annual report for the plan includes the following additional information:
    (a) The name of each regulated financial institution, e.g., brokerage office, holding qualifying plan assets and the amount of such assets held by each institution as of the end of the plan year

(b) The name of the surety company issuing any bond required under the regulations

(c) A notice indicating that participants and beneficiaries may, upon request and without charge, examine or receive copies of evidence of any bond required under the regulation and copies of the statements received from each institution holding qualified assets that describe the assets held by the institution as of the end of the plan year

(d) A notice stating that participants and beneficiaries should contact the Employee Benefits Security Administration if they are unable to examine or obtain copies of the statements or evidence of the bond.

3. When requested by a participant or beneficiary, the administrator makes available for examination, or provides free copies of, the evidence of any bond required by the regulation and the statements of assets from the financial institutions holding qualifying assets.

Qualifying plan assets are defined as:

(a) *Qualifying employer securities* as defined in ERISA Section 407(d)(5), i.e., stock, a marketable obligation or an interest in a publicly traded partnership

(b) Participant loans meeting the requirements of ERISA Section 408(b)(1)

(c) Any assets held by the following institutions:

- A bank or similar financial institution as defined in DOL Regulation Section 2550.408(b)-4(c)
- An insurance company qualified to do business under the laws of the state
- A broker dealer registered under the Security and Exchange Act of 1934
- Any other organization authorized to act as a trustee for individual retirement accounts under IRC Section 408.
- Shares issued by an investment company registered under the Investment Company Act of 1940 (mutual funds)
- Investment and annuity contracts issued by any insurance company qualified to do business under the laws of the state
- In an individual account plan (DC plan), any assets over which the participant or beneficiary exercises control and for which the participant or beneficiary receives, at least annually, a statement from a regulated financial institution (listed in items 3 and 5 in this list), describing the assets held or issued by the financial institution and the amount.

These new rules are effective for plan years beginning on or after April 17, 2001. One of the questions on Form 5500, the annual information return filed by most qualified plans, asks if nonpublicly traded assets have been valued by an outside appraiser. A negative answer to this question may very well trigger an audit of the plan.

For benefit determination, the timing of the asset valuation is essential.

Example 1: As of December 31, 2002, Employee Howard had an account balance of $75,000. Howard terminates employment, whether voluntarily or not, on September 30, 2003. The value of his account on December 31, 2003 is $66,000. How does the plan determine which value to use when it pays out the employee's benefits? Generally, the value of the account as of the end of the plan year in which the employee terminated is used. In this case, Howard would be paid out based on a value of $66,000—and surely would be a very unhappy person who may also have an uncle who is an attorney.

The only way to avoid this problem is to value the plan assets every time an employee terminates and pay them out immediately, which means a guaranteed increase in administrative costs. This is not a practical solution or one that is widely applied. Some plans base the timing on whether the employee has incurred a break in service (BIS). A BIS is a plan year during which the participant has worked less than 500 hours. In the example above, if Howard had terminated on April 3 with fewer than 500 hours worked, he would have been paid based on the account value of $75,000, the value in the plan year before the BIS, if this were the plan's administrative policy. Whatever policy is adopted, it must be applied consistently. Sometimes this can result in what appears to be discrimination. Consider the following:

Example 2: Rachel happens to be a highly compensated employee (HCE). Qualified plans cannot discriminate in favor of HCEs. Rachel terminates with fewer than 500 hours worked and is paid out based on the prior plan year's value. Between the time she terminates and the end of that year, the value of the plan's assets goes down 25%. Fred, a nonhighly compensated employee (NHCE), terminates with more than 500 hours worked and will be paid out based on the lower asset value because Fred's BIS will occur the following year. Is this discrimination? Technically no, if the plan's policy is followed consistently for all employees.

Because the contributions to profit-sharing plans are discretionary, this type of plan is best suited for a company with erratic cash flow. In any year, the employer may make a deductible contribution from zero to 25% of eligible plan compensation (see Chapter 3). This is both an advantage and a disadvantage. The price of the flexibility is the limit of a 25% deduction. What can the employer do in years with unusually high profits? The only alternative would be to adopt a different plan. The only plan that would allow for deductible contributions in excess of 25% of plan compensation would be a defined benefit (DB) plan (see Chapter 6).

Once the contribution is determined, the plan must provide a method of allocating that contribution to the eligible employees. The traditional method is based solely on each participant's compensation. More recent developments in profit-sharing plan design add the participant's age and service to the variables. The next section of this chapter contains sample plans illustrating the various options available to allocate the contributions in a profit-sharing plan.

TRADITIONAL PROFIT-SHARING PLAN

In a traditional profit-sharing plan, allocations are based on compensation (plain vanilla). In the sample plan in Table I, the total contribution is $92,200. All tables in these illustrations list the owners of the company first (the highly compen-

Table I

CONTRIBUTION ALLOCATIONS:
TRADITIONAL PROFIT-SHARING PLAN

	Salary	Age	Employer Contribution	Percent of Total Contribution	Calculation of Allocation
John	$205,000	60	$41,000	44.47%	((205,000 / 461,000) × 92,200)
Stuart	100,000	55	20,000	21.69	((100,000 / 461,000) × 92,200)
	$305,000		$61,000	66.16%	
Carol	$ 25,000	44	$ 5,000	5.42%	((25,000 / 461,000) × 92,200)
David	35,000	38	7,000	7.59	((35,000 / 461,000) × 92,200)
Helen	28,000	29	5,600	6.07	((28,000 / 461,000) × 92,200)
Fred	18,000	25	3,600	3.90	((18,000 / 461,000) × 92,200)
Steve	50,000	45	10,000	10.85	((50,000 / 461,000) × 92,200)
	$156,000		$31,200	33.84%	
	$461,000		$92,200	100.00%	

sated employees) and list the remaining employees separately (the nonhighly compensated employees).

This type of allocation provides a true employee benefit plan, in which employees share in the contribution based only on their compensation, i.e., the relative value of the work they do and their impact on the company's bottom line. This is consistent with the original purpose of profit-sharing plans, i.e., for employees to share in company profits created by their efforts. The next step up the ladder is an allocation integrated with Social Security, otherwise referred to as permitted disparity (vanilla fudge). The result is illustrated in Table II.

Using John as the example, here is the process:

Step 1: 3% × $205,000, +

Step 2: 3% × ($205,000 − $ 87,900) +

Step 3: 2.7% × ($205,000 + $87,900) +

Step 4: ($205,000/$461,000) × remaining total contribution (after steps 1 through 3 for all employees)

Table II

CONTRIBUTION ALLOCATIONS:
PLAN INTEGRATED WITH SOCIAL SECURITY

	Salary	Age	Employer Contribution	Percent of Total Contribution
John	$205,000	60	$41,000	48.5%
Stuart	100,000	55	17,434	20.6
	$305,000		$58,434	69.1%
Carol	$ 25,000	44	$ 4,186	5.0%
David	35,000	38	5,860	6.9
Helen	28,000	29	4,688	5.5
Fred	18,000	25	3,014	3.6
Steve	50,000	45	8,372	9.9
	$156,000		$26,121	30.9%
	$461,000		$84,554	100.0%

There are other options in designing a plan integrated with Social Security (permitted disparity). The application of these rules is as follows:

1. If the integration level is the taxable wage base (TWB), $87,900 in the previous table, the excess percentage can be up to 5.7% (step 2 plus step 3).
2. If the integration level is more than 80% but less than 100% of the TWB, the excess contribution percentage is reduced to 5.4%. (The 2.7% in step 3 would be reduced to 2.4%.)
3. If the integration level is more than 20% but less than or equal to 80% of the TWB, the excess contribution is reduced to 4.3%. (The 2.7% in step 3 would be reduced to 1.3%.)
4. The excess contribution percentage cannot exceed the base contribution percentage by more than the base contribution percentage.

AGE-WEIGHTED PLAN PROFIT-SHARING PLAN

The newer profit-sharing plan designs, including age-weighted plans and "comparability" plans, satisfy the nondiscrimination rules (see Chapter 9) based on cross testing, i.e., testing a DC plan based on benefits as in a DB plan (see Chapter 6) rather than contributions. If the plan sponsor takes the approach that they would like to provide each employee with a retirement income benefit of 1% of compensation, that plan would be nondiscriminatory because all participants are receiving the same benefit as a percentage of compensation.

Because each participant is a different age and is paid a different salary, those variables would have to be considered in determining the amount necessary to fund a participant's benefit. The issue would be to determine what amount would have to be deposited today, at x% rate of return, to accumulate to a value sufficient to pay a monthly benefit of 1% of current-year monthly compensation at the testing age (usually retirement age, e.g., 65). The interest rate to be used must be between 7.5% and 8.5% and the testing age is defined in regulations. Once funding is calculated for each participant, the profit-sharing plan contribution is allocated in proportion to each participant's amount as determined. The issue is really one of determining the present value of a monthly retirement benefit of 1% of the participant's compensation payable at the testing age, at 7.5%. Participants in the plan who are very young may have a contribution of less than 3% of compensation. If the plan is top-heavy (see Chapter 9), contributions will have to be increased to the top-heavy minimum contribution of 3%.

Applying this to the employee census in the earlier tables, Table III shows the result.

Table III

CONTRIBUTION ALLOCATIONS:
AGE-WEIGHTED PLAN

	Salary	Age	Present Value of 1% of Salary	Contri- bution Allocation	Top- Heavy Minimum	Adjusted Employer Contri- bution	Percent of Total
John	$205,000	60	1,427.9452	$41,000		$41,000	65.4%
Stuart	100,000	55	485.1939	13,931		13,931	22.2
	$305,000		1,913.1391	$54,931		$54,931	87.6%
Carol	$ 25,000	44	54.7472	$ 1,572	$ 750	$ 1,572	2.5%
David	35,000	38	49.6638	1,426	1,050	1,426	2.3
Helen	28,000	29	20.7230	595	840	840	1.3
Fred	18,000	25	9.9755	286	540	540	0.9
Steve	50,000	45	117.7066	3,380	1,500	3,380	5.4
	$156,000		252.8161	$ 7,259	$4,680	$ 7,758	12.4%
	$461,000		2,165.9552	$62,190	$4,680	$62,689	100.0%

The contribution for John is calculated as follows:

(PV of 1% of salary) / (Total PV of 1% of salary for all employees) × contribution

$$(1427.9452) / (2165.9552) \times \$62,190 = \$41,000$$

Because the contribution for Helen and Fred is below the top-heavy minimum of 3%, their contribution must be increased to 3%, bringing the total contribution to $62,689.

A comparison of this result to those of the prior sample plans shows two obvious and significant differences. First, the percentage allocated to John and Stuart has gone from 66.16% in Table I to 87.6% here. Second, the total contribution is $29,511 less ($92,200 − $62,689). The higher percentage results from the significant difference in age between John and Stuart and the remaining employees. The reason the contribution has gone down is that although John has reached his limit of $41,000 Stuart has not reached his limit of $25,000. Any additional contribution would have to be allocated to Stuart and the five remaining employees. The result of allocating $25,000 to Stuart is illustrated in Table IV.

Table IV

CONTRIBUTION ALLOCATIONS:
AGE-WEIGHTED PLAN, MAXIMUM FOR OWNERS

	Salary	Age	Present Value of 1% of Salary	Contri- bution Allocation	Top- Heavy Minimum	Adjusted Employer Contri- bution	Percent of Total
John	$205,000	60	1,427.9452	$41,000		$41,000	51.9%
Stuart	100,000	55	485.1939	25,000		25,000	31.6
	$305,000		1,913.1391	$66,000		$66,000	83.5%
Carol	$ 25,000	44	54.7472	$ 2,821	$ 750	$ 2,821	3.6%
David	35,000	38	49.6638	2,559	1,050	2,559	3.2
Helen	28,000	29	20.7230	1,068	840	1,068	1.4
Fred	18,000	25	9.9755	514	540	540	0.7
Steve	50,000	45	117.7066	6,065	1,500	6,065	7.7
	$156,000		252.8161	$13,027	$4,680	$13,053	16.5%
	$461,000		2,165.9552	$79,027	$4,680	$79,053	100.0%

Although John and Stuart end up with a higher total contribution, their share as a percentage of total plan contribution goes down. Another variable can affect the results: the interest rate used to calculate the present values. The interest rate and the present value have an inverse relationship. As the interest rate is increased, the present value of a number decreases.

Example 3: The present value of $10,000 discounted at 7.5% for ten years is $4,851.94, whereas the present value of the same amount for the same time period at 8.5% is $4,422.85, an 8.84% decrease. If the same results were compared over 20 years at 7.5%, the present value would be $2,354.13 and at 8.5% would be $1,956.16—a 16.9% decrease.

So how does this apply to the age-weighted plan? By using the higher rate of interest, the plan gives the younger participants a larger reduction in the present value of a benefit of 1% of salary and therefore a smaller percentage of the total contribution. This is illustrated in Table V, below, using 8.5% instead of 7.5% as in Table III.

Here, the plan was able to allocate the same $41,000 to John with a lower cost for the remaining rank-and-file employees. Although the HCE's share of the total

---

Table V

CONTRIBUTION ALLOCATIONS: AGE-WEIGHTED PLAN (INTEREST RATE CONSIDERATIONS)

	Salary	Age	Present Value of 1% of Salary	Contribution Allocation	Top-Heavy Minimum	Adjusted Employer Contribution	Percent of Total
John	$205,000	60	1,363.3431	41,000		$41,000	67.1%
Stuart	100,000	55	442.2854	13,301		13,301	21.8
	$305,000		1,805.6285	$54,301		$54,301	88.8%
Carol	$ 25,000	44	45.0729	$ 1,355	$ 750	$ 1,355	2.2%
David	35,000	38	38.6781	1,163	1,050	1,163	1.9
Helen	28,000	29	14.8487	447	840	840	1.4
Fred	18,000	25	6.8878	207	540	540	0.9
Steve	50,000	45	97.8082	2,941	1,500	2,941	4.8
	$156,000		203.2957	$ 6,114	$4,680	$ 6,840	11.2%
	$461,000		2,008.9242	$60,415	$4,680	$61,141	100.0%

---

contribution is 88.8% compared to 87.6% in Table III, the total dollars allocated to John and Stuart is slightly lower.

CLASS ALLOCATION PROFIT-SHARING PLAN

The last approach to allocating the contributions in a profit-sharing plan also uses the cross-testing method described earlier in this chapter and then, in accordance with IRS nondiscrimination regulations, limits the results so that the variation in benefits is within prescribed guidelines. One of these methods is referred to as *class allocation*. This allows the employer to define classes of employees and allocate a different percentage contribution to each class. The classes can be defined based on job description, geographic locations, departments within the company or any other objective business criteria. In the most basic form, the plan provides for two job classes: highly compensated employees and nonhighly compensated employees. In a larger company, this method can also be used to reward those employee groups that contribute the most to the bottom line of the company. Using the same employee data as in the preceding tables, Table VI illustrates the result of a class allocation plan.

In Table VI, the contribution is 100% of salary limited to $41,000 for John, 7.17% (rounded) for the NHCEs and whatever contribution can be allocated to

Table VI

CONTRIBUTION ALLOCATION: CLASS ALLOCATION PLAN

	Salary	Age	Contribution Allocation	Percent of Total
John	$205,000	60	$41,000	52.66%
Stuart	100,000	55	25,668	32.97
	$305,000		$66,668	85.83%
Carol	$ 25,000	44	$ 1,793	2.30%
David	35,000	38	2,511	3.22
Helen	28,000	29	2,009	2.58
Fred	18,000	25	1,291	1.66
Steve	50,000	45	3,587	4.61
	$156,000		$11,191	14.37%
	$461,000		$77,859	100.00%

Actual calculations carried to three decimal places. Projections for nondiscrimination testing are using 7.5% preretirement interest and UP84 mortality at 7.5% interest for determination of benefits.

Stuart while still passing nondiscrimination testing. Although there are three classes of employees, John, Stuart and all other employees (NHCEs), the plan could be designed with as many classes as are objective with a different contribution for each. This is used in larger companies to reward departments that are profitable while eliminating or reducing contributions for departments that are not. In this case, we've placed each highly compensated employee in a separate class to maximize John's contribution with as little of a contribution as possible for the NHCEs.

Rather than go through all the supporting calculations (see Chapter 9), let's consider the concept on which the result is based. We begin by making the assumption that our goal is to provide the maximum contribution for John primarily and then Stuart. In summary, that limit is the lesser of 100% of compensation or $41,000 (for the year 2004). For John, the dollar limit applies. For Stuart, although the dollar limit applies, the maximum contribution that would also satisfy the required nondiscrimination testing described below is limited to $25,668.

The first step is to project the contribution to retirement age with interest, in this case, age 65. The resulting amount is then converted to a life annuity payable beginning at the age of 65. The amount of the annuity is compared to the employee's compensation and the resulting percentage is used to determine whether or not the nondiscrimination rules are satisfied. In John's case, the $41,000 is projected to the age of 65 at 7.5%, resulting in a lump sum of $58,861. The lump sum is then converted to an annuity using an annuity purchase rate of $101.49 per monthly dollar of income beginning at the age of 65; i.e., for each $101.49 of accumulated value, a retirement benefit of $1 per month for life can be purchased. The result is $580 per month ($58,861/$101.49) or $6,960 annually. The annual benefit of $6,960 is then represented as a percentage of the employee's salary, resulting in 3.395%. This process is completed for each employee and the results of the highly compensated employees compared to the nonhighly compensated employees. As long as the result is within prescribed IRS guidelines, the nondiscrimination testing is passed.

SUPER-INTEGRATED PROFIT-SHARING PLAN

This method satisfies the nondiscrimination rules in the same manner as the class allocation plan in Table VI. The difference is in the determination of each employee's contribution. Where the class allocation bases contributions on which employee group an employee participates in, this allocation uses the concept of Social Security integration, i.e., different levels of contribution above and below the Social Security integration level (usually defined as the Social Security Wage Base, $89,700 for 2004). Although this is a method that is common in DC plans (see Table II), a super-integrated plan does not comply with IRS rules that must be applied to plans using Social Security integration; therefore, the plan must pass the nondiscrimination rules as described in the class allocation approach. An example of this would be a contribution of 5.37% of total compensation plus 28.25% of compensation in excess of $50,000.

The goal would be to allocate the maximum contribution to the highest paid owner, John, as in Table VI. The result of this allocation method is illustrated in Table VII.

Table VII

**CONTRIBUTION ALLOCATIONS:
SUPER-INTEGRATED PLAN**

	Salary	Age	Contribution Allocation	Percent of Total
John	$205,000	60	$41,000	59.5%
Stuart	100,000	55	19,497	28.3
	$305,000		$60,497	87.8%
Carol	$ 25,000	44	$ 1,343	1.9%
David	35,000	38	1,880	2.7
Helen	28,000	29	1,504	2.2
Fred	18,000	25	967	1.4
Steve	50,000	45	2,685	3.9
	$156,000		$ 8,377	12.2%
	$461,000		$68,874	100.0%

Actual calculations carried to three decimal places. Projections for nondiscrimination testing are using 7.5% preretirement interest and UP84 mortality at 7.5% interest for determination of benefits.

Another approach to allocating the contribution that uses nondiscrimination testing is based on a point allocation. In this approach, points are credited to each employee based on compensation, service and, in some plans, age. Each employee's share of the total plan contribution is based on his or her total points as a percentage of the total points of all the plan participants. The resulting contribution as a percent of salary for the HCEs is compared to the NHCEs and must be within prescribed guidelines (see Chapter 9).

Profit-sharing plans are a great deal more flexible than a discretionary contribution. Depending on the participants' salaries and ages and the employer's goals, several alternate plan designs are available, as illustrated above.

EMPLOYEE STOCK OWNERSHIP PLAN (ESOP)

Employee stock ownership plans (ESOPs) must be part of any discussion of profit-sharing plans. Generally, ESOPs are profit-sharing-based plans that invest primarily in the securities of the employer sponsoring the plan. An ESOP that is combined with a 401(k) plan is referred to as a *KSOP*.

Several studies have shown that ESOPs have a favorable effect on employee motivation and productivity. If the employee's retirement benefit is linked to the performance of the employer, he or she is more likely to be motivated to improve that performance. On the other hand, linking the employee's retirement benefit to company performance is a riskier investment for the employee because a large portion of the employee's retirement benefits are now dependent on one investment. ESOPs can also improve a company's cash position because retirement plan contributions that would otherwise be made in cash are now being made in employer stock.

For privately held companies that have no ready market or will not be passed on to family members, the ESOP provides a market to sell the closely held stock and can solve a liquidity need for estate planning purposes. In some cases, a company can prevent a hostile takeover by adopting an ESOP, which would place a large block of stock in friendly hands. Some courts have taken the position that if the primary reason for adopting the ESOP is to avert a hostile takeover, the plan is not valid because it is not being established for the exclusive benefit of employees and their beneficiaries.

In the traditional ESOP, the sponsoring company contributes stock to the ESOP or the company contributes cash and the ESOP purchases the stock. As an alternative, the ESOP may borrow money, usually from a commercial lender, and purchase a large block of stock from the corporation or a shareholder. The stock serves as collateral for the loan and the employer is usually a guarantor of the loan. This is referred to as a "leveraged ESOP." As the employer makes cash contributions to the ESOP, the loan is repaid and portions of the stock are released and credited to the accounts of the plan participants. Because the contributions are necessary to meet the loan payments, the discretionary nature of a profit-sharing contribution is lost.

Once stock is allocated to a participant's account, the participant must have the right to vote that stock. If the security is a registration-type security, i.e., it is required to be registered under Section 12 of the Securities Exchange Act of 1934, the right to vote must apply to any matter on which a stockholder is entitled to vote. In a plan sponsored by an employer that does not have registration-type securities, the participant must have the right to vote to approve or disapprove a "major change," e.g., corporate merger, liquidation or dissolution. Some plans provide that each employee who holds employer securities in the ESOP has one vote regardless of the number of shares he or she holds. If this is the case, the trustee must then vote the shares in proportion to the result of the "one vote, one participant" rule. If, for example, 70% of the participants vote in favor of a major change, the trustee must then vote 70% of the stock held by the trustee in favor of the major change. If a participant or beneficiary has not given voting directions to the trustee, the trustee may vote those shares in his or her discretion for or against whatever issue is up for a vote.

Because ESOPs are profit-sharing plans, the limitations on contributions are the same as those that apply to any other DC plan. The maximum annual addition to a participant's account is the lesser of 100% of compensation or $41,000 in 2004, including employer contributions, employee contributions and forfeitures. For purposes of determining the annual additions in a leveraged ESOP, the contributions used to pay the loan—not the value of the stock transferred to the employee's account—are included. If the contributions allocated to the HCEs are not more than one-third of the total contributions, contributions applied to pay interest on the loan plus forfeitures of employer securities purchased with the loan proceeds do not count toward the annual addition limit.

Chapter 3 discusses the deduction limit in a profit-sharing plan. Traditionally, the limit is 25% of the compensation of eligible employees (limited to $205,000 in the year 2004) for the tax year of the employer ending with or within the plan year. In a leveraged ESOP, a deduction of up to 25% is available for any principal payments on the loan used to acquire the employer securities and an unlimited deduction is available to pay interest on the loan. In addition, the employer may deduct any dividends:

1. Paid in cash to the plan participants or their beneficiaries
2. Paid to the plan and distributed in cash to participants or their beneficiaries no later than 90 days after the close of the plan year in which paid
3. Paid to the plan and reinvested in qualifying employer securities
4. Used to make payments on loans used to acquire employer securities with respect to which dividends are paid.

VALUATION OF EMPLOYER STOCK

The basis for much of the litigation in the ESOP area is the valuation of the employer's securities. If the security is publicly traded, the value is easily determined. If the employer is a privately held company, the value of the securities must be determined in good faith, based on all relevant factors and reflect the fair market value. This is usually done by an independent appraiser each year.

Fair market value is the price at which an asset would change hands between a willing buyer and a willing seller when neither party is under any compulsion to enter into the transaction. DOL has made it clear that not only must the price of the security and the process by which the price is determined comply with the requirement of fair market value, but also the level of expertise of the parties preparing the valuation will be considered.

Two cases illustrate potential issues in the valuation of closely held stock sold to an ESOP: *Eyler v. Commissioner* and *Chao v. Hall Holding Company, Inc.*

Eyler v. Commissioner

Eyler, a majority shareholder and CEO of Continental Training Services, Inc., sold $10 million ($14.50 per share) worth of Continental stock to a newly adopted ESOP. Based on the facts, IRS determined that the sale to the ESOP was a prohibited transaction; the appropriate excise tax was assessed because Eyler did not establish that the value per share was valid and none of the fiduciaries named in the ESOP had made a good faith determination that the price per share was valid. Eyler appealed.

It was determined that the shares were valued based on an intended initial public offering (IPO) that never went forward as a result of a lack of interest. The underwriters had set a price range for that IPO of between $13 and $16 per share.

Because the IPO did not go forward, Eyler decided to establish an ESOP and sell the stock to the ESOP. An outside financial consultant arranged for a bank loan and the ESOP was formed.

The Seventh Circuit upheld the Tax Court decision that the stock was not sold at fair market value because:

1. The basis for the valuation was not for the purpose of a sale to an ESOP but for an IPO.
2. The valuation was not dated.
3. The valuation by the underwriters was not final but only a suggested range to be finalized at a later date.
4. The lack of interest in the IPO indicated that the share price was incorrect.
5. The value of the stock was lower after the ESOP was adopted: The ESOP reduced the company's cash flow because of contributions required to repay the loan; the company now had debt that it did not have before the ESOP; and the company's ability to borrow for expansion or to pay dividends was hampered.
6. The valuation did not take into consideration a discount for lack of marketability, even though the ESOP included a put option.

Chao v. Hall Holding Company, Inc.

Hall Chemical Company was the primary asset of Hall Holding Company, Inc. An independent appraiser, who was a Wall Street analyst specializing in chemical companies, was engaged to value the stock of Hall Chemical. Although a specialist, he had never performed a valuation for the purpose of establishing an ESOP. A loan was secured and stock of Hall Holding Company, Inc., not Hall Chemical Company, was purchased for the Hall Chemical ESOP.

DOL sued Hall Holding and related parties for breach of fiduciary duty based on their purchase of the stock without adequate investigation and for overpaying. The district court ruled in favor of DOL, holding that the defendants:

1. Failed to conduct a prudent and independent investigation
2. Overpaid for the stock by more than $1 million
3. Failed to provide the expert with complete and accurate information, because the appraiser was not advised as to the purpose of the valuation and that the purchase was of a minority interest; the expert was asked to value the stock of Hall Chemical Company but the ESOP purchased stock of Hall Holding Company Inc.; and last failed to advise the expert that the president of Hall Chemical Company had the rights to acquire 5% of Hall Chemical.
4. Failed to make certain that reliance on the expert's advice was reasonably justified, because Hall Chemical Company was valued but the stock of Hall Holding Company Inc. was purchased by the ESOP.

As a result, the court found that Hall Holding had entered into a prohibited transaction (see Chapter 12) and the fiduciaries were personally liable for any losses, e.g., the overvaluation of the stock.

It should be clear from these cases that an ESOP may not be an appropriate choice for a closely held company because of the difficulty in valuing the stock. In addition, the administrative costs are significantly higher than traditional profit-sharing plans due to the required independent annual valuation of the stock.

DISTRIBUTIONS

Distributions from ESOPs must begin no later than one year after the later of the close of the plan year that is:

1. The year the participant terminates employment upon attaining normal retirement age under the plan, death or disability
2. The fifth plan year following the plan year in which the participant otherwise separates from service.

These distribution options are at the election of the participant and spouse, if required (see Chapter 8). If the distribution is from a leveraged ESOP, this rule can be delayed until the close of the plan year following the plan year in which the ESOP loan is fully repaid. In the event the participant does not make a voluntary election to receive the distribution, benefits must begin no later than the 60th day after the close of the latest plan year in which the participant:

1. Attains the earlier of age 65 or the normal retirement age under the plan
2. Reaches the tenth anniversary of participating in the plan
3. Terminates employment.

Also unique to ESOPs is the distribution period. Unless otherwise elected by the participant and provided for in the plan, the participant's account balance must be distributed in substantially equal periodic payments, at least annually, over no longer than five years. If the participant's account balance exceeds $830,000 (for the year 2004), the distribution period is extended by one year for each additional $165,000 (for the year 2004) or part up to an additional five years.

> **Example 4:** If the participant's account balance is $1 million, the account could be distributed over seven years: five years for the first $830,000, an additional year for the next $165,000 (bringing the total to $995,000) and one additional year for the remaining $5,000.

Although distributions from ESOPs are subject to the same taxation rules as distributions of all other qualified plans, there is special treatment on the unrealized appreciation in the employer securities that are distributed. If a lump-sum distribution is made at the time of termination of employment, the employee has the option of deferring the tax on the unrealized appreciation on employer securities. The tax on the unrealized appreciation would not be due until the employee disposes of the stock. In addition, the withholding rules that usually apply to distributions from qualified plans do not apply to distributions of employer securities or to cash dividend distributions attributable to those securities.

When a distribution is made from an ESOP, the employee has the option of taking employer stock or cash. This is the right of the employee and may not be denied by the plan unless the employer's charter or bylaws restrict the ownership of the employer's securities to employees or to the ESOP. An exception to this rule is an ESOP adopted by an S corporation. In that case, the ESOP is not required to allow participants to demand the distribution in the form of employer securities as long as a cash option is available. Because ESOPs are not adopted only by publicly traded companies, there must be a facility for the employee to dispose of the employer securities at a fair price. In accordance with this rule, the ESOP must include a "put option," the right of the participant to put the employer securities to the employer or the ESOP, although only the employer can be required to purchase the put securities. This requirement adds the burden of maintaining a sufficient cash reserve for redeeming the stock.

DIVERSIFICATION ELECTION

Because an ESOP invests primarily in the securities of the sponsoring employer, each employee's retirement security depends in great part on the financial success of the employer. To guard against the possibility of an employee's account being adversely affected just before retirement, an ESOP must provide qualified participants with an annual diversification election period. Any participant who has attained the age 55 and completed ten years of participation must be given 90 days after the end of the plan year in which he or she attains the age of 55 and completes ten years of participation to make a diversification election. That same election must be offered for each of the next five succeeding plan years. In each of these election years except the last, the participant may elect to diversify up to 25% of his or her account balance reduced by any diversification elections made in prior years. In the last election year, the participant may elect to diversify up to 50% of his or her account balance reduced by any diversification elections made in prior years.

Example 5: Harold has reached age 55 and has ten years of participation in 2004 and is allowed to make the following annual diversification elections:

Participant account balance as of 12/31/2003: $500,000

	Value of Employer Securities	Diversification Limit	Calculation of Maximum Cumulative Diversification	Actual Diversification
2004	$500,000	$125,000 (25%)	($500,000 × 25%)	$100,000
2005	$420,000	$130,000 (25%)	([$420,000 + $100,000] × 25%)	None
2006	$480,000	$145,000 (25%)	([$480,000 + $100,000] × 25%)	None
2007	$560,000	$165,000 (25%)	([$560,000 + $100,000] × 25%)	$ 50,000
2008	$630,000	$195,000 (25%)	([$630,000 + $150,000] × 25%)	None
2009	$700,000	$425,000 (50%)	([$700,000 + $150,000] × 50%)	$275,000
			Total diversified	**$425,000**

BENEFITS TO STOCKHOLDERS

ESOPs adopted by closely held companies offer the stockholders some valuable benefits. A stockholder of a closely held company who sells his or her stock to an ESOP and makes an election on his or her tax return may defer the recognition of capital gains on the sale of that stock. To qualify for tax-deferred treatment, the stockholder must sell "qualified securities" to the ESOP and comply with the following requirements:

1. The stockholder must elect deferral treatment on his or her tax return.
2. The stockholder must have held the qualified securities for at least three years before the sale to the ESOP.
3. The stockholder must purchase "qualified replacement property" within 15 months beginning three months before the sale to the ESOP and ending 12 months after the sale to the ESOP.
4. The ESOP must own at least 30% of each class of outstanding stock or 30% of the total value of all employer securities of the corporation that issued the qualified securities.

If these requirements are satisfied, the gain is deferred to the extent that the proceeds from the sale of qualified securities to the ESOP do not exceed the cost of the qualified replacement property. *Qualified replacement property* is defined as any security issued by a domestic operating corporation that did not have passive investment income in the prior year in excess of 25% of the gross receipts of that company and is not the company that issued the qualified securities that are being replaced. This planning opportunity not only defers the recognition on the gain but also creates a market for closely held stock and allows the exiting stockholder the ability to diversify his or her assets. As an estate-planning tool, this transaction creates liquidity by converting closely held securities to publicly traded securities. Generally, when the qualified replacement property is sold, the gain is recognized. An exception to this rule: At the death of the selling stockholder, no gain is recognized.

NONDISCRETIONARY DC PLANS

As part of the general classification of DC plans, in which the contribution rather than the retirement benefit is defined, the contributions to profit-sharing plans are discretionary. The only exceptions to that rule are SIMPLE plans and safe harbor 401(k) plans (see Chapter 5). Also within the classification of DC plans are money purchase and target benefit plans. The main difference between these plan types and profit-sharing plans is the requirement that contributions to money purchase and target benefit plans are mandatory. If the required contribution to a money purchase or target benefit plan is not made when due, there is an excise tax to the extent minimum funding standards are not satisfied. *Minimum funding standards* define the minimum contribution required to satisfy benefits provided for in a DB plan (see Chapter 6) or contributions to a money purchase or target benefit plan.

Contributions to all "pension" plans (money purchase, target benefit and DB) must be made by 8½ months after the end of the plan year to satisfy minimum funding standards. If the contribution is not made, an excise tax is imposed equal to 10%

of the funding deficiency. If the deficiency is not corrected, the Internal Revenue Service (IRS) has the authority to impose an additional 100% excise tax.

This chapter defines a *profit-sharing plan* in part as a plan "to provide for the participation in his profits by his employees or their beneficiaries." Because a profit-sharing plan was originally established as a facility for employees to receive benefits only when the company was profitable and at the discretion of the employer, it would be inconsistent to make the contribution mandatory.

A pension plan, including money purchase, target benefit and DB plans, must provide for "definitely determinable benefits" for its employees in order to be considered a qualified plan under the Internal Revenue Code (IRC). To be definitely determinable, the benefits must be provided to the employees through fixed (mandatory) contributions that are determined without reference to profits. *Definitely determinable benefits* can be loosely defined as the ability of an outside party to read the plan document and determine the contribution or benefit for the employee given the employee's compensation for the period, i.e., the determination of the benefit in a DB pension plan or the contribution in a DC pension plan is not subject to discretionary control. Consistent with the purpose of pension plans, withdrawals may not be taken before death, disability, retirement, termination of employment or termination of the plan. If the plan allowed for distributions during active employment but before retirement, the benefits would no longer be definitely determinable.

Table VIII is an example of a money purchase plan that provides for a contri-

Table VIII

MONEY PURCHASE PENSION PLAN, 25% OF SALARY

	Salary	Contributions	Percentage of Total Contribution
John	$205,000	$ 41,000	39.05%
Stuart	100,000	25,000	23.81
	$305,000	$ 66,000	62.86%
Carol	$ 25,000	$ 6,250	5.95%
David	35,000	8,750	8.33
Helen	28,000	7,000	6.67
Fred	18,000	4,500	4.29
Steve	50,000	12,500	11.90
	$156,000	$ 39,000	37.14%
	$461,000	$105,000	100.00%

bution of 25% of compensation. This type of plan does not attempt to favor any particular group of employees since the contribution for all employees is the same percentage of salary. After the passage of the Economic Growth and Tax Relief Reconciliation Act of 2001 which increased the maximum contribution in profit-sharing plans to 25% from 15%, the need for money purchase plans has been eliminated. Most of these plans have been merged with existing profit-sharing plans of the same employer or redesigned as profit-sharing plans providing the same contribution limit of 25% but eliminating the fixed nature of the contribution.

A basic money purchase plan does not maximize the benefits for the owners of the company. Because a contribution of 25% of compensation exceeds the maximum contribution (currently the lesser of 100% of compensation or $41,000) for John, this plan should be changed so the contribution percentage allocates the same $41,000 to John but significantly reduces the contributions for the rank-and-file employees. This is accomplished in a money purchase plan with a contribution formula of 20% rather than 25%, as shown in Table IX.

Table IX

MONEY PURCHASE PENSION PLAN, 20% OF SALARY

	Salary	Contributions	Percentage of Total Contribution
John	$205,000	$41,000	44.47%
Stuart	100,000	20,000	21.69
	$305,000	$61,000	66.16%
Carol	$ 25,000	$ 5,000	5.42%
David	35,000	7,000	7.59
Helen	28,000	5,600	6.07
Fred	18,000	3,600	3.90
Steve	50,000	10,000	10.85
	$156,000	$31,200	33.84%
	$461,000	$92,200	100.00%

By changing the contribution formula, John still has $41,000 allocated to his account but the total contribution for rank-and-file employees goes down by $7,800

($39,000 − $31,200). In the preceding plan, forfeitures should be used to reduce contributions even though a plan may allow forfeitures to be reallocated to the remaining participants. If the forfeitures are reallocated, John cannot share in those forfeitures because he is already at the maximum allocation of $41,000.

Earlier in this chapter in Table II, the application of Social Security integration was taken into account when determining the allocation of contributions. That design feature also applies to money purchase plans. If the money purchase plan is designed to be integrated at 80.1% of the 2004 Social Security wage base (this allocates the maximum to John and Stuart with the lowest cost for the remaining employees), or $71,850 (80.1% of $89,700), the result is in Table X.

Money purchase plans cannot be effectively designed to be heavily weighted in favor of the owners, so they are more likely to be used as a supplemental plan with a profit-sharing plan in smaller companies or by larger employers as the primary employer-provided retirement plan.

Table X

MONEY PURCHASE PLAN, INTEGRATED WITH SOCIAL SECURITY

	Salary	Contributions	Percentage of Total Contribution
John	$205,000	$41,000	48.38%
Stuart	100,000	18,013	21.26
	$305,000	$59,013	69.64%
Carol	$ 25,000	$ 4,123	4.87%
David	35,000	5,772	6.81
Helen	28,000	4,618	5.45
Fred	18,000	2,969	3.50
Steve	50,000	8,246	9.73
	$156,000	$25,728	30.36%
	$461,000	$84,741	100.00%

TARGET BENEFIT PENSION PLAN

In the preceding money purchase pension illustrations, the contributions are all allocated based on compensation. If two other variables, age of the participant and length of service, were added, the result would be a target benefit plan. The *target benefit plan* is a hybrid plan. It begins as a DB plan (see Chapter 6), i.e., the plan defines the resulting retirement benefit in the form of monthly retirement income. Once the contributions are calculated, there is no change to those contributions other than as a result of changes in compensation. Consider a parallel financial calculation that is used regularly.

John would like to save for a larger house. He determines that he can afford a monthly mortgage payment of $1,500. To do that, based on the price range of the house he can afford, he would have to put down a deposit of $50,000. John is hoping to accumulate the down payment in five years through an investment in mutual funds that he projects will appreciate by 10% annually after taxes. John has decided that if the mutual fund does not perform as expected, he will adjust his annual deposit so that at the end of the five-year period he will have the $50,000. Here is the result of John's plan:

End of Year	Deposit	End-of-Year Appreciation	Balance	Expected Balance
One	$8,190	$ 819	$ 9,009	$ 9,009
Two	8,190	1,300	18,499	18,919
Three	8,610	2,100	29,209	29,820
Four	8,801	4,560	42,570	41,811
Five	7,431	$50,001	$50,000	

In year two, the investment underperformed. Ten percent of the first year's balance of $9,009 plus 10% of the second year's contribution of $8,190 would be $1,720. The investment appreciated by $1,300, a shortfall of $420. To make up the shortfall, John plans to add to the third year's deposit, bringing it to $8,610 ($8,190 plus $420). In year three, the investments underperformed again. John expected a return of $2,711 (10% of the second year's balance of $18,919 plus 10% of the third year's contribution of $8,610) but only realized a gain of $2,100. The shortfall of $611 is made up in the fourth year's contribution of $8,801 ($8,190 plus $611). In year four, the gain was more than expected, so the fifth year's contribution was reduced and John has his $50,000 at the end of five years.

This situation is similar to the way a DB plan operates (see Chapter 6 for a full discussion of DB plans). A reserve is calculated that is sufficient to fund the employee's retirement benefit and each year the employer's contribution is adjusted based on actual changes in the operation of the plan, including employee salaries, rate of return of the plan investments and employee turnover. A target benefit plan adjusts only for salary. In the above example, the contribution would not change unless the "reserve" of $50,000 was changed. This would be parallel to a salary increase that would increase the benefit and therefore the contribution in a target benefit plan. If the salary does not change, the contribution does not change.

Because a target benefit plan is a hybrid, it must satisfy several conditions to comply with the nondiscrimination rules for benefits:

1. The employee's benefit must be determined based on a straight life annuity beginning at normal retirement age, usually age 65.

2. The employee must earn his or her benefit evenly over future service up to retirement age as adjusted for changes in compensation.
3. Service before the date of participation in the plan may not be credited to the employee for determination of benefits used to satisfy the safe harbor requirements.
4. The retirement benefit must be a flat benefit earned over no less than 25 years or a unit benefit per year of future service up to 25 years.
5. Forfeitures must be used to reduce employer contributions (satisfying definitely determinable benefits).
6. Employee voluntary contributions may not be used to fund the stated retirement benefit.

A *straight life annuity* is a guaranteed payment, usually from an insurance company, that is paid periodically, usually monthly, for the life of the annuitant, in exchange for a lump-sum payment at the inception of the income payment period. At the death of the annuitant, regardless of how many payments have been made, the insurance company retains the lump-sum purchase payment. If the annuitant outlives the assumed life expectancy, the insurance company must make up any shortfall and continue the income payments.

Following these rules creates a safe harbor target benefit plan that is nondiscriminatory by design. In a target benefit plan, the employee's benefit depends on the actual investment return and the contributions. It is not the amount of the benefit formula used in determining contributions. If investment returns are higher than assumed in calculating contributions, the benefit will be higher. If the returns are lower, the benefit will be lower.

TARGET BENEFIT PENSION PLAN FUNDING

Consider the funding of a target benefit plan. This discussion uses the following assumptions for a plan that is effective January 1, 2004:
1. Employee's salary is $45,000.
2. Employee's age is 45; date of birth is January 1, 1959.
3. Employee's date of participation is January 1, 2004.
4. Annuity purchase rate is $109.60 (this factor must be defined in the plan document), i.e., each $109.60 accumulated at retirement age will provide a retirement benefit of one dollar per month for life.
5. Assumed investment rate of return is 8%. If the actual return varies, the employee's benefit will be different than projected.
6. Retirement age is 65; retirement date is January 1, 2024.
7. Retirement benefit formula is 2% per year of service.

This retirement benefit would have the same result if stated as a flat 50% benefit reduced for all service less than 25 years (the safe harbor requirement). The first step in calculating the contribution is to determine the retirement benefit as follows:

(Monthly salary) × (years of participation) × (monthly benefit percentage)

($45,000 / 12) × (retirement date − date of participation) × (2%)

$3,750 × 20 years × 2% = $1,500 per month theoretical benefit

The next step is to calculate the reserve, i.e., the amount necessary to pay the promised benefit:

(Monthly benefit) × (annuity purchase rate)

($1,500) × ($109.60) = $164,400

The last step is to calculate the annual contribution necessary to accumulate $164,400 over the employee's future service, 20 years (January 1, 2004 to January 1, 2024), assuming an 8% return on the investment account. Using a financial calculator, the result is $3,326.39. Once this contribution is determined, it does not change unless the employee's salary changes. If the investments perform better than the assumed investment rate of return, the employee will have a higher benefit. If the investments perform worse, the employee will have a lower retirement benefit.

Suppose that in plan year two, the employee's salary goes up by 10%, to $4,125 per month; the benefit goes up by 10%. The increase in benefits is funded the same as a DB plan (see Chapter 6).

Step 1.

Increase the contribution for the first plan year by the assumed theoretical investment return of 8% to establish the "theoretical allocated assets" for the participant: $3,326.39 + ($3,326.39 × 8%) = $3,592.50.

Step 2.

Calculate the present value of increased benefits as represented by the increased theoretical reserve at retirement from the end of the plan year to retirement age:

[(original reserve) + {(increased benefit) × (annuity rate)}] / (1 + interest rate) ^ (years to fund)

[($164,400 + ($1,500 × 10% × $109.60)] / (1.08 ^ 18 years) = $45,255

Step 3.

Reduce the new present value of benefits by the current allocated assets as determined in step 1 to determine the remaining benefits to be funded: $45,255 − $3,593 = $41,662.

Step 4.

Use a financial calculator to determine the contribution necessary to amortize the remaining benefits to be funded over the future service of the participant as of the first day of the plan year:

Present value	= $41,662
Interest rate	= 8%
Years to fund from the end of the plan year	= 18
Payment	= $4,116.13

Although the employee's salary and therefore benefit went up by 10%, the contribution for that additional benefit went up by more than 20%. As the employee gets closer to retirement, it becomes more costly to fund an increase in the benefit.

The same process would be used if the employee's salary went down. If, for example, the employee in this case was on sick leave and had a $1,200 reduction in his or her annual compensation, the preceding steps would still be followed based on the reduced theoretical reserve at retirement amount. We use "theoretical" because the actual benefit depends on the actual investment experience.

The target benefit plan fits well in a small company with older owners that want to design a plan that benefits primarily the owners. Target benefit plans can also be integrated with Social Security; however, the guidelines for integrating target benefit plans are similar to those for DB plans not DC plans as illustrated previously for the money purchase and profit-sharing plans.

Although target benefit plans have the advantage of benefiting the older and higher paid owners of the company, they have a potential disadvantage in the way contributions are determined. The contributions required to fund higher benefits because of salary increases tend to escalate faster than the salary increases. This trend is called "back loading," i.e., contributions increase as the participant gets closer to retirement age. If not properly monitored, that contribution growth can get out of hand. Consider an employer with a key employee, age 50, whose salary is $75,000. Using the same benefits and assumptions as in the previous example above and assuming a 5% annual increase in salary, here is the schedule of annual deposits:

Year	Salary	Benefit	Deposit	Total % Benefit Increase	Total % Deposit Increase
1	$ 75,000	$ 815	$ 3,414		
2	78,750	855	3,607	5.00%	5.63%
3	82,688	898	3,872	10.25	13.39
4	86,822	943	4,224	15.76	23.72
5	91,163	990	4,684	21.55	37.20
6	95,721	1,040	5,280	27.63	54.65
7	100,507	1,092	6,052	34.01	77.25
8	105,533	1,146	7,058	40.71	106.72
9	110,809	1,204	8,390	47.75	145.73
10	116,350	1,264	10,196	55.13	198.63
11	122,167	1,327	12,744	62.89	273.26
12	128,275	1,393	16,581	71.03	385.64
13	134,689	1,463	23,099	79.59	576.54
14	141,424	1,536	37,962	88.56	1,011.86
15	148,495	1,613		97.99	

The deposit would be limited to the IRC §415(c) amount, currently the lesser of 100% of compensation or $41,000 for 2004. Benefits and salary are rounded to the nearest whole number.

To avoid this potential escalating cost, the plan can provide that there will be a dollar cap on benefits regardless of salary. The positive side of this analysis is that if the employee is properly educated about the operation of a target benefit plan, there is significant incentive for the employee to remain with the employer, reducing turnover and related expenses.

FLEXIBILITY OF CONTRIBUTIONS FOR MONEY PURCHASE AND TARGET BENEFIT PENSION PLANS

Because target benefit plans and money purchase plans are classified as pension plans, contributions are mandatory. What does an employer do during an unexpected business reversal, when it is impossible to meet the minimum funding requirements? If the downturn is recognized early enough, the plan may be amended to reduce contributions or, in the extreme case, the plan may be terminated (see Chapter 15). Any plan amendment must be done before the end of the plan year. If the participant has worked 1,000 hours or more, the contribution due for the year must be based on the benefit before it was reduced by the amendment. If the amendment is executed and effective early in the plan year, before the participants work 1,000 hours, it reduces the contribution for the current year. In addition, all participants must be notified of the reduction in future benefit accruals (contributions) at least 15 days before the effective date of that reduction. IRS privately ruled that a retroactive plan amendment that had the effect of decreasing participants' accrued benefits (contributions they had already earned), was permitted only as it pertained to HCEs participating in the money purchase pension plan, but not as it applied to all other participants.

Another alternative is to apply to IRS for a plan funding waiver. IRS will grant a minimum funding waiver to a DC plan, i.e., a money purchase or target benefit plan, if the following requirements are met:

1. Affected participants must, to the extent reasonably possible, be restored to the position in which they would have been had the waived amount been contributed, i.e., the waived contributions must be made up in the future.
2. The plan must specify how the amounts necessary to amortize the waived funding deficiency (the waiver payments) are to be determined. The waiver payments so specified should provide for an amortization of the waived funding deficiency over 15 years by level payments. The interest rate used to determine the amortization schedule must be reasonable.
3. Shortfalls or excess investment experience compared to the interest rate used in #2 above must be spread over 15 years rather than recognized immediately.
4. The plan must specify what benefit payments are available to participants during the time the waived plan contributions are being funded, i.e., the 15-year amortization period.

Essentially these requirements allow the employer to make up the waived contribution with interest over 15 years, thereby placing the employee in the same position he or she would be in had the contribution not been waived.

As is the case with all qualified plans, the target benefit plan and money purchase plan have their place, as long it is understood how they operate and their advantages and disadvantages.

SIMPLIFIED EMPLOYER PENSION (SEP)

A simplified employee pension (SEP) is intended as an alternative to qualified plans, particularly for small businesses. Other than the maximum limits on the amount of contributions, all IRA rules apply to SEPs since a simplified employee pension plan (SEP) is an individual retirement account (IRA) established and maintained by the employee to which an employer contributes.

The ease of administering these plans and the complete discretion permitted the employer in deciding whether to make an annual contribution are features that are especially attractive. An employer may deduct contributions paid to a SEP in an amount not in excess of 25% of the compensation paid to employees during the calendar year ending with or within the tax year (this is the same deduction basis as for profit-sharing plans, see Chapter 3). In applying the 25% ceiling on the employer's deduction for SEP contributions, the annual compensation of each employee that is taken into account under the plan for any year can be no more than $205,000 for the year 2004. The same participant limits apply as in profit-sharing plans.

Participation requirements for SEPs differ from qualified plans discussed in this chapter (see chapter 2). Eligibility requirements to participate in a SEP are limited to an employee who has attained age 21; has performed service for the employer during at least three of the immediately preceding five years; and has received at least $450 in compensation from the employer for the year. In addition, contributions may not discriminate in favor of the highly compensated employees. The ability to require one year of service and full-time employment, i.e., 1,000 hours annually, does not apply to SEPs making it necessary to include both full-time and part-time employees. Many small employers that sponsor a SEP do not apply the eligibility rules correctly. Consider this example:

> **Example 6:** Dr. Jonathan Jones began his private practice on January 1, 2003. At the same time, he adopted a SEP plan with his broker, signed the necessary IRS forms and made a contribution for that year. On July 15, 2003 he hired a receptionist. He told the receptionist that she would be eligible to participate in his SEP in 2006, the third anniversary of her date of hire. This is not consistent with the requirements that the plan treat all employees the same. If Dr. Jones participated immediately, his employees must also participate immediately requiring a contribution for his receptionist in 2003.

Contributions made by the employer to a simplified employee pension must bear a uniform relationship to total compensation, i.e., the same percentage for each employee (see Table VIII). Social Security integration, also referred to as permitted disparity, may also be used in allocating the contribution (see Table II).

Since a SEP is really an employee IRA that the employer contributes to, employees must have the right to withdraw funds from the SEP account at their discretion. This means that all contributions made by the employer are immediately vested rather than vested over several years as in a qualified plan (see Chapter 2) and may be withdrawn by the employee at any time. This is certainly not an incentive to retain employees.

The advantage of a SEP is simplicity. There is no plan document required, only a one-page IRS form. There is no annual filing required compared to qualified plans that require an annual Form 5500 and there are no administrative fees, since there is no administration. The disadvantage is the liberal eligibility and immediate vesting. If the plan satisfies the needs of the plan sponsor (see Chapter 1), then the advantages outweigh the disadvantages.

401(k) Plan Types and Rules

Chapter 5

During the past several years 401(k) plans have become the plan of choice in most companies. The popularity of 401(k) plans can be attributed to several factors, some of which are beneficial to the employer, whereas others are beneficial to the employee.

Factors beneficial to the employer include:
1. Lower cost of administration compared to some other plans
2. Shifting of investment risk to the employee compared to defined benefit (DB) plans, in which the employer bears the investment risk
3. Reduced contributions for employees compared to plans funded entirely by the employer
4. More flexibility in contribution amounts compared to plans with mandatory employer contributions
5. Higher perceived value by the employees because of ongoing involvement with investments and frequency of reporting to participants.

Factors beneficial to the employee include:
1. Easy-to-understand periodic reports showing contributions, investment gains and account balances
2. Tax-deductible contributions (employee deferrals)
3. Choice of investments to meet his or her needs
4. Ability to coordinate his or her contributions with his or her retirement goals
5. In-service distribution available for hardship
6. Availability of loans.

PLAN REQUIREMENTS

Contrary to common belief, there is no such thing as a 401(k) plan. What is commonly referred to as a 401(k) plan is a cash or deferred option added to a profit-sharing plan, i.e., the ability of each eligible employee to elect to defer a part of his or her compensation or to take it in cash. Because a 401(k) plan is really a profit-sharing plan, it is subject to the same rules and regulations to which profit-sharing plans are subject (see Chapters 3 and 4). The 401(k) option can be added to any of the profit-sharing plan designs discussed in Chapter 4.

To qualify under Internal Revenue Code Section 401(k), a plan must meet the following requirements in addition to the requirements of a profit-sharing plan:

1. The plan must allow an eligible employee to elect to have the employer make contributions to the plan or to pay compensation to the employee directly in cash.
2. The plan may not make distributions to the employee from employee deferrals earlier than separation from service, death, disability, termination of the plan, attainment of age 59½ or hardship of the employee.
3. The employee's right to his or her account balance, derived from the employee's deferrals, must be nonforfeitable.
4. The plan may not require more than one year of service for participation (see Chapter 2 for discussion of effective date of participation).
5. The employer may not condition the availability of any other employer-provided benefits, other than matching contributions in the 401(k) plan, on the employee's election to participate in the 401(k) plan.
6. The employee's elective deferral may not exceed the amount of the dollar limits provided in IRC Section 402(g): $13,000 in 2004, $14,000 in 2005 and $15,000 in 2006.
7. A traditional 401(k) plan must satisfy the nondiscrimination test with respect to deferrals and matching contributions.

Item 1 determines whether the deferral is subject to favorable tax treatment, i.e., a before-tax payment. The election to make the deferral must be made before the funds are currently available. If the employee has already received the funds or may receive them at his or her discretion, the funds are currently available and will be treated as a voluntary employee contribution includable in gross compensation, i.e., an after-tax contribution, and not as a pretax deferral.

In the practical application of this rule, it is essential that each employee who elects to defer a portion of his or her compensation make a *written election* before receiving the compensation. Generally, the plan allows the election to be a percentage of compensation or a fixed dollar amount from each paycheck. If a percentage is chosen, it would apply to all payments, including overtime and bonuses. Most plans allow the employee to change his or her written election during the year. Each time an employee changes the election, a new written election must be executed before the compensation to which the election applies can be withheld from salary. This may be twice annually: on the anniversary of the plan and six months later, e.g., January 1 and July 1 in a calendar-year plan, or more often depending on the plan's administrative rules.

PLAN DISTRIBUTIONS

Distributions from 401(k) plans are more restrictive than from any other qualified defined contribution plans. As indicated in item 2 above, distributions may be made on certain occasions. Some are common to most qualified retirement plans, whereas two of the distribution options are usually unique to 401(k) plans and need additional explanation: distributions relating to plan termination and hardship distributions.

PLAN TERMINATION

Specific rules must be followed when funds are distributed in the event of plan termination. The employer sponsoring the 401(k) plan may not establish a "successor" plan after termination of the 401(k) plan and distribution of the plan assets to employees. A *successor plan* is defined as any other defined contribution plan (see Chapter 4) maintained by the same employer. There is also a narrow exception to this rule. The new plan is not a successor plan if, during the 24-month period that begins 12 months before the termination of the 401(k) plan, less than 2% of the employees covered in the 401(k) plan are eligible in the new defined contribution plan. After 12 months have elapsed from the date the assets are distributed from the terminated plan, the employer may establish a new defined contribution plan with no restrictions.

HARDSHIP DISTRIBUTIONS

Hardship is defined as "an immediate and heavy financial need of the employee." To qualify as a hardship distribution, a distribution must be necessary to satisfy the immediate and heavy financial need (including all income taxes and penalties due on the distribution). Whether the distribution is necessary to satisfy that need is a facts-and-circumstances determination based on whether other assets of the employee and family members are available to satisfy that need. Although the employer may rely on a written statement from the employee regarding the necessity of the distribution, the responsibility still exists to confirm the representations of the employee if the employer has doubts. In addition, it is the responsibility of the employer to confirm the nature of the immediate and heavy financial need. Will the distribution actually be used for the financial need as represented by the employee? If, on audit, the distribution is determined not to satisfy the requirements of a hardship distribution, the plan can be disqualified.

As an alternative, the plan can use a safe harbor provision for hardship distributions. A deemed hardship distribution satisfies the immediate and heavy financial need if the distribution is for:

1. Uninsured expenses for medical care incurred by the employee, the employee's spouse or any dependents of the employee or necessary expenses to obtain medical care

2. Costs directly related to the purchase of a principal residence of the employee excluding mortgage payments

3. Payment of tuition, related educational fees, and room-and-board expenses for the next 12 months for postsecondary education for the employee, the employee's spouse, children or other dependents

4. Payments necessary to prevent the eviction of the employee from the employee's principal residence or foreclosure on the mortgage on that residence.

The distribution is deemed necessary to satisfy the immediate and heavy financial need if the following are satisfied:

1. The distribution is not in excess of the amount of the immediate and heavy financial need, including federal, state or local income taxes or penalties.

2. The employee has obtained all distributions, other than hardship distributions and all nontaxable loans currently available under all plans maintained by the employer.
3. The plan limits the employee's elective contributions for the next taxable year to the applicable limit under IRC Section 402(g) for that year, less the employee's elective contributions for the year in which the hardship distribution occurred.
4. The employee is prohibited from making elective contributions to the plan for at least six months after receipt of the hardship distribution.

Example 1: Susan makes elective deferrals of $2,400 from January through August of 2003. In September, she requests and receives a distribution under the safe harbor definition of hardship. In the year 2004, the IRC Section 402(g) limit is $13,000. The maximum Susan can defer for the year 2004 is $10,600 ($13,000 minus $2,400). She may not make any deferrals before March 2004, following the sixth month after the hardship distribution. If Susan chooses, she may defer the entire $10,600 from March to December if all the appropriate limitations are satisfied.

PLAN DESIGN FEATURES

Even though a 401(k) plan is a defined contribution plan, 401(k) plans have design choices that are unique (see Chapter 2 for general plan designs issues for defined contribution plans). Following is a review of these unique plan design features.
Salary reduction choices:
Each employee may elect to have his or her compensation reduced by:
1. _____%
2. Up to _____%
3. From _____% to _____%
4. Up to the maximum percentage allowable
5. A participant may elect to commence salary reductions as of _____.
   A participant may modify the amount of salary reductions as of _____.
6. Shall cash bonuses paid within 2½ months after the end of the plan year be subject to the salary reduction election?
   ☐ Yes
   ☐ No

These are the basic provisions to activate the cash or deferred election, the ability of a participant to make an elective deferral. The most common choice for the limit on deferrals is option 4, which allows each participant to choose the maximum amount allowed. The limit of IRC Section 401(k) defines the dollar limit as $13,000 for 2004. Prior to January 1, 2002, an employee's elective deferral was considered to be part of the IRC Section 404 deduction limit (see Chapter 3), i.e., 25% of the total compensation of plan participants. Effective with the Economic Growth and Tax Relief Reconciliation Act of 2001 (EGTRRA), for plan years after December 31, 2001, an employee's elective deferral does not reduce the IRC Section 404 limit.

To further encourage participation in 401(k) plans by lower income participants, EGTRRA also introduced a tax credit for elective deferrals up to $2,000. This tax credit is available for years after 2001 and before 2007 and is equal to a percentage of deferrals up to $2,000 based on adjusted gross income:

	Joint Return	Head of Household	Other
50%	$30,000 or less	$22,500 or less	$15,000 or less
20%	$30,001 to $32,500	$22,501 to $24,375	$15,001 to $16,250
10%	$32,501 to $50,000	$24,376 to $37,500	$16,251 to $25,000
0%	Over $50,000	Over $37,500	Over $25,000

Option 3 may be used to establish a minimum deferral to reduce administrative costs. Choosing option 2 in some cases would help the plan to pass the nondiscrimination test unique to 401(k) plans. If deferrals are limited to 6.35% for 2004, a highly compensated employee (HCE) with compensation of $205,000 for 2004, the maximum that can be considered, would be able to defer $13,000, the maximum for 2004. In the absence of that limit, this employee would still be able to defer the maximum, but another HCE with compensation of $80,000 would have to defer 16.25% to reach the same $13,000 limit. That 16.25% would significantly raise the average percentage of the HCEs and could cause the plan to fail the nondiscrimination test. This is discussed in more detail later in this chapter.

Option 5 deals with an election period. When may an eligible employee effectively begin salary deferrals? Most plans coordinate this with the effective date of participation (see Chapter 2). If the date of participation is the January 1 or July 1 after the eligibility requirements are satisfied, the election periods are the same. The election period may be once a year, every day of the year or some other in-between option. Whatever that election period is will apply only to salary earned and received subsequent to the election. This is an administrative decision that ultimately affects the administrative cost of the plan.

Option 6 concerns whether an employee will have the option of applying his or her salary deferral election to a bonus paid after the end of the year but with respect to services performed during the year. Although this may offer some planning opportunities to the employee, it may also increase the administrative costs for record-keeping and nondiscrimination testing.

NEGATIVE ELECTION

A relatively new development in the enrollment for 401(k) plans is the so-called negative election. Although this approach has been around for a while, it was just recently condoned by the Internal Revenue Service (IRS) in Revenue Ruling 98-30. Under a *negative election,* the employer automatically withholds a specified percentage of each employee's compensation when he or she first becomes eligible. Revenue Ruling 98-30 requires that the employee be:

1. Notified of his or her right to make a positive election, other than the automatic election including zero deferral

2. Given a reasonable period of time to make a positive election other than the automatic election
3. Allowed to revoke the negative election at any time in the future.

The notice also requires that the employee have an "effective opportunity" to elect not to have the negative election apply and be provided with "proper notice" of this opportunity. Because *effective opportunity* and *proper notice* are not specifically defined by the revenue ruling, it is the employer's responsibility to interpret these requirements. One possibility might be that the negative election withdrawal does not become effective until the first day of the second month following the month in which the notice is given. If, for example, notice is given on March 28, the employee's date of hire, the employee would have until May 1 to revoke the negative election or change it before it becomes effective.

The advantage of the negative election is a potential increase in the average deferral percentage of the nonhighly compensated employees (NHCEs), which would allow the highly compensated employees (HCEs) to defer higher amounts. In fact, a recent survey by the Profit Sharing/401(k) Council of America of ten companies that added negative elections (also referred to as *automatic enrollment*) shows participation increased significantly. The negative election also forces employees who would otherwise not save for retirement to do so, a positive result not only for the employees but also for the economy. On the other hand, the negative election tends to increase the cost of administration because of an increase in the number of participants, many with small account balances.

The issue of investment direction for those employees who are automatically enrolled and do not actively choose their investment options becomes a fiduciary problem. Should the employer place those employees' deferrals in the most conservative account, in a balanced equity account or in some other diversified portfolio of funds? There is no "right" answer, only the fiduciary guidelines set forth in the Employee Retirement Income Security Act of 1974 (ERISA) requiring diversification to minimize the risk of large losses and prudence, i.e., acting "with the care, skill, prudence, and diligence under the circumstances then prevailing that a prudent man acting in a like capacity and familiar with such matters would use in the conduct of an enterprise of a like character and with like aims."

Consideration must also be given to employee relations. In many cases, employees do not read the material distributed to them regarding their new employer's benefit programs. The employee who finds out that money has been withheld from his or her pay without consent could be upset. Some state laws prevent an employer from withholding any money from an employee's pay without the employee's authorization. It is not absolutely clear whether ERISA may preempt these state laws. One last concern is whether the plan document should specifically provide for negative elections and the amount to be withheld. Revenue Ruling 98-30 does not specifically address this issue. The conservative position is to include the appropriate language and submit the plan to the IRS for a favorable determination letter to protect the plan's qualified status.

EMPLOYER'S MATCHING CONTRIBUTION

The employer may determine matching contributions in a number of ways:

1. N/A. There shall be no matching contributions.
2. The employer shall make matching contributions equal to _____% of the participant's salary reductions.
3. The employer may make matching contributions equal to a discretionary percentage, to be determined by the employer, of the participant's salary reductions.
4. The employer shall make matching contributions equal to the sum of _____% of the portion of the participant's salary reduction that does not exceed _____% of the participant's compensation plus _____% of the portion of the participant's salary reduction that exceeds _____% of the participant's compensation, but does not exceed _____% of the participant's compensation.
5. The employer shall make matching contributions equal to the percentage determined under the following schedule (must also satisfy the general test under IRC Section 401(a)(4)):

Participant's Total Years of Service	Matching Percentage
_____	_____
_____	_____
_____	_____

Option 3 gives the employer the maximum amount of flexibility. Some employers may want the option of changing their match depending on the profitability of the company sponsoring the plan. They may even want to measure that on a quarterly basis. With this option, the employer can change the match as often as desired as long as appropriate notice is given to the employees. For example, the match may be announced by the 15th of the month before the quarter to which it applies. Depending on the change, each employee may increase, decrease or suspend his or her deferrals effective with the first pay period in the quarter affected. The example below compares the employer-matching contributions if option 2, 4 or 5 is used for a group of employees:

Example 2: For a sample plan using the provisions provided at the beginning of this section, assume the following:

- For option 2, assume 50%.
- For option 4, assume 100% up to 4%, 50% in excess of 4% and up to 8%. The blanks in option 4 would be filled in with 100, 4, 50, 4 and 8.
- For option 5, assume John has ten years of service with a match of 100%; Carol has ten years of service with a match of 100%; Dennis has five years of service with a match of 75%; and David has two years of service with a match of 50%.

Using these three options, the employer-matching contribution would be as follows:

	Salary	Deferral	Percentage	Employer Match Option 2	Employer Match Option 4	Employer Match Option 5	Allocation Rate
John	$205,000	$13,000	6.35%	$6,500	$10,600	$13,000	6.35%
Carol	50,000	5,000	10.00	2,500	3,000	5,000	10.00
Dennis	30,000	1,500	5.00	750	1,350	1,125	3.75
David	25,000	2,000	8.00	1,000	1,500	1,000	4.00

Since the match in option 5 is not uniform, it must be tested for nondiscrimination. The allocation rate column indicates the rate to be used in performing the general nondiscrimination test of IRC Section 401(a)(4) for the employer-matching contribution using option 5. To satisfy the test, the number of NHCEs with allocation rates equal to or more than the HCE rate must be 70% or more of the total number of NHCEs. In the example, the test is failed because only one NHCE has an allocation rate equal to or more than the HCE, i.e., 33% (one out of three), not 70%. By no means are these the only match alternatives. There is really no limit to the design variables that can be used. Generally, however, simple is better.

OTHER CONSIDERATIONS
FOR MATCHING CONTRIBUTIONS

Other plan provisions relating to matching contributions can include the following:

1. Matching contributions (a) ☐ shall or (b) ☐ shall not be used in satisfying the deferral percentage tests.
2. Shall a year of service be required in order to share in the matching contributions?
   ☐ Yes   ☐ No
3. In determining matching contributions, only salary reductions up to _____% of a participant's compensation will be matched.
   (a) ☐ N/A
4. The matching contribution made on behalf of a participant for any plan year shall not exceed $_____.
   (a) ☐ N/A
5. Matching contributions shall be made on behalf of:
   (a) ☐ All participants
   (b) ☐ Only NHCEs.

Under option 1, the matching contribution can be used as part of the actual deferral percentage (ADP) test (discussed later in this chapter) if the match is immediately vested. In many cases, this can make the difference in passing or failing the test. The disadvantage is a higher contribution cost if the employer experiences a high turnover because there will be no forfeitures of nonvested balances.

Option 2 relates to whether the plan will require a year of service for the employee to share in the matching contribution. A *year of service* is generally a plan year during which the employee has worked 1,000 hours. If a year of service is required, the plan might not pass the coverage test under IRC Section 410(b) (see Chapter 9). This is more likely for a small plan (fewer than ten participants) than a larger plan.

Option 3 offers a percentage of compensation limit, and option 4 offers a dollar limit on matching contributions if the matching option chosen does not provide for a dollar limit, e.g., a flat 50% match. Lastly, option 5 determines which group of employees will receive the match. A plan can always discriminate *against* HCEs.

QUALIFIED NONELECTIVE CONTRIBUTIONS

Qualified nonelective contributions are usually used to correct a failed non-discrimination test (ADP test). Plan provisions would include:

1. There shall be no qualified nonelective contributions.
2. The employer shall make a qualified nonelective contribution equal to ___% of the total compensation of all participants eligible to share in the allocations.
3. The employer may make a qualified nonelective contribution in an amount to be determined by the employer.

Options 1 and 2 are not practical to correct a failed nondiscrimination test because the amount necessary to correct the test will vary each year. The most common choice here would be option 3.

Consider the possible contribution sources in a 401(k) plan: employee-elective deferrals; employer-matching contributions subject to a vesting schedule; qualified nonelective contributions (QNECs); qualified matching contributions (QMACs), also used to correct a failed nondiscrimination test; employee voluntary contributions (after-tax contributions); and employer discretionary contributions, i.e., traditional profit-sharing contributions. Both QNECs and QMACs must be 100% vested and subject to the same distribution restrictions to which employee-elective deferrals are subject. Both QNECs and QMACs are employer contributions. QNECs are made to all eligible employees based on plan eligibility, e.g., one year of service, full time (1,000 hours) and age 21, whereas QMACs are made only for employees who are making elective deferrals. Employee voluntary contributions are elective after-tax contributions that may be made directly by the employee from a source other than salary deferrals. These contributions are subject to a similar nondiscrimination test as are salary deferrals.

CATCH-UP CONTRIBUTIONS

Although the catch-up contribution provision of EGTRRA was meant to allow women whose careers were interrupted to accelerate their retirement savings, it is an opportunity for any employee to increase retirement savings if he or she meets the eligibility criteria. The additional deferral is available to any participant whose 50th birthday occurs or has occurred by the end of the plan year in which the catch-up contribution is to be made.

It is not necessary to wait until the participant's actual birthday to begin the additional contributions, because the catch-up provisions consider any participant who reaches his or her 50th birthday any time during the year to have reached that birth-day on January 1 of that year. A catch-up contribution is in addition to an employee's maximum salary deferral considering all applicable limits. An example of applicable limits and restrictions would be the 402(g) limit for the year: $13,000 for 2004; a plan limit, e.g., the maximum deferral is 6%; or a limit imposed as a result of a cutback for an HCE necessary to pass the nondiscrimination test in a traditional 401(k) plan (discussed later in this chapter). Because catch-up contributions may be made only if the participant is otherwise restricted in making further deferrals, whether or not a catch-up contribution has been made can usually be determined only after the end of the plan year. The catch-up contributions are in addition to the normal deferral limits under IRC Section 402(g) and are scheduled as follows:

2004	$ 3,000
2005	$ 4,000
2006	$ 5,000

Matching contributions may also be made with respect to catch-up contributions. As with other employee deferrals for plan years beginning on or after January 1, 2002, catch-up contributions do not count toward the deduction limits. In addition, catch-up contributions do not count toward the annual additions limit, i.e., the lesser of 100% of compensation or $41,000; therefore, in the year 2004 in a 401(k) plan, a participant can have a total annual addition of $44,000: $13,000 basic deferral, plus $3,000 catch-up deferral, plus $28,000 employer discretionary contribution (profit-sharing contribution or profit-sharing and other employer contribution, e.g., matching contribution).

NONDISCRIMINATION TESTING FOR TRADITIONAL 401(k) PLANS

All testing for 401(k) plans is based on the definition of HCEs and compares that group's deferrals (ADP) to the NHCE deferrals. An *HCE* is any employee who:

1. Is a 5% owner during the year or the preceding year
2. Has compensation of $90,000 or more in the preceding year (2003 for the 2004 plan year)
3. Is in the top paid group of employees for the preceding year (if elected by the employer).

The top paid group of employees is defined as the top 20% of the employees when ranked on the basis of compensation, excluding certain employees as defined in the Internal Revenue Code. The benefit of electing to include the top paid group in the definition of HCE is most apparent in a company that has a disproportionate number of HCEs compared to NHCEs and tends to limit the number of HCEs considered for testing purposes. Because some of the employees who would otherwise be considered HCEs but for the election of top paid group are now NHCEs, the NHCE average deferral percentage is generally increased.

To pass the ADP test for elective deferrals, the ADP of the HCEs vs. the NHCEs must be within the guidelines shown in Table I.

Table I

ADP LIMITS

NHCE Average	HCE Average
0% to 2%	Twice the NHCE amount
More than 2% up to 8%	2% more than the NHCE amount
More than 8%	1.25 times the NHCE amount

This rule is also true for the actual contribution percentage test (ACP test), which applies to employer-matching contributions that are not immediately vested and after-tax employee contributions. Some plans may provide for eligibility requirements more liberal than the statutory guidelines of one year of service and age 21. For nondiscrimination testing, these plans may be treated as two plans, i.e., one plan that requires one year of service and age 21 for participation, and another plan that has more liberal requirements. The plan with the more liberal eligibility requirements must be tested only if it contains an HCE; otherwise, it may be ignored.

To encourage NHCEs to participate and therefore allow higher deferrals by the HCEs, most plans are designed with matching contributions, accelerated vesting on matching contributions, in-service distributions for hardships and availability of loans. In many plans a match of 100% of the first 3% an employee defers will cost the employer the same as a 50% match on the first 6% but it is more effective in encouraging the lower paid employees to participate.

NONDISCRIMINATION TESTING EXAMPLES

Tables II and III illustrate the nondiscrimination testing requirements. In the plan in Table II, the employer match is 50% of the employee's deferral but not more than 3% of the employee's salary and the employer match is 100% vested. Steve is a 70% stockholder and Michael is a 30% stockholder. Alex is Steve's son. Alex, for purposes of the definition of HCE, is treated as owning the same ownership interest as his parent and is therefore considered to be an HCE (see Chapter 10 for a complete discussion of ownership attribution and controlled groups).

Because the ADP for the NHCEs is more than 2% (see Table I), the greater of the "plus 2" or "1.25 times" test must be used. Multiplying the NHCE percentage of 6.364% by 1.25 yields 7.955%. The plan does not satisfy the 1.25 times test, so the plus 2 test can be tried. Adding 2% to the NHCE percentage of 6.364% results in 8.364%. The HCE percentage is equal to 8.364%, so the test is passed. The calculation of the ADP includes those employees who defer 0% of their salaries.

In Table II the deferral percentages for the NHCEs are added up and divided by ten (not by the number of employees who are actually deferring, i.e., eight).

Table II

MATCH 100% VESTED

	Salary	Employee Deferral	Employer Match	ADP Test	
Steve	$205,000	$13,000	$ 6,150	9.341%	
Michael	75,000	4,755	2,250	9.340	
Alex	60,000	2,564	1,282	6.410	8.364%
	$340,000	$20,319	$ 9,682		
Carol	$ 25,000	$ 750	$ 375	4.500%	
Scott	45,000	2,500	1,250	8.333	
Arthur	22,000	1,000	500	6.818	
Mary Ann	38,000	3,000	1,140	10.895	
Jonathan	55,000	5,000	1,650	12.091	
Rebecca	41,000	—	—	0.000	
Susan	27,000	1,200	600	6.667	
Joan	25,000	1,000	500	6.000	
Stanley	15,000	—	—	0.000	
Stuart	18,000	1,000	500	8.333	6.364%
	$311,000	$15,450	$ 6,515		
	$651,000	$35,769	$16,197		

In Table II the match is 100% vested, so it is treated as part of the employee deferral for testing purposes. This plan option tends to help pass the actual deferral percentage test. In the plan in Table III, the employer match is subject to a vesting schedule, e.g., six-year graded vesting (see Chapter 2). In such a case, the non-discrimination test is done separately for the deferrals and the match.

In Table III the employer-matching contribution is subject to a graded vesting schedule, so the match must pass the ACP test. The calculations are exactly the same as the ADP test. The ADP and ACP both satisfy the plus 2 test: 4.409% plus 2% is equal to the HCE percentage of 6.409% and 1.955% plus 2% is more than the HCE percentage of 2.694%.

Table III

MATCH SUBJECT TO SIX-YEAR GRADED VESTING

	Salary	Employee Deferral	ADP Test	Employer Match	ACP Test
Steve	$205,000	$13,000	6.341%	$ 6,150	3.000%
Michael	75,000	6,540	8.720	2,250	3.000
Alex	60,000	2,499	4.164	1,249	2.082
	$340,000	$22,039		$ 9,649	
	HCE Average Percentage		**6.409%**		**2.694%**
Carol	$ 25,000	$ 750	3.000%	$ 375	1.500%
Scott	45,000	2,500	5.556	1,250	2.778
Arthur	22,000	1,000	4.545	500	2.273
Mary Ann	38,000	3,000	7.895	1,140	3.000
Jonathan	55,000	5,000	9.091	1,650	3.000
Rebecca	41,000	—	0.000	—	0.000
Susan	27,000	1,200	4.444	600	2.222
Joan	25,000	1,000	4.000	500	2.000
Stanley	15,000	—	0.000	—	0.000
Stuart	18,000	1,000	5.556	500	2.778
	$311,000	$15,450		$ 6,515	
	$651,000	$37,489		$16,164	
	NHCE Average Percentage		**4.409%**		**1.955%**

CORRECTION OF FAILED TESTS

Four options that allow a plan to pass an otherwise failed ADP or ACP test are available:

1. Employer QNECs for all eligible NHCEs to raise their average deferral percentage if the match is 100% vested
2. Employer QMACs (qualified matching contributions) for all NHCEs mak-

ing deferrals to raise their average deferral percentage, if the match is 100% vested

3. Refunds to the HCEs to reduce their average deferral percentage
4. Recharacterization of HCE elective deferrals to after-tax employee voluntary contributions.

Each of these options has its advantages and disadvantages. QNECs are easy to administer and do not require the HCEs to reduce their contributions by taking refunds; however, this could be a costly option if there are many NHCEs. Also, because QNECs are made for all eligible employees, even those who do not make elective deferrals, they tend to reward the wrong employees. QMACs are similar to QNECs but at least are directed only to those employees making elective contributions. Refunds to the HCEs are the least costly for the employer but may create dissatisfaction among the HCEs because they will have additional taxable income. Recharacterization costs the employer nothing but usually is not practical, i.e., it usually does not work. The most common correction method is refunds to the HCEs. The method of calculating the refunds is beyond the scope of this book. For detailed examples and discussion of all correction methods see *The Financial Professional's Guide to Qualified Retirement Plans,* Aspen Publishing, 2004.

PRIOR-YEAR ADP AND ACP TESTING

In 1996 the Small Business Job Protection Act (SBJPA), among other changes, added the ability to satisfy nondiscrimination testing in 401(k) plans on a "prior-year" testing method. This allowed employers to use the NHCE ADP or ACP from the prior plan year in determining whether the HCE ADP or ACP for the current plan year satisfied testing. At first this approach appears to solve the problem of maximizing the HCEs' percentage up to the allowable limits required to satisfy testing. Here is the dilemma: The employer can allow all HCEs to defer up to their individual limit, i.e., the lesser of 100% of compensation or the IRC Section 402(g) limit of $13,000 for 2004 and refund any excess after year-end to pass the ADP or ACP test; or the employer can limit the HCEs to a percentage that guarantees satisfaction of the testing based on the prior year but may not effectively allow each HCE to maximize his or her deferrals. In the second case, if the employer limits HCE deferrals to 6% (assuming the prior-year NHCE percentage is 4%) and one or more HCEs elect to defer less than 6%, or zero, the remaining HCEs do not have the option of increasing their deferrals past 6% (the HCE percentage is *the average* of all HCEs, including those who defer 0% of compensation).

Using the employee data from Table II, the HCE's percentage was 8.364%. Under prior-year testing, the NHCE percentage for the prior year would have to be at least 6.364% for the test to be passed in the current year. Although the use of prior-year testing gives the employer advance notice of the limit on the HCE's ADP, it does not solve the problem of how to deal with individual elections of each HCE. Suppose the prior-year NHCE percentage was 6%. How should the employer limit the HCEs in the current year so their average would be 8% rather than 8.364%? Which HCE should be required to cut back? The one with the highest dollar deferral? The one with the highest percentage deferral? Or the one with the highest compensation? Regardless of which the employer chooses, someone will be unhappy, maybe unhappy enough to seek other employment. If a new plan uses the prior-year method, SBJPA allows the plan to assume that the NHCE ADP and ACP percentage for the prior year is the greater of 3% or the actual ADP or ACP percentage of the NHCEs for the current year. In the author's experience, prior-year testing does not result in any significant benefits to the employer, with all the limitations and restrictions on its use, the complexities added to the corrective employer contribution options and the added potential for error.

In an attempt to simplify the rules and regulations for 401(k) plans, Congress, in SBJPA, introduced a new type of 401(k) plan: the SIMPLE 401(k) and the SIMPLE IRA. As a further incentive to the small business community, the same legislation introduced the safe harbor 401(k) plan to be effective in 1999. With the introduction of the SIMPLE IRA and SIMPLE 401(k), SBJPA has eliminated the availability of salary reduction simplified employee pension plans (SARSEPs) for years after December 31, 1996, although plans in existence on that date may continue to receive contributions and newly eligible employees may participate after that date. Each of these relatively new plan designs has its advantages and disadvantages.

SIMPLE IRA PLAN

Effective beginning in 1997, a SIMPLE plan can be adopted as a SIMPLE individual retirement account (IRA) or a SIMPLE 401(k). The SIMPLE IRA is not a qualified plan, but a type of IRA plan. Eligibility to sponsor a SIMPLE IRA is limited to an employer having no more than 100 employees who received at least $5,000 of compensation from the employer in the preceding year. If an employer adopts a SIMPLE IRA and in a subsequent year cannot satisfy the 100-employee rule (i.e., the employer has more than 100 employees), under some circumstances, a two-year grace period is provided, allowing the employer to continue the SIMPLE IRA for two years. For purposes of the 100-employee limitation, all employees employed at any time during the calendar year are taken into account, regardless of whether they are eligible to participate in the SIMPLE IRA plan.

An employer that adopts a SIMPLE IRA may not maintain any other "qualified plan" for which contributions are made or benefits accrued (DB plan) beginning in or ending in the year the SIMPLE plan is maintained. A newly established SIMPLE IRA may be adopted effective on any date between January 1 and October 1 if the employer did not sponsor a SIMPLE plan previously. A newly formed employer may establish the plan as soon as administratively feasible after coming into existence. The employer may use Form 5305-SIMPLE to adopt the plan with a "designated financial institution" or Form 5304-SIMPLE to adopt the plan if each employee selects his or her own financial institution.

Employees of an eligible employer are eligible to make elective deferrals in a SIMPLE IRA if they:
1.   Receive at least $5,000 in compensation from the employer during any two preceding years
2.   Are reasonably expected to receive at least $5,000 in compensation during the current year.

An employer may impose less restrictive eligibility requirements by eliminating or reducing the prior-year compensation requirements, current year compensation requirements, or both. For example, an employer can allow participation for employees who received $3,500 in compensation during any preceding calendar year or for all employees regardless of compensation.

The employer must notify each eligible employee of his or her option to make a deferral election or to modify an existing election. Notification must occur 60 days before the beginning of the plan year, or 60 days before the first day the employee is eligible if the effective date of the plan is not the first day of the plan year (plan adopted during the year). During the 60-day election period, employees have the right to modify their salary reduction agreements without restrictions.

As in the case of qualified plans, union employees and nonresident aliens may be excluded from participation in the SIMPLE IRA; however, it appears that union employees must be counted as employees of the employer for purposes of the 100-employee requirement. This has the effect of preventing an employer from adopting a SIMPLE IRA for its nonunion employees if the total of union and nonunion employees is more than 100, even though there are fewer than 100 nonunion employees.

SIMPLE plans eliminate the need to satisfy the nondiscrimination tests common to 401(k) plans, the ADP and ACP tests (see above). In exchange for the reduced testing and elimination of top-heavy rules (see Chapter 9), the amount that can be deferred pretax by each employee is limited to $9,000 for 2004 increased by $1,000 each year up to $10,000 in 2005 (thereafter adjusted in $500 increments for cost of living), compared to the $13,000 (for 2004) that can be deferred to a traditional or safe harbor 401(k).

The employer may not make any contributions to the plan other than those that are specifically allowed. SBJPA provides for two types of employer contributions: a matching contribution and a nonelective contribution, both of which must be immediately vested. The matching contribution is equal to 100% of the employee's deferral up to 3% of compensation. One of the advantages of the SIMPLE IRA compared to the SIMPLE 401(k) is the ability to reduce the matching contribution in any two of the five years ending in the current year. The reduced match cannot be any lower than 100% of the employee's deferral, up to 1% of compensation. This means that the employer, for the first two plan years, can reduce the match to 1%. For a new plan that has not been in effect for five years, it is assumed the prior-years' match was 3%.

As an alternative, the employer may make an elective contribution of 2% of compensation to all employees who are eligible to participate and have compensation of at least $5,000 for the year. Whichever employer contribution is chosen, the employer must notify the employees within a reasonable period before the 60-day election period. This notice is also required if the employer elects to make a reduced match for any year.

A SIMPLE IRA is not required to file Form 5500. In addition, the employer is not subject to fiduciary liability resulting from the employee exercising control over the assets in the SIMPLE account. Regarding the SIMPLE IRA accounts, the 60-day election notice must also disclose the employee's ability to select the financial institution that will serve as the trustee for the employee's SIMPLE IRA account. If several employees are participating and each chooses a different trustee, a separate check must be sent to each trustee for that employee's deferrals. This could create quite an administrative cost and burden for the employer. To avoid this problem, the employer may require that all contributions be made to a specific financial institution, a "designated financial institution." To qualify, the financial institution must:

1. Agree that if a participant requests, his or her contribution must be transferred *without cost or penalty* to another SIMPLE IRA account at a different financial institution of his or her choice
2. Provide each participant with written notification describing the procedure under which that transfer will be executed.

Certain financial institution products, such as front- or back-loaded mutual funds, variable or fixed annuities with surrender charges and certificates of deposits with surrender penalties, may not be eligible for use as SIMPLE IRA accounts. Check with the financial institution to determine whether it has the appropriate products that satisfy this requirement.

SIMPLE 401(k) PLAN

Most of the SIMPLE 401(k) provisions are the same as those for the SIMPLE IRA, although the underlying IRC sections are different. The SIMPLE 401(k) is a variation of the traditional 401(k) plan, which is regulated under IRC Sections 401(k) and 401(a), and regulations relative to those Code sections.

Certain provisions of the SIMPLE 401(k) are guided by the same rules and under the same IRC sections as those of a SIMPLE IRA. These include:

1. Eligible employers
2. Plan year must be calendar year.

On the other hand, some rules are different for SIMPLE 401(k) plans because they are considered qualified plans under IRC Section 501(a):

1. The employer may require one year of service, a minimum age of 21 and minimum compensation of $5,000 to participate.
2. Early distributions are subject to a 10% penalty, including the first two years of participation, not the higher 25% applied to the SIMPLE IRA.
3. The employer cannot require employment on the last day of the plan year or completion of a specific number of hours to receive a matching contribution or an employer nonelective contribution.
4. The plan must file an annual Form 5500 with attachments.
5. An IRS-approved plan document must be prepared and executed to adopt the SIMPLE 401(k) plan as is required for any other qualified retirement plan under IRC 501(a).

SAFE HARBOR 401(k) PLAN

The primary benefit of the safe harbor 401(k) plan is automatic satisfaction of the nondiscrimination tests required for traditional 401(k) plans (see above) and the availability of the higher traditional 401(k) deferral limits as compared to the SIMPLE plans. A safe harbor 401(k) plan automatically satisfies the testing if it complies with either of two employer contributions: a matching contribution or a nonelective contribution. Both of these employer contribution options must be immediately vested, are subject to the same withdrawal restrictions that apply to traditional 401(k) plans and must be contributed to the plan no later than 12 months after the plan year to which the contributions relate.

The statutory match requires the employer to contribute 100% of the employee's deferrals up to 3% of compensation and 50% of the employee's deferrals in excess of 3%, but not more than 5%; therefore, the next 2% the employee defers will be matched at a rate of 50%. An alternate matching option or "enhanced matching formula" may be used as long as it is as liberal as the statutory matching contribution, i.e., provides the same or higher match at any level of employee deferral. In addition to meeting the statutory rate, the enhanced match may not be based on deferrals in excess of 6% of compensation. In addition to the statutory matching contributions and the enhanced matching contributions, the employer may also make discretionary matching contributions. The discretionary matching contributions may not be used to satisfy the safe harbor requirements and may not exceed an amount equal to 4% of the employee's compensation.

The other alternative for employer safe harbor contributions is a nonelective contribution of 3% for all "eligible employees." In this context an *eligible employee* is one who has satisfied the eligibility requirements of the plan, i.e., the statutory requirements: generally age 21, one year of service and full-time employment (1,000 hours). Similar to traditional 401(k) plans, if the eligibility is more liberal, employees who are eligible but have not satisfied the age 21 and one-year-of-service requirement are treated as participating in a separate plan and may be excluded from the required safe harbor contribution. Clearly, an employee is eligible to receive the nonelective contribution whether or not the employee makes an elective deferral.

Table IV provides a comparison of the various 401(k) plans.

CATCH-UP CONTRIBUTIONS

	401(k) Plans	SIMPLE Plans
2004	$3,000	$1,500
2005	$4,000	$2,000
2006	$5,000	$2,500

Together with the 402(g) deferrals, a participant would be able to defer and contribute $20,000 in the year 2006. The limit for SIMPLE plans would be $12,000 in 2005; however, for 2006, although the catch-up limit is known, the deferral limit would be the 2005 deferral limit of $10,000, adjusted for inflation. Matching contributions may also be made with respect to catch-up contributions. As with other employee deferrals for plan years beginning on or after January 1, 2002, catch-up contributions do not count toward the deduction limits or the annual additions limit, i.e., the lesser of 100% of compensation or $41,000 for 2004. In a 401(k) plan it is therefore possible for a participant to have a total annual addition in the year 2004 of $44,000: $13,000 basic deferral, $3,000 catch-up deferral and $28,000 employer discretionary contribution (profit-sharing contributions).

Table IV

COMPARISON OF 401(k) PLANS

	Traditional	SIMPLE IRA	SIMPLE 401(k)	Safe Harbor
ADP/ACP	Yes	No	No	No testing
Top-heavy	Yes	No	No	Yes, can be satisfied by safe harbor contributions
Match	Flexible	100% of first 3%, no cap on salary	100% of first 3%	100% of first 3% and 50% of next 2%
Flexibility of match	Yes	With notice reduce to 1% for two out of five years	No	Enhanced match if result is same or better than required match
Nonelective option	QNEC	2%	With notice 2%	With notice 3%, can be used in nondiscrimination testing
Taxation	10% early withdrawal penalty	25% penalty in first two years, then 10% penalty	10% early withdrawal penalty	10% early withdrawal penalty
Deferral limit	$13,000 indexed	$9,000 indexed, 25% limit does not apply	$9,000 indexed	$13,000 indexed
Effective	N/A	After 12/31/96	After 12/31/96	After 12/31/98
5500 Filing	Yes	No	No	Yes
Maintain other plan	Yes	No	Yes, but not for same employees	Yes
Other contributions	Yes	No	No	Yes
Vesting	Traditional options	Full	Full	Full
Rollovers	Existing rules	After two years in plan or to another SIMPLE	Existing rules	Existing rules
Election period	N/A	60 days	60 days	30 days
New plan	Can be adopted any time during year	No later than October 1 unless newly established employer	No later than October 1 unless newly established employer	No later than October 1 unless newly established employer
Plan year	Calendar year	Calendar year	Calendar year	Calendar year

Understanding Defined Benefit (DB) Plans

Chapter 6

The discussion of target benefit plans (see Chapter 4) uses an analogy of saving to buy a house.

> **Example 1:** John would like to save for a larger house. He determines that he can handle a monthly mortgage payment of $1,500. To do that, based on the price range of the house he can afford, he would have to put down a deposit of $50,000. John is hoping to accumulate the down payment in five years through an investment in mutual funds that he projects will appreciate by 10% annually after taxes. John has decided that if the mutual fund does not perform as expected, he will adjust his annual deposit so that at the end of the five-year period he will have the $50,000. Here is the result of John's plan:

End of Year	Deposit	End of Year Appreciation	Balance	Expected Balance
1	$8,190	$ 819	$ 9,009	$ 9,009
2	8,190	1,300	18,499	18,919
3	8,610	2,100	29,209	29,820
4	8,801	4,560	42,570	41,811
5	7,431		50,001	50,000

In year two the investment underperformed. Ten percent of the sum of the first year balance of $9,009 and the second year's contribution of $8,190 would be $1,720. The investment appreciated by $1,300, a shortfall of $420. To make up the shortfall, John's plan is to add to the third year's deposit, bringing it to $8,610 ($8,190 plus $420). In year three the investments underperformed again. John expected a return of $2,711 (10% of the second year's balance of $18,919 plus 10% of the third year's contribution of $8,610) but realized a gain of only $2,100. The shortfall of

$611 is made up in the fourth year's contribution of $8,801 ($8,190 plus $611). In year four the gain was more than expected so the fifth year's contribution was reduced and, as you can see, John has his $50,000 at the end of five years.

In a DB plan, a retirement benefit, usually in the form of monthly income, is determined by the plan's benefit formula. A reserve is then calculated based on the life expectancy of the participant at retirement age and the expected investment return that is sufficient to pay the employee's retirement benefit under the plan's benefit formula beginning at retirement age for life. The employer then makes a contribution each year for the participant until retirement age so the contributions plus investment earnings accumulate to the reserve determined above. Each year the employer's contribution is adjusted based on actual changes in the operation of the plan, including employee salaries, actual rate of return of the plan investments and employee turnover.

A DB plan is not an individual account plan. Although many small DB plans report a contribution for each participant to the plan sponsor, this number is a theoretical contribution. In actual operation the plan's liability is calculated as a total liability and is funded as a total liability. When a participant is entitled to a distribution due to termination of employment, his or her payout is calculated based on his or her individual benefit based on the plan's benefit formula and the funds are paid from the "plan assets," not his or her individual account.

Example 2: Consider the following example in a one-person plan:

Date of birth:	September 1, 1950
Date of retirement:	January 1, 2015 (age 65)
Date of hire:	January 1, 1998
Effective date of the plan:	January 1, 1999
Employee's salary:	$48,000
Benefit formula:	2% of salary per year of service

Step 1. Calculate the monthly retirement benefit:

Total service:	17 years (date of retirement − date of hire)
Benefit per year:	2%
Total benefit:	34% (17 years × 2%)
Monthly benefit:	$1,360 per month for life ($48,000 ÷ 12 × 34%)

Step 2. Calculate the reserve necessary at retirement age:

Monthly benefit:	$1,360
Annuity purchase rate:	$137.52 per dollar per month retirement benefit
Reserve at retirement:	$187,027 ($1,360 × $137.52)

The annuity purchase rate is the amount necessary to pay $1 per month for the life of the participant beginning at retirement age (65 in this example) taking into consideration life expectancy at age 65 and an assumed investment rate of return beginning at retirement age.

Step 3. Calculate the annual contribution necessary to accumulate the reserve:

Reserve at retirement:	$187,027
Assumed investment rate of return:	7.5% preretirement, i.e., accumulation years
Years to contribute:	16 (retirement date – employee's date of participation)
Annual contribution:	$5,983.33 (from financial calculator)

Assuming this employee's salary does not change and the contributions made actually earn 7.5% each year, this contribution will not change. To the extent that actual experience varies from these assumptions, the contribution will change each year.

BASIC PLAN DESIGN FEATURES

This section discusses the basic design features unique to DB plans (see Chapter 2 for a discussion of universal design features).

Average Monthly Compensation

The following options are used in the sample calculations in this subsection: Average monthly compensation shall be based on:

1. ☐ Plan years of service

2. ☐ Total years of service.

And compensation shall be averaged over:

3. ☐ The _____ consecutive year period within the last ten years to date of termination of employment that produces the highest average

4. ☐ The _____ consecutive year period that produces the highest average

5. ☐ All years

6. ☐ The _____ final years to date of termination of employment.

Options 1 and 2 refer to the time choices to which options 3 through 6 will be applied. Option 1 considers only years from the effective date of the plan, whereas option 2 considers years from date of hire, including years before the plan effective date. In all cases compensation must be averaged over no less than three years, which is the basis for statutory benefit limitations. Usually the shorter the period over which compensation is averaged, the higher the average compensation of the participant, all else being equal.

Example 3: Consider a professional medical practice with one employee in addition to the professional with the following compensation history and a plan that was effective on January 1, 2000. Further assume the professional cut down on her working hours as she approached retirement.

	Professional	Employee		Professional	Employee
1996	$175,000	$26,000	2003	$75,000	$55,000
1997	$190,000	$25,000	2004	$50,000	$60,000
1998	$180,000	$30,000	2005	$75,000	$70,000
1999	$100,000	$30,000	2006	$50,000	$58,000
2000	$ 75,000	$40,000	2007	$50,000	$50,000
2001	$ 75,000	$42,000	2008	$50,000	$38,000
2002	$ 75,000	$45,000			

If option 1, plan years of service, and a three-year averaging period were used, the result would be:

	Professional	Employee
Option 3	$ 75,000 (years 2000-2002)	$62,667 (years 2004-2006)
Option 4	$ 75,000 (years 2000-2002)	$62,667 (years 2004-2006)
Option 5	$ 63,889 (years 2000-2008)	$50,889 (years 2000-2008)
Option 6	$ 50,000 (years 2006-2008)	$48,667 (years 2006-2008)

If option 1, plan years of service, and a five-year averaging period were used, the result would be:

	Professional	Employee
Option 3	$ 70,000 (years 2000-2004)	$58,600 (years 2003-2007)
Option 4	$ 70,000 (years 2000-2004)	$58,600 (years 2003-2007)
Option 5	$ 63,889 (years 2000-2008)	$50,889 (years 2000-2008)
Option 6	$ 55,000 (years 2004-2008)	$55,200 (years 2004-2008)

If option 2, total years of service, and a three-year averaging period were used, the result would be:

	Professional	Employee
Option 3	$ 83,333 (years 1999-2001)	$62,667 (years 2004-2006)
Option 4	$181,666 (years 1996-1998)	$62,667 (years 2004-2006)
Option 5	$ 93,846 (years 1996-2008)	$42,385 (years 1996-2008)
Option 6	$ 50,000 (years 2006-2008)	$48,667 (years 2006-2008)

If option 2, total years of service, and a five-year averaging period were used, the result would be:

	Professional	Employee
Option 3	$ 80,000 (years 1999-2003)	$58,600 (years 2003-2007)
Option 4	$144,000 (years 1996-2000)	$58,600 (years 2003-2007)
Option 5	$ 93,846 (years 1996-2008)	$42,385 (years 1996-2008)
Option 6	$ 55,000 (years 2004-2008)	$55,200 (years 2004-2008)

There is quite a difference in average compensation depending on the definition of average monthly compensation in the plan. For the professional key employee, the best definition with the illustrated compensation history is option 2, total years of service, because her compensation was higher before the plan was adopted, and three-year averaging. Since benefits are based on compensation, this choice can have a significant effect on the determination of retirement benefits and therefore plan costs.

Normal Retirement Age

Although the choices for DB plans are the same as for defined contribution (DC) plans, the effect is not the same. In a DB plan, the benefit is funded over the working life of the participant. If the retirement age is lower, the contributions will be higher because there is less time to accumulate the necessary reserve to fund the promised benefit. In Example 1, the annual contribution to fund a benefit of $1,360 per month at age 65 was $5,983.33. To fund that same benefit at age 60, the contribution would be $10,734.04, almost double.

In addition, the maximum benefit that can be provided in a DB plan (the lesser of 100% of average compensation or $165,000 annually for 2004) is payable at age 62 and must be reduced if payable before that date. If the age at which the benefit is payable is greater than age 65, the age-adjusted dollar limit is determined by increasing the maximum benefit to recognize the shorter period over which the benefit will be paid.

Normal Form of Benefit

This choice determines how long the promised benefit will be paid. There are numerous annuity choices including payments for life only; joint life payments usually for participant and spouse; payments for life with a guarantee period, e.g., payments for life with a ten-year guarantee; and many variations of these, e.g., a 50% joint life payment, i.e., the surviving spouse receives 50% of the benefit the participant was receiving. In addition, the benefit may be paid in a lump-sum equivalent rather than in monthly benefits.

If any benefit form other than a life annuity is the "normal form," i.e., the standard form provided for and funded in the plan, the monthly benefit may have to be reduced. This adjustment is based on the value of the alternate form. An annuity for ten years certain is more valuable than a life-only annuity; a 50% J&S annuity is more valuable than a ten-year-certain annuity (depending on the age of the participant and beneficiary); and a 100% J&S annuity is more valuable than a 50% J&S annuity. Consider a plan that provides a benefit equal to 100% of the high three-year average compensation beginning at retirement age 65. The participant's high three-year average compensation is $48,000. The maximum benefit that can be paid as a life-only annuity is $4,000 per month (the lesser of 100% of high three-year average compensation or the dollar limit, which for the year 2004 is $13,750 per month).

Actuarial Equivalent

This is the section of the document where the assumptions are defined for calculating alternate forms of distribution as discussed previously. These assumptions can be changed only by plan amendment. The combination of the mortality assumption and the interest assumption creates an annuity purchase rate (see Example 2) used to make adjustments to the normal form of benefit including the determination of the amount of lump-sum distributions.

Benefit Formula

This is the section of the plan that determines each participant's benefit based on the definition of average monthly compensation. Just as in DC plans, a DB plan may take into consideration benefits the employer is providing through Social Security (see Chapter 4) or, as referred to in qualified retirement plans, "permitted disparity." Generally the benefit formula is in the form of a flat benefit or a unit benefit. A flat benefit formula provides for a flat percentage of average compensation or a flat dollar amount, e.g., 50% of average monthly compensation, 75% of compensation, or $1,000 per month. A unit benefit formula provides for a specific percentage or dollar amount per year of service or participation, e.g., 2% of high three-year average compensation per year of service, 1.5% of high five-year average compensation per year of plan participation, $100 per month per year of service, or $50 per month per year of plan participation. In this type of benefit formula, the plan can limit the number of years that will be taken into account to calculate the benefit.

Credited Service

This design feature determines what service is to be included in calculating the benefit amount. For this purpose service can be counted from date of hire, possibly before the plan was adopted, or from date of participation.

Reductions and Limitations

This section applies to any adjustment to the benefit calculated by the benefit formula. It allows for adjustments to the benefit for years of service or participation, minimum benefits and caps on benefits. Some common choices are:
1. No reductions or limitations
2. The benefit shall be reduced by _____ (e.g., one-tenth) for each year of credited services less than _____ (e.g., ten) that the participant is credited with at his or her normal retirement date.
3. Years of credited service before _____ shall not be recognized.

4. A participant's monthly benefit shall not exceed $ _____.
5. A participant's monthly benefit shall not be less than _____.

Accrued Benefits

In concept, the accrued benefit in a DB plan is roughly equivalent to the account balance in a DC plan. A participant in a DB plan earns his or her projected retirement benefit over credited service, either participation service or total service. The most common method of accrual is referred to as the *fractional rule*. In this method the accrued benefit payable to a participant at separation from service is (a) the normal retirement benefit calculated under the plan benefit formula, times (b) a fraction, the numerator of which is the number of years of participation (or total service) at separation from service and the denominator of which is the number of years of participation (or total service) the participant would have at normal retirement age. A participant with a normal retirement benefit of $1,000 per month, eight years of participation at separation from service, and 16 years of participation had the employee stayed until normal retirement date would have an accrued benefit of $500 per month at termination of employment ($1,000 times [8 years / 16 years]).

Death Benefits

All qualified plans, with some exceptions, are required to provide, at a minimum, a qualified preretirement survivor annuity (QPSA). This is an immediate annuity for the life of the surviving spouse of a participant who dies before benefit payments begin. The amount of the benefit must be 50% of the actuarial equivalent (see above) of the benefit payment that would have been made to the participant based on his or her accrued benefit at the time of death. Some plans pay death benefits in addition to the required minimum. Common options found in DB plans include:

1. 100% vesting of the accrued benefit paid as an equivalent qualified joint and survivor annuity or in the form of a lump sum
2. An insured death benefit funded with life insurance.

Since the primary purpose of the DB plan is to provide retirement benefits, Internal Revenue Service (IRS) regulations require that the death benefit be "incidental" to the retirement benefit. This requirement is generally satisfied if the insured death benefit is no more than 100 times the monthly retirement benefit. For example, if the monthly retirement benefit is $2,500, then the maximum insured death benefit would be $250,000. The premium paid for the insurance becomes part of the pension contribution, and the cash value of the insurance policy becomes part of the retirement benefit. If a qualified retirement plan provides for an insured death benefit, IRS regulations take the position that the plan is providing a current "economic benefit," compared to a future benefit, the retirement benefit. Since the benefit is current, the taxation must also be current. Each year the participant will include in income the value of the insured death benefit, usually measured by the term insurance rates of the insurance company issuing the policy or rates from an IRS table referred to as the PS-58 Table. In some cases it is desirable to include an insured death benefit in a DB plan since the premium is deductible as part of the pension contribution (other than the PS-58 cost). Depending on the age of the participant, the limit of 100 times the monthly retirement benefit may be insufficient for the participant's needs. In that case a higher amount may be purchased based on an old Revenue Ruling (74-307) allowing the plan to purchase as much insurance as possible using approximately two-thirds of the pension contribution. The actual calculation is somewhat more complex but a guideline of two-thirds is sufficient for this discussion.

Example 4: Assume the following plan and participation information:

Participant's age:	50
Participant's salary:	$60,000
Normal retirement benefit at age 65:	Life annuity of 50% of three highest years' average consecutive salary ($2,500 monthly)
Annuity purchase rates:	$117.68 per dollar per month
Annual contribution to fund benefit:	$10,478
Premium for $250,000 variable life policy:	$3,025
Maximum insurance:	
Premium	$6,985
Death benefit	$577,273

PLAN FLEXIBILITY: REDUCING PLAN CONTRIBUTIONS

Even though the contribution is mandatory in a DB plan, the plan sponsor may reduce that contribution if done so in a timely manner. This can be accomplished by:

1. Amending the plan to a reduced benefit
2. Freezing all future benefit accruals
3. Changing funding assumptions
4. Funding waiver
5. Terminating the plan (see Chapter 15).

Amending the plan to a lower benefit, after funding the plan at a higher benefit for several plan years, would have the effect of reducing the contribution. Usually the contribution goes down by a higher percent than the benefit; i.e., if the benefit is reduced to half, the contribution would go down by more than half if the plan were funded at a higher level for several years. The longer the plan has been funded at the higher level the greater the variation. Any plan amendment must be done before the end of the plan year and, if the participant has worked 1,000 hours or more, the accrued benefit as of the end of that plan year must be based on the benefit before it was reduced by the amendment. If the amendment is executed and effective early in the plan year, before the participants work 1,000 hours, it would affect the accrued benefit for that year but could not reduce the prior accrued benefit. In addition, all participants must be notified of the reduction in future benefit accruals at least 15 days before the effective date of that reduction.

The second option is to freeze all future benefit accruals. This would be equivalent to the retirement benefit being reduced to the current accrued benefit. If, for example, the projected monthly retirement benefit at age 65 was $2,500 and the accrued benefit at the time future benefit accruals were frozen was $2,000 per month, the projected monthly benefit for that participant would now be $2,000 per month. In some cases freezing benefit accruals will cause the contribution to go to zero. The same rules apply for notice to participants as if the plan were amended.

The next alternative is to change the assumptions used to calculate the contributions. Consider changing the preretirement interest rate (the rate at which contributions are accumulated to fund future benefits) from 7.5% to 8.5%.

> **Example 5:** A participant's retirement benefit is $2,500 per month requiring a reserve of $294,200 at retirement age. The contribution necessary to fund that reserve from age 45 to age 65 at 7.5% is $6,320 while at 8.5%, the contribution is $5,605. If this change is made after funding the plan at the lower rate for several years, the effect on the contribution will be more proportional than the change in the interest rate. Increasing the interest rate from 7.5% to 8.5% is a 13.3% increase; however, the contribution would go down by more than 13.3% depending on the number of years of funding at the lower interest rate.

If all else fails, the plan sponsor may apply to IRS for a funding waiver. To be eligible for a funding waiver, the plan sponsor must show that satisfying the funding requirement of the plan would create a temporary business hardship and would be adverse to the best interests of the plan participants. IRS will consider the following in determining whether a business hardship exists:
1. The employer is operating at a loss.
2. There is substantial unemployment or underemployment in the trade or business and the industry.
3. The sales and profits of the industry are depressed or declining.
4. It is reasonable to expect that the plan will be continued only if the waiver is granted.

If the funding waiver is granted, the waived contribution must be amortized and made up over no more than five years and no more than three waivers will be granted in a 15-year period.

The last option available to reduce contributions to a DB plan is to terminate the plan. This should be used only as a last resort when it becomes clear that the employer will not be able to continue the plan in later years because of irreversible changes in its financial ability to fund the plan. Plan terminations are covered in detail in Chapter 15.

PENSION BENEFIT GUARANTY CORPORATION (PBGC)

Because DB plans promise a retirement benefit that depends on the solvency and funding level of the plan, there is always a possibility that the plan sponsor may not be able to fund the plan because of financial difficulty or, worse yet, insolvency or bankruptcy. In 1974, the Employee Retirement Income Security Act (ERISA) established PBGC, a government-owned corporation that is responsible for overseeing terminations of DB plans and insuring benefits under those plans. Benefits payable with respect to a plan participant are guaranteed up to a specified dollar limit. For the year 2003 the PBGC guarantees benefits up to $3,664.77. This amount is adjusted annually. DB plans subject to PBGC rules must pay an annual premium of $19 per participant plus a variable premium based on the funding level of the plan compared to the plan's benefit liabilities. The variable portion has no limit. Exempt are DB plans that cover only owners, or professional service employers, e.g., medical practitioners, that do not have more than 25 participants.

No discussion of DB plans would be complete without considering alternate types of DB plans: the 412(i) plan and the cash balance plan.

FULLY INSURED 412(i) PLANS

The 412(i) refers to Internal Revenue Code Section 412(i), which sets forth the guidelines for fully insured DB plans. Requirements include:

1. A fully insured plan is funded exclusively by individual or group insurance (whole life policies) or fixed annuity contracts.
2. The funding contracts must provide for level annual premiums from the date of participation until retirement as defined in the plan.
3. A fully insured plan provides only the benefits provided by the funding contract and is guaranteed by an insurance carrier, i.e., the retirement benefits are funded totally by the guaranteed cash values in the life insurance policies and/or fixed annuity policies.
4. A fully insured plan must pay all premiums before the contracts funding the benefits lapse.
5. No rights under the contracts have been subject to a security interest at any time during the plan year.
6. A fully insured plan may not allow for policy loans.

The greatest advantage of the 412(i) plan is the high level of contributions necessary to fund the plan compared to traditional DB plans. This high level of contributions results from the highly conservative assumptions that underlie the insurance or annuity contracts used to fund the benefits. Many insurance companies have developed special products for 412(i) plans. Generally, these products pay dividends in later years because of excess earnings but allow the plan sponsor to fund very large amounts in the early years, i.e., front-loaded funding. This is perfect for a mature company where the owner began funding retirement benefits late in his or her career and would like to semiretire in a few years, just as the contribution for the pension plan is reduced because of increasing dividends. A typical annuity contract used in fully insured plans would assume 4% to 5% preretirement interest, 3% to 4% postretirement interest and 1971 individual annuity mortality—very conservative assumptions. Compare this to typical assumptions that must be reasonable in the aggregate in a traditional DB plan: 7% to 8% preretirement interest, 5% to 6% postretirement interest and 1983 individual annuity mortality.

The most common application of 412(i) plans is to develop very high contributions and deductions in the early years, higher than would be possible in a traditional DB plan because of the reluctance to use extremely conservative assumptions that the IRS may challenge as unreasonable. Because the products that fund the 412(i) plans are usually participating, i.e., the contract issued by the insurance company participates in excess investment income, the premiums would be reduced by that excess income (dividends). Depending on the extent of the excess income, it is possible for the premiums in later years to be less than the contribution would be in a traditional DB plan. The 412(i) plan can therefore be described in that situation as a front-loaded plan, i.e., the contributions are high in the early years and lower in the later years as compared to a traditional DB plan.

The price the plan sponsor pays is a higher cost to fund the benefits. If the product funding the plan guarantees a return of 4.5% and it is possible to earn an investment return well in excess of 4.5%, the higher deduction is really a higher cost to pay benefits. The extent to which this is true depends on the excess earnings of the product (the dividends that reduce premiums in later years), which would determine the true cost of providing benefits, the timing of the contributions and the investment climate for alternate investments. As discussed in Chapter 1, the goals of the sponsoring company should drive the design of the retirement plan. The same is true for the 412(i) plan.

Over the last few years several insurance companies have developed marketing programs to promote fully insured plans. These plans are seen as an opportunity for the insurance companies to market their products in large quantities. Unfortunately, there are many sales representatives selling 412(i) plans that do not understand their mechanics relative to overall IRS rules and regulations for DB plans. Although these issues are technical in nature, there is one that is worthy of discussion.

Since 412(i) plans use very conservative assumptions, the reserve that is accumulated at retirement age to fund the promised benefit is significantly larger than the reserve accumulated in a traditional DB plan to fund the same benefit. If the participant chooses to take his or her benefit in the form of a lump-sum distribution, the amount of the distribution will be limited based on IRS-promulgated interest rates. Upon plan termination the excess assets in the plan that could not be distributed to the participants due to this limitation on lump-sum distributions will revert to the plan sponsor and is subject to an excise tax of 50% and income tax at the income tax rate of the plan sponsor. A total tax rate approaching 90%. Although 412(i) plans have their place, use of these plans without extensive knowledge of the rules governing DB plans is dangerous.

CASH BALANCE PLANS

Another form of nontraditional DB plan is the cash balance plan. Cash balance plans were introduced in 1985 when BankAmerica Corporation adopted the first cash balance plan. These plans have been the topic of a great deal of debate recently because several well-known public companies announced the conversion of their traditional DB plans to cash balance plans. These companies were accused of age discrimination and misleading employees. The issues became so widely publicized that the IRS issued a field directive on September 15, 1999, instructing field offices to stop reviewing determination letter applications for cash balance plans.

A *cash balance plan* is a DB plan that defines benefits for each participant by reference to that employee's hypothetical account. This hypothetical account is established based on contribution credits, e.g., a contribution of 5% of compensation, and interest credits, e.g., 8%, as provided in the plan, not actual investment experience. The contribution credits must satisfy the same nondiscrimination requirements that a DC plan would be required to satisfy, i.e., the same percentage of compensation for each participant or the same dollar amount for each participant. Furthermore, the plan may take permitted disparity into consideration in determining the contribution credits (see Chapter 4). The amount of the contribution credits is based on several issues:

1. What are the employer's retirement income replacement targets for the employees?
2. What is the benefit being provided in the current plan that is being replaced?
3. Are benefits available from other plans, such as 401(k)s?
4. Will there be any grandfather provisions guaranteeing prior benefits to employees closer to retirement?
5. Will there be a minimum benefit?
6. What cost levels are acceptable to the employer to provide retirement benefits?
7. What do other employers in the same industry offer their employees?

In addition to the basic contribution credits, the plan sponsor may offer early retirement supplements. This can be accomplished by increasing the account balance of an employee electing early retirement by a stated percentage or by increasing annuity purchase rates (providing a higher income per dollar of account balance) to supplement early retirement benefits. The employer may increase opening balances for older employees with fewer years to retirement to make up for lower accrual (contribution) rates in the cash balance plan or offer higher contribution credits for older employees. Some companies may increase their contribution to savings plans, e.g., 401(k) plans, to make up part of the reduced accruals in the cash balance plan.

The actual funding of the cash balance plan is based on the projected benefit, as in a traditional DB plan. The projected benefit is based on the hypothetical account balance projected to retirement age based on the contribution credit and interest credit and converted to an annuity, e.g., $500 per month for life beginning at retirement age. Once the benefit is determined, the contribution is calculated as in a traditional DB plan, explained earlier in this chapter. To illustrate the differences, Example 6 compares the relative results of cash balance plans vs. those of traditional DB plans.

Example 6: The data for three employees is used to illustrate the differences between cash balance plans and traditional DB plans:

	Salary	Age	Retirement Age
Employee 1	$18,000	25	65
Employee 2	$35,000	38	65
Employee 3	$50,000	45	65

In this case, the traditional DB plan provides a benefit of 1.5% of high three-year average compensation times years of service up to 25 years. The traditional plan uses 7.5% preretirement interest, 5% postretirement interest and the 1983 individual annuity mortality male rates (an accepted standard mortality table). The cash balance plan credits contributions at the rate of 6.44% (rounded) and interest at 8%. Each employee's salary is assumed to increase by 3% annually, and all contributions are made at the end of the year. Each employee's retirement benefit and reserve at retirement for both the traditional plan and the cash balance plan follow. For comparison purposes, the two plans were designed so Employee 2 would receive the same benefits in each plan:

	Traditional Plan		Cash Balance Plan	
	Monthly Retirement Benefit	Reserve at Retirement	Monthly Retirement Benefit	Reserve at Retirement
Employee 1	$1,729.57	$237,845	$3,111.88	$427,937
Employee 2	$2,502.42	$344,125	$2,502.42	$344,125
Employee 3	$2,128.04	$292,642	$1,336.64	$183,810

Employee 1, the youngest, will receive an increased benefit from the cash balance plan. Employee 2 will receive the same benefit. Employee 3, the oldest, will receive a reduced benefit.

Because the retirement benefit depends on the hypothetical account balance, which has the attributes of a DC plan, the benefits for a younger employee will be higher as a result of the longer period of compounding. Many older employees voiced this objection when their employers converted their traditional DB plan to a cash balance plan. Many government agencies became involved in this issue, including the Department of Labor under the Age Discrimination in Employment Act and the Equal Employment Opportunity Commission. Assuming this to be the first plan year, the funding of the two plans is compared and the cost for the cash balance plan is determined to be lower than for the traditional DB plan:

	Traditional Plan	Cash Balance Plan
Employee 1	$ 1,047	$ 1,883
Employee 2	$ 4,268	$ 4,268
Employee 3	$ 6,758	$ 4,245
	$12,073	$10,396

The lower cost for the cash balance plan is caused mainly by the lower benefit for Employee 3, the oldest employee. Because each employee's retirement benefit is based on the compounding effect of the hypothetical account, the less time an employee has to retirement, the lower the retirement benefit compared to a traditional DB plan and the lower the cost to fund.

Plans for Nonprofits and Nonqualified Plans

Chapter 7

PROFIT-SHARING PLANS

In Chapter 4 we said that a *profit-sharing* plan is:
A plan established and maintained by an employer to provide for the *participation in his or her profits* by the employees or their beneficiaries. The plan must provide a definite predetermined formula for allocating the contributions made to the plan among the participants and for distributing the funds accumulated under the plan after a fixed number of years, the attainment of a stated age or upon the prior occurrence of some event such as layoff, illness, disability, retirement, death or severance of employment.

It is clear that a nonprofit organization does not produce profits. That being the case, profit-sharing plans were not available to nonprofit organizations since profit-sharing contributions could be made only from current or accumulated profits. Although the original concept and basis for profit-sharing plans was for employees to share in profits, that was changed by the Technical and Miscellaneous Revenue Act of 1988 (TAMRA). TAMRA eliminates the need for contributions to be based on profits and allows for the adoption of profit-sharing plans by tax-exempt organizations. As a result of that change, a *profit-sharing* plan is really a discretionary defined contribution plan. In addition, 401(k) plans (see Chapter 5) were not available to nonprofit organizations prior to 1997.

SECTION 457 PLANS

In application, a 457 plan is not a qualified plan but instead is a plan of deferred compensation. These plans are not subject to the general qualification requirements of qualified retirement plans under Internal Revenue Code Sections 401(a) and 501(a) and therefore are not funded in a tax-exempt trust. The deferral made by an employee is includible only in income for the taxable year in which payments are paid to the employee or other beneficiary, or the funds are otherwise made available to the participant or other beneficiary.

An eligible deferred compensation plan means a plan established and maintained by an eligible employer (nonprofit or government employer) in which only individuals who perform service for the employer may be participants. The plan must provide that the maximum amount that can be deferred under the plan for the year does not exceed the lesser of the applicable dollar amount ($13,000 for 2004) or 100% of the participant's compensation. As a special limit the plan may also provide that in one or more of the participant's last three taxable years ending before attaining normal retirement age under the plan, e.g., age 65, the limit above can be:

1. The lesser of twice the dollar amount (two times $13,000 for 2004) or
2. The sum of the current year's limitation ($13,000) plus any unused contributions in prior years.

Example 1: Harry White, a participant in an eligible 457 plan, will turn 62 on April 1, 2007. The 457 plan provides a normal retirement age of 65. Harry's compensation in 2007 is $40,000. In 2006 Harry elected to defer $2,000 under the 457 plan. The plan provides limitations on annual deferrals up to the maximum permitted, allowing both special Section 457 catch-up and age 50 catch-up (see Chapter 5). The applicable basic dollar limitation for eligible 457 plans in 2006 and 2007 is $15,000, and the additional dollar amount of permitted age 50 catch-up for 2007 is $5,000. Since Harry will turn 65 within the next three years, he elects to defer the maximum amount permissible. Assume that before 2006 Harry had no underutilized amounts. In 2006 he had an underutilized amount of $13,000 (i.e., the $15,000 plan ceiling minus the $2,000 deferred under the plan). Therefore, Harry's special Section 457 catch-up for 2007 is $28,000, the lesser of: (1) $30,000 (two times the basic annual ceiling for 2007), or (2) $28,000 ($15,000, the annual ceiling + $13,000, the underutilized amount from prior tax years). The age 50 limit including the catch-up for 2007 is $20,000: $15,000 (the annual ceiling) + $5,000 (the additional dollar amount). The limit on Harry's deferrals for 2007 is $28,000, the greater of (1) $20,000, the current year's dollar limit plus the age 50 catch-up, or (2) $28,000, the special Section 457 catch-up.

The plan must also provide that compensation will be deferred for any calendar month only if a written agreement providing for the deferral has been entered into before the beginning of the month. Unlike a trust created under a qualified plan all compensation deferred under the plan and all investment income on those investments remain solely the property and rights of the employer, subject to the claims of the employer's general creditors, until the account is made available to the participant or other beneficiary as provided above.

Distributions from 457 plans are subject to some of the same requirements as qualified plans but not all of these requirements. Generally, the funds in a 457 plan cannot be made available to the employee before:

1. The calendar year in which the participant attains age 70½

2. When the participant has a severance from employment with the employer or
3. When the participant is faced with an unforeseeable emergency, similar to hardship distributions in a qualified plan.

In addition, the plan must meet the minimum distribution requirements (distributions beginning at age 70½) the same as qualified retirement plans (see Chapter 8).

For purposes of Section 457 plans, an eligible employer includes a state, political subdivision of a state and any agency or instrumentality of a state or political subdivision of a state, and any other organization (other than a governmental unit) exempt from tax. For purposes of this book, we are addressing only tax-exempt employers other than government entities. Unlike a *qualified* plan, which requires that benefits be provided only to *employees* of the plan sponsor, a 457 plan may include individuals that perform service as an independent contractor or an employee.

Section 457 also allows for *ineligible* plans. These plans are nonqualified and therefore are not subject to any of the rules of qualified plans including limitations on deferrals, distributions requirements and nondiscrimination requirements. In this case if an eligible employer provides for a deferral of compensation under any agreement or arrangement that is not an eligible deferred compensation plan, the compensation deferred under the ineligible plan is included in the gross income of the participant or beneficiary for the first tax year in which there is no substantial risk of forfeiture of the rights to the compensation deferred. The rights of a person to receive compensation that has been previously deferred including investment gains on those deferrals are subject to a substantial risk of forfeiture if the person's rights to the compensation are conditioned on the future performance of substantial services by that individual.

Wages deferred by an employee to a 401(k), SIMPLE IRA or 403(b) plan are generally subject to FICA taxation when they are deferred. However, certain nonqualified deferred compensation is subject to FICA tax when the services for which it is paid are performed or, if later, when the amounts payable are no longer subject to a substantial risk of forfeiture. In the case of an ineligible 457 plan the FICA taxes are due when the amounts are no longer subject to substantial risk of forfeiture. A trap for the unwary requires that if the substantial risk of forfeiture lapses, even though the participant has not received the funds, those funds are subject to taxation.

Since an ineligible 457 plan is not a qualified plan, the employer cannot submit a plan document to the Internal Revenue Service (IRS) for review and approval resulting in a favorable letter of determination. Instead the plan can be submitted for a favorable letter ruling. IRS will issue a favorable letter ruling on an unfunded deferred compensation plan only under the following conditions:

(1) If a plan provides for an election to defer the payment of compensation, the election must be made before the beginning of the period of service for which the compensation is payable. Except as described below, the deferral election cannot be made after the beginning of the period of service, regardless of any forfeiture provisions in the plan. The exceptions to this rule are that:

(a) In the year in which the plan is first implemented, an eligible participant may make an election to defer compensation for services to be performed after the election within 30 days after the date the plan is effective for eligible employees.

(b) In the first year in which a participant becomes eligible to participate in the plan, the newly eligible participant may make an election to defer compensation for services to be performed after the election within 30 days after the date the employee becomes eligible.

(2) If any elections (other than the initial election in (1) above) may be made by an employee after the beginning of the service period, the plan must set forth substantial forfeiture provisions that must remain in effect throughout the entire period of deferral before a ruling will be issued. A *substantial forfeiture provision* is one that imposes on the employee a significant limitation or duty, which requires a meaningful effort on his part to fulfill. There must also be a definite possibility that the event which will cause the forfeiture could occur.

(3) The plan must define the time and method for payment of the deferred compensation for each event (e.g., employment termination, regular retirement, disability retirement or death) that entitles a participant to receive benefits. The plan may specify the date of payment or provide that payments will begin within 30 days after the occurrence of a stated event. However, the plan may provide for payment of benefits in the case of an "unforeseeable emergency," which must be defined in the plan as an unanticipated emergency that is caused by an event beyond the control of the participant or beneficiary and that would result in severe financial hardship to the individual if early withdrawals were not permitted. The plan must also provide that any early withdrawals approved by the employer are limited to the amount necessary to meet the emergency.

(4) The plan must provide that participants have the status of general unsecured creditors of the employer and that the plan constitutes a mere promise by the employer to make benefit payments in the future. The plan must also state that it is the intention of the parties that the arrangements be unfunded for tax purposes and for purposes of Title I of ERISA.

(5) The plan must provide that a participant's rights to benefit payments under the plan are not subject in any manner to anticipation, alienation, sale, transfer, assignment, pledge, encumbrance, attachment or garnishment by creditors of the participant or the participant's beneficiary.

Another major difference between a qualified retirement plan and an ineligible 457 plan is the status of the plan assets. In a qualified plan, all plan assets must be segregated in a qualified trust as provided in Internal Revenue Code Section 501(a). In an ineligible 457 plan the plan assets, i.e., participant's deferred compensation and investment gains, remain part of the assets of the sponsor of the plan, the employer that establishes the plan as unfunded. These assets are available to creditors. If the assets were otherwise segregated, the employee would be taxed. In some cases the participant's deferrals are not invested in specific investment vehicles but remain part of the employer's general assets with investment gains based on actual investment vehicles, e.g., a specific financial index. The participant's account, in this case, would be a theoretical account maintained for reporting purposes to the participant only. When the account is due to be distributed, the payments would be made from the general assets of the employer. Since the security of the assets depends on the financial solvency of the employer in an ineligible 457 plan, employees will participate in this type of plan only if their employer's financial condition is sound.

In many cases, both an eligible and an ineligible 457 plan are sponsored by the same employer. Deferrals are first made to the eligible plan to the extent of the allowable limit with excess deferrals deposited to the ineligible plan.

> **Example 2:** Howard Smith is the director of ABC Non Profit Association. His salary is $225,000 annually. ABC adopts an eligible and an ineligible 457 plan. Howard elects to defer 20% of his salary each year or $45,000. The deferral would be allocated as follows:
>
> | | | |
> |---|---|---|
> | Eligible plan: | $13,000 | (for 2004) |
> | Ineligible plan: | $32,000 | |

Because of a quirk in the rules for 457 plans, the limit for eligible 457 plans, $13,000 for 2004, is not coordinated with any other plans that allow for deferred compensation. In practice this would allow an individual to defer $13,000 to an eligible 457 plan and an additional $13,000 to a 403(b) plan or a 401(k) plan.

> **Example 3:** In 2004, Carol Jones, who has compensation of $78,000, participates in the eligible Section 457 plan of XYZ Company. The plan permits a maximum deferral of the lesser of $13,000 (which is the maximum annual deferral for 2004) or 100% of includible compensation. In 2004, Carol defers the full $13,000 under the plan. In addition she also makes a salary reduction contribution of $13,000 to a Code Sec. 403(b) annuity with the same employer. Because of the repeal of the coordination limitation, Carol's salary reduction deferrals under the Code Sec. 403(b) annuity are not considered in determining her applicable deferral limitations under the eligible Section 457 plan.

TAX-SHELTERED ANNUITIES (403(b) PLANS)

A tax-sheltered annuity may be offered by a corporation and any community chest, fund or foundation, organized and operated exclusively for religious, charitable, scientific, testing for public safety, literary or educational purposes, in addition to other less common tax-exempt entities, to an employee who performs services for that organization. All employees must be eligible to make salary deferrals except students performing services and employees who normally work less than 20 hours per week.

The current limit for deferrals to a tax-sheltered annuity is the same as the limits for 401(k) plans, i.e., $13,000 for the year 2004 plus a $3,000 catch-up contribution for any employee who has or will reach his or her 50th birthday during the year. In the case of a tax-sheltered annuity, the limit is coordinated with 401(k) deferrals. Prior to 2002, the limitations in a 403(b) plan were based on the *exclusion allowance*. The exclusion allowance was:

20% of the employee's "includible compensation" times the employee's number of years of service reduced by the amount contributed by the employer on behalf of the employee for annuity contracts and excludable from the employee's gross income in years before the tax year for which the exclusion is being determined.

Includible compensation for a tax year is the amount of compensation received from the employer (the exempt organization or public school), and includible in the employee's gross income, for the most recent period, which can be counted as a full "year of service" (generally the calendar year) and which precedes the current tax year by no more than five years.

Includible compensation includes:

Any elective deferral to a 401(k) plan, to a salary reduction simplified employee pension plan (SARSEP), a Code Sec. 403(b) annuity contract, to a savings incentive match plan for employees individual retirement account (SIMPLE IRA) plan, and any amount contributed or deferred by the employer at the election of the employee, a Code Sec. 125 cafeteria plan; a Code Sec. 132(f)(4) qualified transportation fringe benefit plan; or a Code Sec. 457 deferred compensation plan of a state or local government or a tax-exempt organization.

If an employee is covered by a qualified pension, profit-sharing or stock bonus plan maintained by one organization and is also covered by a tax-sheltered Code Sec. 403(b) annuity to which another employer contributed (i.e., remitted the employee's deferrals), the contributions by both employers to both plans would have to be aggregated to determine whether the overall limitation on allocations to the employee's account have been exceeded. A common example of the application of this limit is the medical professional in private practice who also participates in a hospital's 403(b) plan.

Although tax-sheltered annuities are not subject to most of the rules for qualified plans, many of the tax qualification requirements that apply to qualified employer plans are also applied, with modifications, to tax-sheltered annuities. These include required distribution rules (age 70½ distributions, see Chapter 8), direct rollover rules from other plans and nondiscrimination rules with respect to eligibility to participate in the tax-sheltered annuity plan.

Tax-sheltered annuities are treated as being adopted by the employee, not the employer. The employer's only function in a tax-sheltered annuity plan is to act as a conduit to facilitate remitting the employee's salary deferral to the financial institution that will be holding the funds. Over the last three to five years, the Internal Revenue Service has been conducting test audits on tax-sheltered annuity plans to determine whether or not the various guidelines are being followed. The result of these audits indicated several defects: organizations offering tax-sheltered annuity plans that were not eligible to do so, employee deferrals in excess of allowable limits and employer involvement in these plans other than acting as a conduit. In the event of employer involvement, e.g., making a matching contribution, severely limiting which financial institutions will be made available to employees to hold the employees' deferrals or including eligibility requirements more restrictive than indicated above, the plan is then subject to all of the same requirements as a qualified plan, including:

1. The plan and trust must be a definite written program that sets forth all the provisions necessary for qualification. In the absence of employer involvement, a 403(b) plan does not require a plan document.
2. The plan must be communicated to the employees. This is accomplished by preparing a summary plan description (see Chapter 2).
3. The plan must be for the exclusive benefit of employees and their beneficiaries.
4. Contributions or benefits provided by the employer must not discriminate in favor of the highly compensated employees (see Chapter 9).
5. The plan must satisfy the minimum vesting rules (see Chapter 2).
6. The plan must satisfy minimum coverage requirements (see Chapter 9).
7. Plan assets cannot be diverted or used for any purpose other than providing benefits to employees.
8. The plan must provide automatic survivor benefits providing that, in the event of death, distributions to a surviving spouse will be paid in the form of a 50% joint-and-survivor annuity unless the surviving spouse elects an alternate form, e.g., lump sum. In addition, periodic notices explaining the survivor benefit must be distributed to all married participants.
9. The plan may not provide contributions or benefits in excess of statutory limitations (see Chapter 3).
10. The plan must provide for required distributions (see Chapter 8).
11. The plan must provide that, in the event of partial or total termination, the employees' right to benefits or contributions accrued will become 100% vested (see Chapter 15). This requirement would apply if the employer were making a matching contribution subject to a vesting schedule.
12. The plan must provide that benefits may not be assigned or alienated.
13. The plan must provide that only the first $205,000 (as adjusted) of an employee's compensation may be taken into account to determine contributions or benefits.
14. The plan must comply with the top-heavy rules (see Chapter 9).
15. The plan must file an annual Form 5500 with all applicable attachments (see Chapter 13). If the employer is unaware of the fact that the plan is subject to the Employee Retirement Income Security Act (ERISA) and the prior Form 5500s were not filed, the plan can submit the past-due forms under the Delinquent Filer Voluntary Compliance Program (DFVC). Under DFVC, for small plans, fewer than 100 participants, the applicable penalty is $10 per day for each day that the annual report is filed late, without regard to any extensions. However, the maximum penalty for a single submission, including submissions that cover more than one year's delinquent annual report filing for the plan, is $750 rather than $1,500. If there is a delinquent or late annual report due for a plan year in which the plan was not a small plan, then the plan is ineligible for the reduced maximum penalty and must pay the otherwise applicable penalty.

16. If the plan has more than 100 participants, an outside audit must be attached to the annual Form 5500.

Many of these requirements have minimal impact on the operation of the plan while others will add significant administration and cost on the part of the employer. For example, the cost of a plan document ranges from $1,500 to $2,500 and annual administration, including the annual filing of the Form 5500, can be in the thousands depending on the number of eligible employees. The message here is to make sure, as an employer, not to exercise any control over the plan but to maintain status only as a facilitator.

For those plans that have uncovered defects, the Internal Revenue Service has established a program allowing for correction of those defects. The program is called the Employee Plans Compliance Resolution System (EPCRS) and provides for correction of:

- Operational failure
- Employer eligibility failure
- Demographic failure.

An *operational failure* includes:

1. A failure to satisfy the requirements relating to the availability of salary reduction contributions, i.e., availability is nondiscriminatory
2. A failure to satisfy the nondiscrimination requirements (actual contribution percentage test) for matching contributions (see Chapter 5)
3. A failure to satisfy the compensation limitation requirements, $205,000 for 2004
4. A failure to satisfy the distribution restrictions on salary deferrals
5. A failure to satisfy the incidental death benefit rules
6. A failure to pay minimum required distributions, the age 70½ rules
7. A failure to give employees the right to elect a direct rollover, including the failure to give meaningful notice of the right to a rollover
8. A failure of the annuity contract or the custodial agreement to provide participants with a right to elect a direct rollover
9. A failure to satisfy the limit on elective deferrals, $13,000 for 2004
10. A failure of the annuity contract or custodial agreement to provide the limit on elective deferrals
11. A failure involving contributions or allocations of excess amounts, i.e., the lesser of 100% of compensation or $41,000 for 2004
12. Any other failure to satisfy requirements under Code Sec. 403(b) that:
    (a) Results in the loss of Code Sec. 403(b) status for the plan or the loss of Code Sec. 403(b) status for the custodial account(s) or annuity contract(s) under the plan
    (b) Is not a "demographic failure" or "eligibility failure," or a failure related to contributions on behalf of individuals who are not employees of the employer.

An *employer eligibility failure* is any of the following:

1. The adoption of a plan intended to satisfy the requirements of Code Sec. 403(b) by an employer that is not:
   (i) A Code Sec. 501(c)(3) tax-exempt organization or
   (ii) A public educational organization

2. A failure to satisfy the nontransferability requirement of the annuity contract prohibiting the transfer to an ineligible person
3. A failure to initially establish or maintain a custodial account
4. A failure to buy (initially or thereafter) either an annuity contract from an insurance company or a custodial account from a regulated investment company utilizing a bank or an approved nonbank trustee/custodian.

A *demographic failure* is a failure to satisfy the Code's nondiscrimination and coverage requirements. Nondiscrimination requirements prohibit discrimination in favor of highly compensated employees (see Chapter 9). The coverage rules require that the ratio of nonhighly compensated employees that are covered by the plan to highly compensated employees covered by the plan be equal to or more than 70%.

Example 4: Midtown Hospital offers a 403(b) plan to their employees; however, the employees of their lab are excluded. There are no highly compensated employees employed in the lab. The employee profile of Midtown Hospital is as follows:

Highly compensated employees	10
Lab employees	12
Other nonhighly compensated employees	29

Nonhighly compensated employees covered $= 29 / 41 = 70.73\%$

Highly compensated employees covered $= 10 / 10 = 100.00\%$

$70.73\% / 100.00\% = 70.73\%$

This plan passes the coverage test since the ratio is 70.73%, equal to or more than 70%.

Here are some of the more common defects and the correction methods.

CORRECTION PRINCIPLES THAT ARE APPLICABLE TO THE TREATMENT OF "EXCESS AMOUNTS"

An *excess amount* under a 403(b) plan means any contributions or allocations that are in excess of: (1) the Code Sec. 415 limits, the lesser of 100% of compensation or $41,000 for 2004, or (2) for years before January 1, 2002, the exclusion allowance (see above).

Excess amounts may be corrected through distribution or retention. To correct excess contributions or excess allocations by distribution, excess amounts for a year, adjusted for earnings through the date of distribution, must be distributed to affected participants and beneficiaries, and are includible in their gross income in the year distributed. The distribution must be reported on Form 1099-R for the year of distribution with respect to each participant or beneficiary receiving a distribution. The distribution of excess amounts is not an eligible rollover distribution. In addition, the plan sponsor must inform affected participants and beneficiaries that the distribution of excess amounts is not eligible for rollover.

As an alternative, if either the employer or the funding agent is unable to make a correcting distribution, excess amounts will be treated as corrected even where the excess amounts have been retained in the 403(b) plan, if excess amounts arising from an Internal Revenue Code Section 415 contributions limitation failure, adjusted for earnings through the date of correction, reduce the affected participants' applicable Internal Revenue Code Section 415 contributions limit for the year following the year of correction, and later years, until the excess is eliminated.

Example 5: Dr. Johnson participates in the Midtown Hospital 403(b) plan. Due to an oversight the total of all contributions made for Dr. Johnson for 2004 was $45,000 although the Internal Revenue Code Section 415 limit was $41,000. For 2005, assuming the limit remains the same, i.e., $41,000, Dr. Johnson's limit for 2005 would be $37,000 ($41,000 − $4,000 the excess from the prior year).

The permitted EPCRS correction of an employer eligibility failure requires:
(1) The discontinuance of all contributions (including salary reduction and after-tax contributions) beginning no later than the date the application under the Voluntary Correction Program is filed
(2) That plan assets
    (a) Remain in the trust, annuity contract or custodial account
    (b) Be distributed no earlier than the occurrence of one of the applicable distribution events, i.e., dies, reaches age 59½, separates from service, becomes disabled or, in the case of contributions made under a salary reduction agreement, encounters financial hardship.

Even though an employer may not be eligible to maintain a 403(b) plan, the correction for eligibility failure above does not allow the employer to simply terminate the plan. After correction, an employer would still have to incur the expense and administrative burden of maintaining a separate plan until all the assets are distributed as provided above.

A submission under the Voluntary Correction Program requires a fee for submission determined in accordance with the following table, which is based on the number of employees:

Number of Employees	Fee
20 or fewer	$ 750
21 to 50	1,000
51 to 100	2,500
101 to 500	5,000
501 to 1,000	8,000
1,001 to 5,000	15,000
5,001 to 10,000	20,000
Over 10,000	25,000

Although a 403(b) plan is commonly referred to as a tax-sheltered annuity, an alternate form of establishing a 403(b) account is through the use of a custodial account with a regulated investment company (mutual fund). The funds held in the custodial account may not be paid or made available to any distributee before the employee dies, attains age 59½, has a severance from employment, becomes disabled or, in the case of contributions made pursuant to a salary reduction agreement, encounters financial hardship. These restrictions are the same as those applied to accounts established using an annuity contract.

Amounts held in either a 403(b) annuity or custodial account may be rolled over to an eligible retirement plan including:

1. An individual retirement account described in Section 408(a)
2. An individual retirement annuity described in Section 408(b)
3. A qualified trust, e.g., profit-sharing plan
4. An annuity plan described in Section 403(a)
5. An eligible deferred compensation plan described in Section 457(b)
6. An annuity contract described in Section 403(b).

DISTRIBUTION REQUIREMENTS

Distributions may not begin before age 59½, severance from employment, death or disability. A hardship distribution may not be made from any income attributable to salary deferrals but only the salary deferral amount. Similar to qualified plans, distributions must begin under the age 70½ distribution rules. Generally, distributions must begin over life expectancy on the April 1 following retirement (see Chapter 8).

NONQUALIFIED PLANS

Under some conditions it is in the best interest of the employer to provide employer-funded benefits to a select group of employees without the need to comply with all the rules and regulations of qualified plans. On the plus side nonqualified plans may pick and choose who will participate, the level of benefits to be provided for each participant and when and under what conditions those benefits will be paid. This sounds like the ideal plan. On the negative side, however, the contributions used to fund the nonqualified benefits are not deductible by the employer. The tax benefit is not realized until the benefits are actually paid to the employee at which time the employer takes a deduction for the amount paid and the employee pays tax on the amount received. Nonqualified plans are sometimes used to retain key employees and in other cases to provide benefits to highly paid employees in excess of the maximum benefits that may be paid in a qualified plan. The popular forms of nonqualified plans are reviewed below.

SUPPLEMENTAL EXECUTIVE RETIREMENT PLAN (SERP)

The purpose of a supplemental executive retirement plan (SERP) is to provide benefits for salaried employees in excess of the limitations imposed by the Internal Revenue Code.

Example 6: Howard Redding, the CEO of Warren Manufacturing Inc., is a participant in Warren's defined benefit (DB) plan. The plan provides a benefit for Howard of the lesser of 100% of his high three-year average compensation or $165,000 annually (2004 limit). Howard's annual compensation for 2004 is $460,000 and his high three-year average compensation is $400,000. To provide Howard with 100% of his total compensation as a retirement benefit, Warren adopts a SERP that provides a benefit of 100% of the high three-year average compensation, without limit, offset by the benefit provided in Warren's qualified DB plan. If Warren Manufacturing Inc. informally funds the SERP, the contributions are not deductible and the investment gains are taxed to Warren. When the additional benefits are paid to Howard, most likely in the form of monthly retirement benefits, Warren will take a deduction for those payments, and Howard will include the payments in his taxable income.

The funds set aside to provide the additional benefits remain assets of Warren and are subject to Warren's creditors. If those assets were segregated for the sole purpose of funding the additional benefit, Howard would be taxed currently.

The creation or adoption of a rabbi trust to protect the diversification of the assets to other business use (other than to pay creditors) does not result in income to the employee. A *rabbi trust* is an irrevocable trust in which an employer deposits deferred compensation or employer contributions for the benefit of an employee, which is treated as a grantor trust where the trust's assets are subject to the claims of the employer's creditors. An employer's deposit into a rabbi trust is not taxable to the employee as long as the rabbi trust requirements, e.g., the trust's assets are subject to the claims of the employer's creditors, are met. The crediting of deferred amounts does not result in the constructive receipt of income by an employee using the cash method of accounting, because participants in the deferred compensation plan have only the rights of unsecured creditors.

Benefits from a rabbi trust are includible in the income of the employee for the year in which the benefits are paid or the year in which the benefits are made available, whichever is earlier.

An executive who is the beneficiary of an existing rabbi trust, and who is offered an opportunity to transfer rabbi trust funds to a secular trust, must include the amount that can be transferred, even if no transfer is made. IRS' position is that the executive would be in constructive receipt of the income that could be transferred in the year that the offer is made.

A *secular trust* is an irrevocable trust in which the employee's interest and his or her right to the trust's assets are vested from the trust's inception, and the trust's assets are not subject to claims of the employer's creditors. The employee's deferred compensation is paid to, and held by, the trustee for the benefit of the employee until the occurrence of specified events, e.g., retirement, death, disability or passage of specified time period, requiring distribution of the trust's assets to the employee. Secular trusts provide the employee with a greater degree of protection than a rabbi trust because a secular trust is not revocable and its assets cannot be appropriated by the employer or its creditors. Consequently, the protection provided for the employee's deferred compensation by a secular trust is similar to that provided by a tax-qualified retirement plan. However, unlike a tax-qualified retirement trust, the secular trust cannot protect the employee against current taxation on the employer's contributions to the trust.

TOP-HAT PLANS

Top-hat plans are maintained by an employer primarily for the purpose of providing deferred compensation for a select group of management or highly compensated employees and are excluded from coverage under ERISA's (a) participation and vesting provisions, (b) funding requirements and (c) fiduciary responsibility rules. In addition, the plan is unfunded similar to a SERP, i.e., the assets are part of the general assets of the employer.

To qualify for exclusion from ERISA's participation, vesting, funding and fiduciary responsibility provisions as a top-hat plan, the plan's primary purpose must be to provide deferred compensation for a select group of management or highly compensated employees. For this purpose, the definition of *highly compensated* as used in the qualified plan context does not determine which employees are considered a select group of management or highly compensated employees. Although plans offered to a very small percentage of an employer's workforce may qualify as a top-hat plan, there is no specific guideline that establishes when a plan is too large to be deemed select. A plan offered to 15.34% of a bank's employees was held to have been established for a select group because all plan participants were selected officers of the bank, in management positions and were highly compensated in comparison to bank employees at large. An employee in one case was part of a select group of management or highly compensated employees where he was the highest earning nonowner employed by the company and received almost twice as much as the compensation of the next highest employee.

Plans funded by employer deposits can also be used as golden handcuffs to lock a key employee to the employer. This type of arrangement is designed in such a way that the value of the benefits given up due to termination of employment are well in excess of any monetary benefit the employee may realize as a result of a change in employment. For example, the plan may say that, when the employee's youngest child begins college, the plan will pay $10,000 per year for four years for each child entering college. In addition, the plan will pay a retirement benefit to the employee beginning at age 55 of $50,000 annually for 15 years, and will pay the same benefit to the employee's beneficiary in the event of death before retirement. If, however, the employee leaves before any of these payments are made, any unpaid benefits are forfeited. The benefit amounts and timing of payments can be different for each employee. Generally, the employer will enter into an agreement with the employee, setting out the benefits and what is expected of the employee, e.g., performance. In addition, the benefits can be linked to a performance guideline on a money purchase basis, i.e., the annual deposit made by the employer would vary based on the employee's performance relative to a guideline.

In many cases, this type of plan is funded with life insurance products. The product is designed so that the death benefit is as low as possible allowing higher cash accumulations to fund the lifetime benefits as described above. The growth of

---

cash value in a life insurance policy is not taxable until distributed, providing a tax-advantaged facility to fund the benefits. In the event of death, the insurance proceeds are available to the employer to fund the survivor benefits and/or to recoup some of the contributions made to fund the benefits during the employee's working years.

Voluntary and Mandatory Distributions From Qualified Plans

Chapter 8

The availability of distributions from a qualified retirement plan depends on:
1. The type of plan
2. Whether the distribution is voluntary or involuntary
3. The event that triggers the distribution
4. The provisions in the plan document
5. The age of the participant.

VOLUNTARY DISTRIBUTIONS

For purposes of voluntary distributions and the rules guiding *in-service* voluntary distributions of employer-funded accounts, qualified plans are classified as profit-sharing or pension plans. Pension plans include defined benefit (DB) (see Chapter 6), target benefit (see Chapter 4), money purchase (see Chapter 4) and cash balance plans (see Chapter 6). The rules governing profit-sharing plans, in part, state, "The plan must provide . . . for distributing the funds accumulated under the plan after a fixed number of years, the attainment of a stated age or upon the prior occurrence of some event such as layoff, illness, disability, retirement, death or severance of employment."

Relying on the preceding Treasury regulations statement, a profit-sharing plan can provide in the plan document that in-service distributions of accumulated vested funds are available after a fixed number of years. It has been determined that a minimum of two years would satisfy this requirement. In addition to allowing distributions of funds accumulated after two years, a profit-sharing plan may also include a provision in the plan document allowing for distributions of all vested funds after five years of plan participation. The basis for the availability of in-service distributions in profit-sharing plans goes back to the original purpose of profit-sharing plans: A profit-sharing plan is a plan established and maintained by an employer to provide for the participation in his profits by his employees or their beneficiaries. A plan that allows for in-service distributions is also allowing the employees and beneficiaries to share some of the company profits.

Pension plans cannot, however, allow for in-service distributions before the normal retirement age defined in the plan. Regulations state, "A pension plan within the meaning of section 401(a) is a plan established and maintained by an employer primarily to provide systematically for the payment of *definitely determinable* benefits to employees over a period of years, usually for life, after retirement" (emphasis added). A definitely determinable benefit or contribution is provided if the amount, duration and the person's eligibility to receive it are ascertainable from the plan document or other instrument.

If a pension plan allowed for the withdrawal of employer contributions before retirement distributions began, the benefits would not be definitely determinable. The amounts would not be ascertainable because of the unknown effect of potential withdrawals. The prohibition on in-service distributions in a pension plan does not prevent distributions from being made to participants who have reached the retirement age as defined in the plan but who choose to continue employment past retirement age.

In addition to voluntary in-service distributions, qualified plans may provide for statutory voluntary distributions including loans, hardship distributions and early retirement, in addition to statutory-triggering events, such as participant termination, attainment of retirement age, death, disability and court-issued divorce decrees. The availability of some of these distributions depends on the type of plan. In some cases the distribution may cause adverse tax consequences for the participant receiving the distribution.

PLAN LOANS

A qualified plan can restrict the availability of loans to financial hardship, can be liberal and can allow loans for any purpose or may not include a loan provision at all at the option of the employer sponsoring the plan.

To avoid adverse tax consequences, all loans from qualified plans must comply with the following rules:

1.   *The loan must be available to all participants and beneficiaries on a reasonably equivalent basis.* To satisfy this requirement, loans must be available to all participants without regard to race, color, religion, sex, age or national origin. Factors considered in making the loan can be only those that a commercial lender would consider in making a similar loan and may include, e.g., creditworthiness and financial need. The facts and circumstances surrounding the operation of the loan program must indicate that loans are not unreasonably withheld from any applicant.

     Example 1: The Connors Manufacturing Company profit-sharing plan provides for loans only to those participants whose account balance is at least $100,000. This provision would not comply with the above requirement since it is unlikely that any of the employees other than the highly compensated would have an account balance that high.

2.   *The loan does not discriminate in favor of highly compensated employees (HCEs).* This requirement is satisfied if the facts and circumstances do

not indicate that a large number of nonhighly compensated employees (NHCEs) are excluded from receiving loans.

> **Example 2:** An example of this would be a provision that security for a loan may only be the participant's vested benefits and the minimum loan is $25,000. In the plan under review, only HCEs have sufficiently high enough vested benefits to secure a loan.

3. *The loan is made in accordance with specific plan provisions.* To satisfy this requirement, the plan must contain provisions specifically authorizing the establishment of a loan program. The loan program can be part of the plan document or it can be a separate document and must include:
   (a) The identity of the person authorized to administer the loan program
   (b) A procedure for applying for a loan
   (c) The basis on which loans will be approved or denied if, for example, loans are only available for specific purposes
   (d) Limitations on the types and amounts of loans
   (e) The procedure for determining a reasonable rate of interest
   (f) The events constituting default and the steps that will be taken to collect the balance of the loan in the event of default.
4. *The loan bears a reasonable rate of interest.* A loan bears a reasonable rate of interest if it is commensurate with the rates charged by those in the business of lending money for loans under similar circumstances. Generally, this requirement is satisfied if two or three local banks are polled to determine the rate on a similar loan with respect to amount, security and duration.
5. *The loan is adequately secured.* A loan is adequately secured if the security pledged may be sold, foreclosed upon or otherwise disposed of upon default of the loan, and the value and liquidity of the security is sufficient so that a default will not result in loss of principal or interest. The participant's vested benefits most commonly serve as security for the loan.

Loans from qualified plans to participants must comply with the following Internal Revenue Code (IRC) guidelines to avoid being treated as taxable distributions:

1. The maximum amount of a loan available to a plan participant is the lesser of $50,000 or 50% of the participant's vested benefit.
2. The dollar limit of $50,000 is further reduced by the highest outstanding loan balance for the participant during the prior one-year period. The purpose of this provision is to prevent participants from avoiding #4 below by renewing a maximum loan annually for an indefinite period of time.

> **Example 3:** Jonathan takes a $50,000 loan on January 1, 2004, payable over 12 months. On January 1, 2005, he requests a new loan for $50,000. The plan administrator denies that loan since the maximum loan available (see #1) reduced by the highest outstanding balance over the prior year ($50,000) results in zero. In the absence of this rule Jonathan could continue renewing his loan annually to avoid the five-year limit in #4 below.

3. The loan amount may exceed 50% of the vested benefit but is then limited to $10,000. If the participant's account balance is less than $10,000, additional security would have to be provided to the plan. This option is not recommended for most plans since the need for additional security adds to the administrative costs of operating the plan.
4. The loan must be repaid over no more than five years, with level amortization payments, including interest and principal payable, at least quarterly. The loan term and periodic payments must be part of the loan request.
5. The loan may be for a period in excess of five years if its purpose is to acquire a primary residence of the participant. This option is not recommended for most plans because of the additional administrative costs.
6. The loan must be evidenced by a legally enforceable agreement in writing specifying the amount of the loan, the term of the loan and the repayment schedule.

If the requirements above to avoid taxation are not satisfied, the loan or a part of the loan will be considered a deemed distribution. A *deemed distribution* is an amount considered, for income tax purposes, to be distributed to the participant at the time the loan fails to satisfy the preceding requirements to avoid taxation.

This would apply to a loan that is issued for a period in excess of the maximum period allowable, that does not comply with the level amortization requirement or that is not evidenced by an enforceable agreement and would cause the entire amount of the original loan to be considered a deemed distribution taxed to the participant. If the only defect in the loan is that the amount is in excess of the maximum allowable, only the excess is treated as a deemed distribution. An exception to the requirement of level amortization payments is available for a participant on leave of absence for up to one year. A leave of absence due to military service allows for the suspension of loan payments for the entire period of the military service.

A deemed distribution may also occur if the participant fails to make a scheduled amortization payment. The plan may allow for a grace period for payment through the end of the calendar quarter following the quarter in which the payment was due.

Example 4: If, for example, a payment is due on February 10, the grace period would expire on June 30, after which the entire outstanding balance of the loan would be a deemed distribution.

Because a deemed distribution is in fact a taxable distribution, it is also subject to a 10% early distribution penalty if the participant has not yet reached age 59½.

HARDSHIP DISTRIBUTIONS

Hardship distributions are customary in 401(k) plans because of the limited availability of in-service distributions but may also be included in profit-sharing plans. The amounts available for hardship distributions are also limited, and the availability of a hardship distribution must be specifically provided for in the plan document. This amount can include the following:
1. Employee elective contributions plus investment earnings

2. Qualified matching contributions (QMACs) used to satisfy the actual deferral percentage (ADP) test plus investment earnings (see Chapter 5)
3. Qualified nonelective contributions (QNECs) used to satisfy the ADP test plus investment earnings (see Chapter 5).

Items 2 and 3 are further limited to their value as of the last day of the 1988 plan year, e.g., December 31, 1988, in a calendar-year plan. Additions to these balances after the last day of the 1988 plan year are not available for hardship distributions. A hardship withdrawal must also satisfy a two-part test:

1. The withdrawal must be made because of the participant's immediate and heavy financial need. The determination of immediate and heavy financial need is based on the facts and circumstances. This requirement focuses more on the nature of the need. The regulations indicate that payment of funeral expenses would qualify, but the purchase of a boat would not.
2. The withdrawal must be necessary to satisfy that need. Whether the withdrawal is necessary to satisfy the need depends on the amount of the withdrawal, i.e., whether it is in excess of the financial need and whether funds are available elsewhere to satisfy the need. The amount of the withdrawal may also include applicable income taxes and penalties allowing the distribution to be grossed up.

Example 5: Carol has established an immediate and heavy financial need of $30,000. Her actual hardship withdrawal will be a larger amount, after applicable taxes are taken into account:

Financial need:	$30,000
Participant's age:	50
Income tax due:	30%
Excise tax due:	10% (distribution before age 59½)
Total distribution:	$50,000
Less:	
Income tax	($15,000)
Excise tax	($ 5,000)
Net distribution:	$30,000

The rules governing hardship withdrawals offer two ways of satisfying this two-part test. One is based on a facts-and-circumstances determination by the plan administrator (generally the employer), and the other is a safe harbor approach, which guarantees compliance if the safe harbor rules are followed. Either approach may be used for each of the two parts of the test. In most cases, particularly in small- to medium-sized companies, the safe harbor approach is used for both parts of the test.

Although the facts-and-circumstances method offers more flexibility in determining what constitutes a hardship, it also creates the possibility of noncompliance if the plan administrator makes an incorrect judgment on the validity of the application for the hardship withdrawal. This is possible because the administrator must secure documentation from the applicant to support compliance with the two-part test:

Is the indicated need valid? Is the amount requested appropriate to satisfy the need (i.e., not inflated)? Does the applicant have other assets that can be used to satisfy the immediate and heavy financial need? Also, the administrator must ask whether any part of the financial need was satisfied by insurance. If so, that part is ineligible for a hardship withdrawal. Unless the employer has knowledge to the contrary, the employee's written representation that the distribution is necessary to satisfy an immediate and heavy financial need may be accepted.

The more common approach to hardship withdrawals in smaller companies is to use the safe harbor definition. Using the safe harbor guidelines, the hardship withdrawal is deemed to satisfy the two-part test. To satisfy the immediate and heavy financial need the withdrawal can be made for:

1. Payment of medical care for the participant, the participant's spouse or dependents not otherwise covered by insurance
2. Purchase and costs relating to the participant's primary residence (not including mortgage payments)
3. Payment of tuition and related educational expenses, including room and board, for the next 12 months for postsecondary education for the participant, the participant's spouse or other dependents
4. Payments necessary to avoid the eviction of the participant from the primary residence or foreclosure on the mortgage of the participant's primary residence.

To comply with the amount necessary to satisfy the financial need:

1. The amount of the withdrawal does not exceed the amount of the financial need. (Although, as previously discussed, the withdrawal may also include any applicable federal, state or local income taxes and penalties incurred in taking the withdrawal.)
2. The participant has made all other withdrawals, other than hardship withdrawals, e.g., loans currently available from any plan sponsored by the employer. If the plan allows for loans, the participant must take the maximum loan available to satisfy the financial hardship and, then to the extent the loan cannot satisfy the amount needed, the balance may be taken as a hardship distribution. The same is true if the plan allows for in-service distributions with respect to the employer's discretionary profit-sharing contributions.
3. All plans sponsored by the employer must provide that the participant will not be allowed to make any elective contributions to any plan sponsored by the same employer for at least six months after electing a hardship withdrawal.

EARLY DISTRIBUTIONS

Generally, all taxable distributions from qualified plans made before the participant's age 59½ are subject to a 10% excise tax in addition to the appropriate income taxes. The exceptions to this rule in part include:

1. Distributions made to a beneficiary on or after the death of the participant
2. Distributions made to a participant because of the participant's disability
3. Part of a series of substantially equal periodic payments made for the life of

the participant or the joint lives of the participant and beneficiary. In accordance with the Internal Revenue Service (IRS) guidelines, any one of the three following methods would be acceptable in determining the amount of the periodic payments:

(a) Following the method used to determine mandatory distributions beginning at age 70½ (see Mandatory Distributions below)

(b) Amortizing the participant's account balance over the participant's or the participant's and beneficiary's life expectancy using a reasonable interest rate.

> **Example 6:** Rita, aged 52, has a profit-sharing account balance of $800,000. Her life expectancy from an IRS table is 31.3 years and, using an interest rate of 8%, the annual payment would be $70,323.17.

(c) The third method is based on annuity purchase rates, i.e., the lump sum required when payments begin, for each dollar of monthly benefit payable for life using a reasonable mortality table and reasonable interest rates.

> **Example 7:** Using the same assumptions as in item b, the account balance would be divided by the monthly annuity purchase rate of $121.26 (based on the UP84 Mortality Table at 6%). The resulting annual payment would be $79,168.73 ($800,000 divided by $121.26 times 12).

Once the periodic payment amount is determined, that amount cannot be modified before the later of five years from the date of the first payment or attainment of age 59½, if later. If the amount is modified for reasons other than death or disability, the 10% excise tax plus interest will be due on all payments made that would have otherwise been subject to the 10% excise tax.

4. Made to an employee after separation from service after age 55 (early retirement). If a distribution is made to a participant during or after the calendar year in which the participant reaches age 55, the distribution is not subject to an early withdrawal penalty.

5. Allowable deductible medical expenses described in IRC Section 213 if provided for in the plan document

6. Payments to an alternate payee pursuant to a qualified domestic relations order (due to a divorce decree).

MANDATORY DISTRIBUTIONS

Most qualified plans would not be in place if not for the tax benefits: the deductibility of the contributions, both employer and employee, and the tax-deferral of the investment gains. As always, all good things come to an end. The tax benefits created through qualified plans are one of the largest income losses to the U.S. Treasury.

In 1987, IRS issued proposed regulations to guide the determination of the timing and amount of required distributions from qualified retirement plans. These regulations were complex and difficult for plan participants to understand. Over the years, many comments were submitted to the IRS in an attempt to have the regulations simplified. Finally, on January 12, 2001, proposed regulations were issued that simplified many aspects of these rules. The proposed regulations are effective with plan years beginning on or after January 1, 2002.

If the following Internal Revenue Code (IRC) rules are not satisfied, a 50% excise tax is levied on the difference between the required distribution and the actual distribution. The IRC states:

> A trust shall not constitute a qualified trust under this subsection unless the plan provides that the entire interest of each employee, (i) will be distributed to such employee not later than the *required beginning date,* or (ii) will be distributed, beginning not later than the required beginning date, in accordance with regulations, over the life of such employee or over the lives of such employee and a designated beneficiary (or over a period not extending beyond the life expectancy of such employee or the life expectancy of such employee and a designated beneficiary).

The *required beginning date* is April 1 of the calendar year following the later of the calendar year in which the employee attains age 70½ or the calendar year in which the employee retires. The required beginning date for a 5%-or-more owner (of the plan sponsor) is April 1 of the calendar year following the calendar year in which the employee-owner attains age 70½.

Example 8: Mike, whose date of birth is March 23, 1925, and who is not a 5% owner, had a required beginning date of the later of April 1, 1996, or April 1 of the calendar year following the year of actual retirement. Mike reached age 70½ on September 23, 1995, so the following April 1 was 1996. Darryl, whose date of birth is August 20, 1925, and who is not a 5% owner, had a required beginning date of the later of April 1, 1997 or April 1 of the calendar year following the year of actual retirement. Darryl reached age 70½ on February 20, 1996, and the following April 1 was in 1997.

The distribution made by the following April 1 is with respect to the prior calendar year (i.e., the distribution made on April 1, 1996, in Example 8 is for the 1995 calendar year, the first *distribution calendar year)*. A second distribution must be made by December 31, 1996, for the 1996 calendar year, and all future distributions must be made by December 31 of each year.

A *distribution calendar year* is a calendar year for which a minimum distribution is required. The first distribution calendar year is the calendar year a 5%-or-more owner reaches age 70½ or the calendar year an employee who is not a 5%-or-more owner retires.

BENEFICIARY DESIGNATION

If the goal of distribution planning is to defer taxation as long as possible, clearly the participant must name a designated beneficiary; otherwise, the benefit must be paid out in a lump sum soon after death (see below). The regulations provide that the designated beneficiary is determined as of September 30 of the year *following the year of the employee's death*. Deferred distribution techniques to children or grandchildren have been changed under the new regulations. It is now easier to plan for deferred distributions at the time the distribution must begin (the year following the death of the employee) with the use of disclaimers. The employee's spouse, if named as primary beneficiary, can disclaim to the children or grandchildren or, if the children are named beneficiary, they can disclaim to the grandchildren.

To take advantage of a qualified disclaimer by one or more beneficiaries, that disclaimer must satisfy IRC Section 2518, which provides:

> . . . the term "qualified disclaimer" means an irrevocable and unqualified refusal by a person to accept an interest in property but only if:
> 1. That refusal is in writing
> 2. That writing is received by the transferor of the interest, his or her legal representative, or the holder of the legal title to the property to which the interest relates not later than the date that is 9 months after the later of:
>   (a) The day on which the transfer creating the interest in that person is made, or
>   (b) The day on which that person attains age 21;
> 3. That person has not accepted the interest or any of its benefits; and
> 4. As a result of that refusal, the interest passes without any direction on the part of the person making the disclaimer and passes either:
>   (a) To the spouse of the decedent, or
>   (b) To a person other than the person making the disclaimer.

If the employee has more than one designated beneficiary as of the end of the year following the year of the employee's death, the beneficiary with the shortest life expectancy is considered the designated beneficiary. This rule is the same as the 1987 proposed regulations. To avoid this result, the account should be separated into several accounts, naming a single beneficiary for each so that the distribution from each account is based on that beneficiary's life expectancy. As an alternative, if there are two beneficiaries as of the date of death, one can be paid out in the year of death and one can be paid out as of the determination date, the last day of the year following the year of death. If, for example, the beneficiaries are the spouse and a charity, the charity can be paid out in the year of death and the spouse can be the sole beneficiary in the following year. This is particularly important if the spouse is more than ten years younger, so the longer Life Expectancy Table (see Table II) rather than the Uniform Table (see Table I) may be used.

If the account owner dies before the required beginning date, there are two ways to satisfy the minimum distribution requirements. The first method, the five-year rule, requires that the entire interest of the account owner be distributed within five years of death, i.e., by December 31 of the year in which the fifth anniversary of death occurs. This rule would be followed if the account owner did not name a beneficiary. If a beneficiary has been named, the applicable distribution period is the remaining life expectancy of the employee's designated beneficiary.

For tax purposes, the employee's spouse is the only beneficiary who can inherit a qualified pension benefit before the employee's required beginning date and defer taxation to a later date, i.e., the deceased employee's required beginning date, or

Table I

REQUIRED DISTRIBUTIONS UNDER NEW REGULATIONS FOR SINGLE LIFE OR SPOUSE TEN YEARS OR LESS YEARS YOUNGER THAN EMPLOYEE (UNIFORM TABLE)

Age	Life Expectancy	Percentage Distribution
71	26.5	3.77%
72	25.6	3.91
73	24.7	4.05
74	23.8	4.20
75	22.9	4.37
76	22.0	4.55
77	21.2	4.72
78	20.3	4.93
79	19.5	5.13
80	18.7	5.35

treat the benefit as his or her own and roll it to his or her own IRA rollover account. A spousal beneficiary is also the only one for whom the actual age of the beneficiary may be used to determine life expectancy if the employee's spouse is more than ten years younger than the employee.

The employee may also name a trust as beneficiary. In that case all beneficiaries of the trust are treated as beneficiaries of the employee for determination of the required minimum distribution. For purposes of determining the life expectancy of the beneficiary when the trust has multiple beneficiaries, the beneficiary with the shortest life expectancy is used, i.e., the oldest beneficiary.

DETERMINATION OF THE DISTRIBUTION PERIOD

For lifetime required distributions, the regulations provide a uniform distribution period for all employees of the same age. The Uniform Distribution Period Table is illustrated in part here in Table I. (The entire table can be found in Treasury Regulation 1.72-9, Minimum Distribution Incidental Benefit.) An exception applies if the employee's sole beneficiary is the employee's spouse and the spouse is more than ten years younger than the employee. In that case, the employee is permitted to use the longer distribution period measured by the joint life expectancy of the employee and spouse, as under the old rules using Table VI in Treasury Regulations Sec-

Table II

Table II

JOINT LIFE EXPECTANCY

Employee Age	Beneficiary Age	Life Expectancy	Percentage Distribution
71	60	27.2	3.68%
72	61	26.3	3.80
73	62	25.4	3.94
74	63	24.5	4.08
75	64	23.6	4.24
76	65	22.7	4.41
77	66	21.8	4.59
78	67	21.0	4.76
79	68	20.1	4.98
80	69	19.3	5.18

tion 1.72-9 (see Table II). Using Table I, most employees will be able to determine their required minimum distribution for each year based on their current age and their account balance as of the end of the prior year.

Tables I and II illustrate two important concepts. First, life expectancy is not reduced by one year for each year an individual ages. This is based on the premise that, the longer you live, the longer you are expected to live—generally referred to as recalculation of life expectancy. Second, the column headed "Percentage Distribution" indicates the rate of return necessary to maintain the principal balance and satisfy the required distribution with investment gains only. If, for example, an account owner began distributions based on a life-only table (see Table I), he or she would have to earn the rate of return on his or her account shown here to avoid depleting the principal. For example if, at age 80, the rate of return were only 4%, the balance of the required distribution, 1.35%, would have to be withdrawn from principal. The older the individual becomes, the higher the rate necessary to maintain the account balance.

DEATH OF EMPLOYEE AFTER
THE REQUIRED BEGINNING DATE

The distribution period to be used if an employee dies after distribution has begun is either:

1. If the employee has a designated beneficiary, the remaining life expectancy of the employee's designated beneficiary or
2. If the employee does not have a designated beneficiary, the remaining life expectancy of the employee.

For a nonspouse beneficiary, the applicable distribution period measured by the beneficiary's remaining life expectancy is determined using the beneficiary's age as of the beneficiary's birthday in the calendar year immediately following the calendar year of the employee's death. In subsequent calendar years, the applicable distribution period is reduced by one for each calendar year that has elapsed since the calendar year immediately following the calendar year of the employee's death (recalculation is not permitted for a nonspouse beneficiary).

For a spousal beneficiary using the Uniform Table (see Table I), if the surviving spouse of the employee is the employee's sole beneficiary, the applicable period is measured by the continuing life expectancy in the Uniform Table. If the spouse is more than ten years younger than the employee, the spouse's remaining life expectancy is the life expectancy of the spouse using the age of the spouse as of the spouse's birthday in the calendar year following the employee's death (recalculation can be used).

If there is no beneficiary, the applicable distribution period measured by the employee's remaining life expectancy is the life expectancy of the employee using the age of the employee as of the employee's birthday in the calendar year of the employee's death. In subsequent calendar years, the applicable distribution period is reduced by one for each calendar year that has elapsed since the calendar year of death (the straight-line method).

INDIVIDUAL RETIREMENT ACCOUNT (IRA) REPORTING

Because the new regulations significantly simplify the calculation of required minimum distributions, IRA trustees (banks, brokerage offices, insurance companies, mutual fund companies) determining the account balance as of the end of the year can, in most cases, also calculate the following year's required minimum distribution for each IRA if they know the age of the account owner. To improve compliance with distribution rules, the proposed regulations require the trustee of each IRA to report the amount of the required minimum distribution from the IRA to the IRA owner or beneficiary and to the IRS. This reporting would be required whether the IRA owner is planning to take the required minimum distribution from that IRA or from another IRA and would indicate that the IRA owner is permitted to take the required minimum distribution from any other IRA of the owner. If a required distribution is reported by an IRA custodian or plan trustee and the distribution is not reflected on the participant's tax return, the IRS will levy the appropriate 50% excise tax.

Beginning in 2004, trustees and custodians of IRAs will be required to report to the IRS on Form 5498 each IRA that requires a distribution. Although the amount of the distribution does not have to be reported to the IRS, the trustee or custodian must advise the IRA owner of the need to make the distribution and offer to calculate the amount or actually provide the calculation and notify the IRA owner.

ILLUSTRATIONS

Example 9: John was born on March 5, 1934. He has accumulated $500,000 in his profit-sharing account and has named his wife Sarah as his beneficiary. Sarah was born on April 10, 1935. John's youngest grandson Michael was born on May 4, 2001. John's required beginning date is April 1, 2005, the April 1 following the year in which John reaches age 70½ (September 5, 2004). John's accountant advises him that the distribution for 2004 can be made by December 31, 2004 rather than waiting until the following year requiring two distributions to be made in the same year. Assuming John's account earns 8.0% annually the required distributions are illustrated in Table III.

Table III

1	2	3	4	5	
		Uniform Life	Required	Account	
Year	Age	Expectancy	Distribution	Balance	
(Lifetime or Spousal Beneficiary)					
2004	71	26.5	$18,867.92	$519,622.64	($500,000 / 26.5) = $18,867.92
2005	72	25.6	20,297.76	539,270.87	($500,000 − $18,867.92) * (1.08) = $519,622.64
2006	73	24.7	21,832.83	558,833.09	
2007	74	23.8	23,480.38	578,180.92	
2008	75	22.9	25,248.08	597,167.47	
2009	76	22.0	27,143.98	615,625.38	
2010	77	21.2	29,038.93	633,513.36	
2011	78	20.3	31,207.55	650,490.27	
2012	79	19.5	33,358.48	666,502.34	
2013	80	18.7	35,641.84	681,329.34	
2014	81	17.9	38,063.09	694,727.55	
2015	82	17.1	40,627.34	706,428.23	
2016	83	16.3	43,339.15	716,136.20	
2017	84	15.5	46,202.34	723,528.57	
2018	85	14.8	48,887.07	728,612.82	
2019	86	14.1	51,674.67	731,093.21	

Since the assumed rate of return is 8%, the account balance will continue to grow until the life expectancy factor is less than 12.5 (100% / 8%). At that point the 8% rate of return will not be sufficient to satisfy the required minimum distribution and the account balance will begin to be depleted. Whether the distribution is being made over the employee's lifetime or as a result of his death, and payable to his spouse as beneficiary, the distributions will continue as illustrated.

Example 10: The facts are the same as in Example 9. However, John dies in 2007 and has named a nonspouse beneficiary. (See Table IV.)

Table IV

1	2	3	4	5
		Uniform Life	Required	Account
Year	Age	Expectancy	Distribution	Balance
			(Nonspouse Beneficiary)	
2004	71			
2005	72			
2006	73			
2007	74			
2008	75	22.8	$25,358.81	$597,047.88
2009	76	21.8	27,393.00	615,356.43
2010	77	20.8	29,597.37	632,910.24
2011	78	19.8	31,995.62	649,639.16
2012	79	18.8	34,600.55	665,160.90
2013	80	17.8	37,443.95	679,383.06
2014	81	16.8	40,555.32	692,035.95
2015	82	15.8	43,970.10	702,818.05
2016	83	14.8	47,731.64	711,392.32
2017	84	13.8	51,893.93	717,381.65
2018	85	12.8	56,525.67	720,363.13
2019	86	11.8	61,746.85	720,215.25

Since John has chosen a nonspouse beneficiary, in the year following his death the life expectancy factor reverts to the straight-line method, i.e., the factor is reduced by one for each year that elapses. In addition, in 2019 the account balance begins to go down since the life expectancy factor is less than 12.5 as discussed in Example 9.

Example 11: The facts are the same as in Example 9. However, John's wife Sarah disclaims the inheritance so the benefits are payable to John's grandson, the contingent beneficiary. (See Table V.)

Since the grandson's life expectancy is so long, it will be several years before the account begins to go down. This is a very effective method of passing on substantial assets to later generations.

Table V

1	2	3	4	5	6
		Uniform Life	Grandson	Required	Account
Year	Age	Expectancy	Age	Distribution	Balance
				(Disclaimer to Grandson)	
2004	71				
2005	72				
2006	73				
2007	74				
2008	75	50.4	7	$11,471.84	$ 612,045.80
2009	76	49.4	8	12,389.59	647,628.71
2010	77	48.4	9	13,380.76	684,987.79
2011	78	47.4	10	14,451.22	724,179.49
2012	79	46.4	11	15,607.32	765,257.95
2013	80	45.4	12	16,855.90	808,274.21
2014	81	44.4	13	18,204.37	853,275.43
2015	82	43.4	14	19,660.72	900,303.88
2016	83	42.4	15	21,233.58	949,395.92
2017	84	41.4	16	22,932.27	1,000,580.74
2018	85	40.4	17	24,766.85	1,053,879.01
2019	86	39.4	18	26,748.20	1,109,301.27

Nondiscrimination Rules

The Internal Revenue Code (IRC), in Section 401(a)(4), states:

> Requirements for Qualification—A trust created or organized in the United States and forming part of a stock bonus, pension or profit-sharing plan of an employer for the exclusive benefit of his employees or their beneficiaries shall constitute a qualified trust under this section—
>
> ... if the contributions or benefits provided under the plan do not discriminate in favor of highly compensated employees (within the meaning of Section 414(q)). For purposes of this paragraph, there shall be excluded from consideration employees described in Section 410(b)(3)(A) and (C).

This short paragraph has probably generated more regulations, revenue rulings, revenue procedures, private letter rulings and commentary than any other section of the IRC relating to qualified plans.

The position of the Internal Revenue Service (IRS) is that, in exchange for the considerable tax benefits afforded to sponsors of qualified retirement plans, those plans must benefit employees across all levels of status: owners, highly paid employees, management, and rank-and-file employees. In all cases of discrimination, the highly compensated employees (HCEs) are compared to the nonhighly compensated employees (NHCEs). A *highly compensated employee* is defined as a 5%-or-more owner of the company or companies (see Chapter 10) that sponsors the plan or has received compensation in excess of $90,000 in the previous year.

When addressing nondiscrimination, the following specific rules must be satisfied:

1. Benefits/contributions must be nondiscriminatory in amount. Unless specific nondiscrimination tests are passed, benefits and/or contributions must be uniform across all employee groups. Uniformity may be as a percentage of compensation or a uniform dollar amount.
2. The effects of plan amendments, terminations and grants of past service must be nondiscriminatory on their face and in operation. If plan benefits are based on service, e.g., defined benefit (DB) plans (see Chapter 6),

recognition of past service must be nondiscriminatory. If the only employee with significant past service is an HCE, the recognition of past service must be limited; generally, five years is a safe harbor.

3. The plan must provide nondiscriminatory coverage (the coverage test under IRC Section 410(b)). This test generally provides that at least 70% of the otherwise eligible NHCEs (those that satisfy the age and service requirements) must be covered by the plan and its benefits/contributions (see examples later in this chapter).

4. The plan must provide for the adjustable compensation limit of $150,000 as adjusted for cost of living ($205,000 in the year 2004) to be taken into account to determine contributions or benefits. If an HCE's compensation is in excess of the limit that excess cannot be considered in determining benefits or contributions.

5. The plan must define compensation so as not to discriminate in favor of HCEs (see Chapter 2).

6. The plan must comply with the rules for considering Social Security as part of the retirement benefit funded by the employer (see Chapter 4, Table II).

7. The plan must satisfy the minimum participation rules under IRC Section 401(a)(26) requiring that the lesser of 40% or 50 employees who satisfy the statutory eligibility rules, i.e., one year of service, age 21 and full-time employment, participate in any DB plan sponsored by the employer.

8. The benefit, rights, and features provided in the plan must be nondiscriminatory in both "current availability" and "effective availability." This refers to structural provisions in the plan. For example, a provision that allows loans only for employees with an account balance of over $100,000 may be currently available but not effectively available if it is unlikely that most of the NHCEs will have an account balance of that magnitude.

NONDISCRIMINATION IN BENEFITS AND CONTRIBUTIONS

The amount of benefits and/or contributions represents the heart of nondiscrimination compliance. In a defined contribution (DC) plan (see Chapter 4), i.e., profit-sharing, money purchase and target benefit plans, the nondiscriminatory amount rule may be satisfied in any one of the following three ways:

1. Safe harbor testing
2. The general nondiscrimination test
3. Cross-testing, where contributions are converted to equivalent benefits as in a DB plan (see Chapter 4).

Safe Harbor Testing

Safe harbor testing offers two alternative methods to satisfy the non-discrimination-in-amount test. The first is a traditional uniform allocation formula, where contributions and forfeitures are allocated to participants in proportion to their compensation, i.e., the same percentage of compensation or the same dollar amount is allocated to each participant (see Chapter 4, Table I). This percentage allocation would be:

$$\text{Plan Contribution} \times \frac{\text{Participant's compensation (as limited in item \#4 above)}}{\text{Total plan compensation (as limited in item \#4 above)}}$$

This allocation is most common in profit-sharing plans, whereas a money purchase plan usually satisfies the safe harbor by defining a specific and uniform percentage of each participant's compensation to be contributed on his or her behalf (see Chapter 4, Table VIII).

The second safe harbor is a uniform allocation formula weighted for age and/or service and salary. This safe harbor is available to plans that use a uniform point allocation, not to be confused with age-weighted DC plans as illustrated in Chapter 4, which satisfy the non-discrimination-in-amount rule by use of the more complex general test.

A point allocation plan must:
1. Provide points to participants on a uniform basis considering compensation, age (optional) and service or participation
2. Allocate the plan contribution based on each participant's points as a percentage of the total points of all participants.

Table I allocates ten points for each year of service and one point for each $100 of compensation. Once the contribution is allocated, the average of the allocation rates for the HCEs may not be more than the average allocation rate for the NHCEs. The plan in Table I passes since the average rate for the HCEs is 15.12%, which is not more than the average rate for the NHCEs of 15.37%.

Table I

POINT ALLOCATION

	Years of Service	Salary	Age	Service Points	Salary Points	Total Points	Contri- bution	Percent of Salary
John	25	$205,000	60	250	2,050	2,300	$29,951.98	14.61%
Stuart	20	100,000	55	200	1,000	1,200	15,627.12	15.63
S TOTAL		$305,000		450	3,050	3,500	$45,579.10	15.12%
Carol	4	$ 25,000	42	40	250	290	$ 3,776.55	15.11%
David	2	35,000	38	20	350	370	4,818.36	13.77
Helen	8	28,000	29	80	280	360	4,688.14	16.74
Fred	5	18,000	25	50	180	230	2,995.20	16.64
Steve	6	50,000	45	60	500	560	7,292.66	14.59
S TOTAL		$156,000		450	1,560	1,810	$23,570.90	15.37%
TOTAL		$461,000		700	4,610	5,310	$69,150.00	

General Nondiscrimination Test

If neither of the safe harbor approaches is satisfied, the next option is to satisfy the nondiscrimination-in-amount requirement by use of the general nondiscrimination test. Generally, this test establishes rate groups for each HCE and all other employees with equal or higher rates. These rate groups must pass the same test that is used to test for nondiscriminatory coverage (item #3 above), the so-called 70% test. In a DC plan, the rate group is equivalent to the allocation rate including employer contributions and forfeitures.

In Table II, John, Carol and Fred receive an allocation of 20% of compensation, while all other participants receive an allocation of 10.5% of compensation. This variable allocation rate may be based on job description, specific departments within the business, geographical location for businesses with multiple locations or any other valid business guideline. All forfeitures are allocated as part of the total compensation.

Table II

VARIABLE ALLOCATION RATE

	Salary	Employer Contribution	Forfeitures	Allocation Percent
John	$205,000	$35,000	$ 6,000	20.00%
Stuart	100,000	8,000	2,500	10.50
S TOTAL	$305,000	$43,000	$ 8,500	
Carol	$ 25,000	$ 4,375	$ 625	20.00%
David	35,000	2,800	875	10.50
Helen	28,000	2,240	700	10.50
Fred	18,000	3,150	450	20.00
Steve	50,000	4,000	1,250	10.50
S TOTAL	$156,000	$16,565	$ 3,900	
TOTAL	$461,000	$59,565	$11,400	

Table II has two HCEs, which means one rate group for each HCE must be tested. The basis for this approach is that if each rate group were a separate plan, it would be tested under the coverage test of IRC Section 410(b), item #3 above. If different contribution rates can be provided in two plans without being discriminatory, those same two contribution rates should be nondiscriminatory if provided in one plan.

The first rate group includes John, Carol and Fred, remembering that each rate

---

group is based on one HCE and all participants, including other HCEs, that have an equal or higher allocation rate. In this rate group, John has an allocation rate of 20%. The only other participants who have allocation rates equal to or higher than that are Carol and Fred. The next step is to test the rate group as if it were a separate plan covering only those three employees. The ratio percentage test (IRC Section 410(b)) provides that the percentage of NHCEs covered must be at least 70% of the percentage of HCEs covered. The same guidelines apply in this test. Because only John is in the first rate group, the rate group covers 50% of the HCEs (one out of two). With two NHCEs included in the first rate group, Carol and Fred, 40% of the NHCEs are covered (two out of five). The result of dividing the NHCE percentage (40%) by the HCE percentage (50%) is 80%, and the test for the first rate group is passed (the ratio must be at least 70%).

The second rate group (one for each HCE) includes all employees because the allocation rate for Stuart is 10.5% and all other participants, including John, have an allocation rate equal to or higher than Stuart's allocation rate of 10.5%. The plan includes 100% of the HCEs and 100% of the NHCEs. When the NHCE percentage is divided by the HCE percentage, the result is 100% again, and the test is passed for the second rate group.

With only two HCEs to consider, this is a simplified application of the general test; however, the same test works for a plan with five or ten HCEs and 30, 40 or 50 NHCEs. The approach is the same but the process is much longer and more time-consuming. This approach can be used when a plan allocates different percentages based on profit centers, geographical locations, or other business or employee groups (see cross-testing example in Chapter 4, Tables VI and VII). This test must be passed each year based on the participants in that year. If there is a major change in the profile of the employees because of turnover, the makeup of the individual groups change and the test may fail. In that case, the plan contribution allocation has to be amended to satisfy the test.

Cross-Testing

The last option available to satisfy the nondiscriminatory-in-amount requirement is cross-testing. This approach projects contributions with investment gains to retirement age and then converts that accumulated sum to annuity payments, similar to benefits in a DB plan (see Chapter 6). It then uses the annual annuity payments as a percent of compensation in place of allocation rates and the rules for the general test above (the 70% test) to compare rate groups.

This method involves the following steps:

1. Determine the allocation taken into account, including employer contributions and forfeitures only.
2. Project the allocation amount to retirement age with investment gains. (Table III uses 7.5%.)
3. Convert the amount calculated in #2 above to annuity payments (the accrual) at the testing age (usually age 65).
4. Divide the annuity payment by plan year compensation (as limited, i.e., $205,000 for 2004) to determine the accrual rate.
5. Adjust the accrual rate for Social Security integration (optional).

6. Determine whether each rate group (each HCE and all other employees with equal or higher accrual rates) satisfies the coverage test of IRC Section 410(b), the 70% test.

Table III shows how a cross-tested plan passes the nondiscrimination rules. This type of plan is often referred to as a class allocation plan, i.e., where a different rate of contribution is allocated to different classes of employees. The classes must have a business basis, e.g., job description, geographical location or business division. Table III has two classes: (1) HCEs with a contribution of 25% up to the dollar limit of $41,000 and (2) all other employees with a contribution of 7.17% (rounded).

Table III

CROSS-TESTED PLAN WITHOUT SOCIAL SECURITY
(PERMITTED DISPARITY)

	Salary	Age	Employer Contribution	Percent of Total Contribution	Annual Annuity Payment*	Accrual Rate
John	$205,000	60	$41,000	52.50%	$6,790	3.395%
Stuart	100,000	55	25,000	32.81	6,092	6.092
	$305,000		$66,000	85.31%		
Carol	$ 25,000	44	$ 1,793	2.35%	$ 968	3.872%
David	35,000	38	2,511	3.30	2,092	5.977
Helen	28,000	29	2,009	2.64	3,209	11.461
Fred	18,000	25	1,291	1.69	2,755	15.306
Steve	50,000	45	3,587	4.71	1,802	3.604
	$156,000		$11,191	14.69%		
	$456,000		$76,191	100.00%		

Rate Group #1		Coverage Ratio	Rate Group #2		Coverage Ratio
Stuart	6.092%	50.0%	John	3.395%	
			Stuart	6.092	100.00%
Helen	11.461		Carol	3.872	
Fred	15.306	40.0%	David	5.977	
			Helen	11.461	
			Fred	15.306	
			Steve	3.604	100.00%

PASS
Must be => 70%   80.0%
(40% divided by 50%)

PASS
Must be => 70%   100.00%
(100% divided by 100%)

---

*Based on UP84 mortality at 7.5% pre- and postretirement interest.

This plan maximizes the contribution for John and Stuart, the two HCEs. In keeping with the above procedures, the rate groups are tested based on each HCE's accrual rate (accrual divided by salary) and all employees, including other HCEs, with equal or higher accrual rates, as if each rate group were a separate plan required to pass the coverage rules of IRC Section 410(b).

The first rate group consists of Stuart, Helen and Fred. The second rate group consists of all the employees in the plan. Referring to the determination of the rate groups above, Stuart's accrual rate is 6.092%. Employees, including other highly compensated employees, with an accrual rate equal to or more than Stuart's include only Helen and Fred at 11.461% and 15.306%, respectively. If we treat the rate group as if it were an independent plan, does it satisfy the coverage test (the 70% test)? Since we are covering one out of two highly compensated employees, the HCE coverage ratio is 50%. We are also covering two out of five nonhighly compensated employees, or 40%. The result of dividing the nonhighly compensated percentage by the highly compensated percentage is 80%, and the test is passed. The same process is followed for Rate Group #2.

The use of cross-testing in DC plans is very sensitive to the age of the HCEs. In Table III the HCEs are 55 and 60, giving the plan a great deal of leverage because the NHCEs are much younger. Table IV shows the effect of a younger HCE.

In Table IV, the two HCEs are age 60 and 45. Using the same approach to testing as in Table III, Rate Group #1 does not pass the coverage test. This is due to Stuart's age. In Rate Group #1 there are not a sufficient number of NHCEs with an accrual rate equal to or more than Stuart's.

Because Rate Group #1 fails the coverage test, the plan fails nondiscrimination testing. Luckily, there is one more option in the cross-testing approach. Rate groups that do not pass the ratio test (the 70% test for coverage) can then be tested under the average benefit test. Although it may not be appropriate to go this deeply into the technical aspects of nondiscrimination testing, I include the procedure for the average benefit test since it is part of cross-testing.

This test has two parts to it: the nondiscriminatory classification test and the average benefit ratio test. Under the classification test, the coverage ratio of the rate group, 40% in Rate Group #1 in Table IV, must be at least at the midpoint between the safe harbor percentage and the unsafe harbor percentage in accordance with IRS guidelines. Under the average benefit ratio test, the average accrual rates of the NHCEs must be equal to at least 70% of the average accrual rates of the HCEs. These rules as applied to Rate Group #1 in Table IV are as follows:

1. *Determine the concentration percentage.* Divide total NHCEs by total employees (five divided by seven); percentage equals 71.4%.
2. *Determine the midpoint from IRS guidelines* (see below).

Safe harbor percentage	41.75%
Midpoint percentage	36.75%
Unsafe harbor percentage	31.75%

If the midpoint percentage is less than or equal to the coverage ratio (40% in Rate Group #1 in Table IV) in the failed rate group, the first part of the average benefit test is passed. Because the coverage percentage in the failed Rate Group #1 is 40%, this part of the test is passed.

3. *Compare the average accrual rate of the NHCEs to that of the HCEs.* If the ratio of the NHCE average to the HCE average is equal to or more than 70%, the second part of the average benefit test is passed.

NHCEs (3.872 + 5.977 + 11.461 + 15.306 + 3.604) ÷ 5 NHCEs = 8.044%
HCEs   (3.395 + 12.556) ÷ 2 HCEs = 7.976%
Ratio NHCE % ÷ HCE %
       8.044% ÷ 7.976% = 100.85%

The average benefit test is passed and the plan qualifies.

Table IV

CROSS-TESTED PLAN WITH YOUNGER HCE

	Salary	Age	Employer Contribution	Percent of Total Contribution	Annual Annuity Payment*	Accrual Rate
John	$205,000	60	$41,000	53.11%	$ 6,960	3.395%
Stuart	100,000	45	25,000	32.39	12,556	12.556
	$305,000		$66,000	85.50%		
Carol	$ 25,000	44	$ 1,793	2.32%	$ 968	3.872%
David	35,000	38	2,511	3.25	2,092	5.977
Helen	28,000	29	2,009	2.60	3,209	11.461
Fred	18,000	25	1,291	1.67	2,755	15.306
Steve	50,000	45	3,587	4.65	1,802	3.604
	$156,000		$11,191	14.50%		
	$461,000		$77,191	100.00%		

Rate Group #1		Coverage Ratio	Rate Group #2		Coverage Ratio
Stuart	12.556%	50.0%	John	3.395%	
			Stuart	12.556	100.00%
			Carol	3.872	
Fred	15.306	20.0%	David	5.977	
			Helen	11.461	
			Fred	15.306	
			Steve	3.604	100.00%

FAIL
Must be => 70%   40.0%
(20% divided by 50%)

PASS
Must be => 70%   100.00%
(100% divided by 100%)

---

*Based on UP84 mortality at 7.5% pre- and postretirement interest.

This is certainly a lot of work for a seven-person plan but, as a result of the extra work, the two HCEs have been allocated a total contribution of $66,000 at a cost for the employees of $11,191. Even if the administrative cost to maintain this plan were $2,000 annually—which is on the high end of the likely fees—the result is highly favorable. In addition to using the cross-testing method to leverage a plan for owners and key employees, this method may also be used to reward specific departments within a company, a division of a midsized company or any other business unit that significantly contributes to the success of the business.

A typical application of the cross-testing rules is to combine a class allocation profit-sharing plan (see Chapter 4) with a safe harbor 401(k) plan (see Chapter 5). The results are illustrated in Table V.

Table V

SAFE HARBOR 401(k) PLAN WITH CLASS ALLOCATION PROFIT-SHARING PLAN

	Salary	Age	Employer Contri- bution	Employee Salary Deferral	Employer 401(k) Safe Harbor	Annual Annuity Payment	Accrual Rate
John	$205,000	60	$21,850	$16,000	$ 6,150	$4,753	2.319%
Stuart	100,000	55	22,000	13,000	3,000	6,092	6.092
	$305,000		$43,850	$29,000	$ 9,150		
Carol	$ 25,000	44	$ 500	$ 0	$ 750	$ 675	2.700%
David	35,000	38	700	0	1,050	1,458	4.166
Helen	28,000	29	560	0	840	2,237	7.989
Fred	18,000	25	360	0	540	1,920	10.667
Steve	50,000	45	1,000	0	1,500	1,256	2.512
	$156,000		$ 3,120	$ 0	$ 4,680		
	$461,000		$46,970	$29,000	$13,830		

Rate Group #1		Coverage Ratio		Rate Group #2		Coverage Ratio
Stuart	6.092%	50.0%		John	2.319%	
				Stuart	6.092	100.00%
Helen	7.989			Carol	2.700	
Fred	10.667	40.0%		David	4.166	
				Helen	7.989	
				Fred	10.667	
				Steve	2.512	100.00%

PASS			PASS		
Must be => 70%	80.0%		Must be => 70%	100.00%	
(40% divided by 50%)			(100% divided by 100%)		

The illustration in Table V is based on a safe harbor employer contribution of 3% of compensation (see Chapter 5) plus a 2% employer profit-sharing contribution for the nonhighly compensated employees, which will satisfy the new nondiscrimination rules for cross-testing as long as the rate groups pass the coverage test (the 70% test). In this case both rate groups pass at 80% and 100%, respectively. The calculation of the accrual rate is not required to include the salary deferrals to the 401(k) account.

AMENDMENTS, TERMINATIONS AND PAST SERVICE

As stated in item 2 in the list of nondiscrimination rules at the beginning of this chapter, "The effects of *plan amendments, terminations and grants of past service* must be nondiscriminatory on their face and in operation." Plan amendments include the establishing of a plan, termination of a plan, and any changes that affect benefits or allocations under the plan. Whether a plan satisfies this requirement is a facts-and-circumstances determination. The issues to be considered are the relative number of HCEs and NHCEs affected by the amendment, the relative benefits for the HCEs and NHCEs before and after the amendment, the relative service of the HCEs and the NHCEs, the length of time the plan has been in effect and the turnover of the employees before the effective date of the plan.

> **Example 1:** Atlas Manufacturing Inc. has sponsored a money purchase pension plan for the last 15 years. The plan has always been integrated with Social Security (see Chapter 4) at the current year's Social Security wage base, using a contribution formula of 5.7% in excess of the wage base plus 11.4% of total compensation. The company is in the process of liquidating its business. After terminating all NHCEs but before terminating the plan, Atlas amends the plan to a 25%-of-pay money purchase plan that benefits only the remaining HCEs. This plan does not satisfy nondiscrimination rule 2 because the timing of the amendment is discriminatory.

> **Example 2:** Potter Pharmaceuticals is about to adopt a DB plan. The plan provides that benefits are 2% of compensation times years of total service. Alfred Potter began the company 25 years ago while the most past service of any nonhighly compensated employees is nine years. The maximum past service that can be considered without discrimination is five years, the safe harbor, unless the facts and circumstances support that if nine years is used the result would not be discriminatory, i.e., there are a sufficient number of nonhighly compensated employees with nine years of service so the result is nondiscriminatory.

TOP-HEAVY PLANS

The Internal Revenue Code defines a *top-heavy* plan as:
1. Any DB plan if, as of the determination date, the present value of the cumulative accrued benefits (see Chapter 6) under the plan for key employ-

ees exceeds 60% of the present value of the cumulative accrued benefits under the plan for all employees

2. Any DC plan if, as of the determination date, the aggregate of the accounts of key employees under the plan exceeds 60% of the aggregate of accounts of all employees under such plan.

Generally, the IRC definition of *top-heavy* includes both employer- and employee-funded benefits and, in some cases, rollovers from other plans. For example, employee deferrals in a 401(k) plan and voluntary after-tax employee contributions are included in the determination of top-heavy status. The rules for including rollovers and transfers depend upon whether they are unrelated, i.e., both initiated by the employee and made from a plan maintained by one employer to a plan maintained by another nonrelated employer in which case the rollover or transfer is not included in the top-heavy test, or related, i.e., a rollover or transfer either not initiated by the employee or made to a plan maintained by the same employer in which case the rollover or transfer is included in the top-heavy test.

In the case of unrelated rollovers and transfers:

1. The plan making the distribution or transfer must count the distribution in its determination of top-heavy status.

2. The plan accepting the rollover or transfer does not consider the rollover or transfer as part of the accrued benefit if the rollover or transfer was accepted after December 31, 1983, but must consider it as part of the accrued benefit if the rollover or transfer was accepted before January 1, 1984.

In the case of related rollovers and transfers, the plan making the distribution or transfer does not count the distribution or transfer in determining top-heavy status, and the plan accepting the rollover or transfer does count the rollover or transfer in the value of the accrued benefits. Rules for related rollovers and transfers do not depend on whether the rollover or transfer was accepted before January 1, 1984.

Determination Date

The determination date is the last day of the preceding plan year or, in the case of the first plan year, the last day of the first plan year. For a plan in its first plan year, the determination of top-heavy status in that year causes the plan to be top-heavy for the first two years. A plan established on January 1, 2004, has a determination date of December 31, 2004, in its first year and December 31, 2004, in its second year in accordance with the preceding definition of *top-heavy*.

Value of Accrued Benefits

DB plans do not have account balances for employees but provide true retirement benefits in the form of monthly retirement income. To value these benefits for determination of top-heavy status, the accrued benefits must be converted to lump sums. The present value of accrued benefits answers the question, "What is the lump sum necessary today, so that its future value at x% annual growth, at retirement age, is sufficient to pay the accrued monthly retirement benefit beginning at retirement age defined in the plan and has been totally depleted by the death of the annuitant?"

The portion of the total retirement benefit earned in a DB plan based on years of service or years of participation (see Chapter 6), or the account balance in a DC plan as of a specific date, is the accrued benefit.

Example 3: Following are data for an employee in a DB plan as of December 31, 2004:

Salary:	$30,000
Date of hire:	January 1, 1994
Date of plan participation:	January 1, 1995
Date of birth:	January 1, 1960
Date of retirement:	January 1, 2025 (age 65)
Plan benefit:	60% of average compensation

Assuming level compensation to retirement age, this employee's retirement benefit at age 65 will be $1,500 per month for life ($30,000 × 60% / 12 months). The funding calculations of this plan determine that $206,275 will be needed at age 65 to be able to provide the promised benefit. (See Chapter 6 for a full discussion of DB plans.) To say this another way, the plan needs $137.52 (the annuity purchase rate) at age 65 to fund each dollar of monthly benefit promised ($206,275 / $1,500). Further assume that benefit accruals are based on participation; therefore, the employee's accrued benefit would be:

$$\text{Retirement benefit} \times (\text{years of participation to } 12/31/04 / \text{years of participation to } 1/1/2025)$$

$$\$1,500 / \text{month} \times (10 \text{ yrs} / 30 \text{ yrs}) = \$500 / \text{month}$$

The lump sum necessary to fund the accrued benefit, i.e., the amount necessary to pay the accrued benefit of $500 per month beginning at age 65, for life, would be $68,760 ($500 per month × $137.52). The next question is how much is necessary today, December 31, 2004, so that if invested at x%, that amount will grow to $68,760 at the employee's age 65? A financial calculator will show that at 7.5% the answer is $16,187, the present value of the participant's accrued benefit as of December 31, 2004. The determination of top-heavy status in a DB plan follows the same procedure for each employee.

Key Employee

A *key employee* is any employee who, at any time during the plan year containing the determination date, is:

1. An officer of the employer having an annual compensation greater than $130,000, adjusted for inflation in $5,000 increments
2. A 5% owner of the employer or
3. A 1% owner of the employer having an annual compensation from the employer of more than $150,000.

When identifying key employees under items 2 and 3, the ownership attribution rules of IRC Section 318(a) apply (see Chapter 10).

Officer

Within the definition of *key employee,* the term *officer* must be clarified. Does the title *vice president* qualify as an officer for purposes of top-heavy status? Is a 100% owner of a business who is not an officer considered an officer for determination of top-heavy status? The determination about whether employees are officers is based on the facts, including the source of their authority, the term for which they are serving in the position, whether elected or appointed, and the nature and extent of their duties. There is a limit on the number of officers who must be taken into account depending on the number of employees in the group being tested for top-heavy status. Keeping in mind that the term *officer* refers to the facts and circumstances and not the title, entities other than corporations can have officers for purposes of top-heavy status. A partner in a partnership with the authority of an officer would be considered an officer for top-heavy purposes.

Years of Service/Vesting Schedule

If a plan becomes top-heavy, it must satisfy the following plan requirements.

First, an employee who has completed at least three years of service with the employer maintaining the plan must have a nonforfeitable right to 100% of his or her accrued benefit, or the employee must have a nonforfeitable right to a percentage of his or her accrued benefit under the following example:

Years of Service	Nonforfeitable Percentage
2	20%
3	40
4	60
5	80
6	100

In a year in which the plan is not top-heavy, the vesting schedule can revert to the non-top-heavy vesting schedule as provided in the plan. When the vesting schedule changes for the non-top-heavy year, the nonforfeitable percentage of the accrued benefit for the employee cannot be reduced below the prior year's nonforfeitable percentage. In addition, any employee with three or more years of service must be given the option of remaining with the top-heavy vesting schedule.

Example 4: The plan's top-heavy vesting schedule was a six-year graded schedule as illustrated previously, but the plan's non-top-heavy vesting schedule was a seven-year graded vesting schedule (zero vesting for the first two years, and then 20% per year thereafter until 100% in year seven). An employee who was 20% vested after two years (the six-year schedule) could not be reduced to zero vesting but would continue to be 20% vested when the plan went back to the seven-year graded vesting in the third year, when the plan was not top-heavy.

Second, the plan must provide minimum benefits as follows:

1. In a DB plan, an accrued benefit equal to the lesser of 2% multiplied by the number of years of service (excluding service when the plan was not top-heavy) but not more than 20% of the employee's average compensation (averaged over the highest five or fewer consecutive years of service as provided in the plan) payable for life beginning at the retirement age as provided in the plan.

    Example 5: Assume an employee has the following compensation and work history:

		Compensation
1999	Top-heavy	$25,000
2000	Top-heavy	$27,500
2001	Not top-heavy	$30,000
2002	Not top-heavy	$30,000
2004	Top-heavy	$35,000

    This employee's benefit accrual for top-heavy purposes for the 2004 plan year would be:

    [($25,000 + $27,500 + $30,000 + $30,000 + $35,000) / 5] × 2% = $147.50

2. In a DC plan, a contribution of the lesser of 3% of the employee's compensation or the highest percentage contribution made for any key employee (including elective deferrals in a 401(k) plan). Applying this to a typical traditional 401(k) plan with no profit-sharing contribution if the only key employee makes a salary deferral of 2% of compensation than the top-heavy minimum is 2%. If the key employee makes a salary deferral equal to or more than 3%, the top-heavy minimum is 3% of compensation.

Hours of Service

In determining which non-key employees must accrue a benefit in a DB plan, hours of service must be considered. Any non-key eligible employee (one who has satisfied the eligibility requirements of the plan) who has at least 1,000 hours of service must accrue the top-heavy minimum benefit. In a DC plan, those participants employed on the last day of the plan year must receive a contribution regardless of whether they have 1,000 hours of service during that plan year.

Over the past several years, 401(k) plans have become the plan of choice for many employers. Unfortunately, in small plans this becomes a trap. On the one hand, the employer wants to offer a 401(k) plan to its employees; on the other hand, it cannot afford the added cost of top-heavy minimum contributions. The Economic Growth and Tax Relief Reconciliation Act of 2001 (EGTRRA) amended the top-heavy rules to provide that the matching contribution will be counted toward the employer's minimum contribution requirement. For employees that do not make salary deferrals or for employees for whom the match is less than 3%, the top-heavy minimum or the balance of the top-heavy minimum must still be deposited by the employer.

As a further incentive to establish a 401(k) plan, EGTRRA amended the top-heavy rules to provide that a plan will not be considered top-heavy if it provides only for safe harbor contributions (see Chapter 5, Safe Harbor 401(k) Plans). This means the plan could not allow for profit-sharing contributions in addition to the safe harbor employee deferrals and safe harbor employer contribution.

Effect of Distributions on Top-Heavy Status

When determining whether a plan is top-heavy, all distributions to terminated employees made during the one-year period ending on the determination date are added back as either key employee or non-key employee accrued benefits except for in-service distributions to current participants, which are subject to a five-year look back ending on the determination date.

Example 6: Following is a calendar year plan for the plan year ending December 31, 2004 (the determination date is 12/31/2003):

	Key Benefits/ Distributions	Non-Key Benefits/ Distributions
As of 12/31/2003	$410,000	$465,000
Distributions: 12/31/2003	450,000	15,000
Total	$860,000	$480,000

Top-heavy status: ($860,000) / ($860,000 + $480,000) = 64.2%

For the plan year ending December 31, 2005, here is the same calculation.

	Key Benefits/ Distributions	Non-Key Benefits/ Distributions
As of 12/31/04	$475,000	$515,000
Distributions: 12/31/04	None	5,000
Total	$475,000	$520,000

Top-heavy status: ($475,000) / ($475,000 + $520,000) = 47.7%

In this case, the distribution to a key employee, probably because of that employee's retirement, caused the plan to continue to be top-heavy for only one year whereas under prior law (for plan years beginning prior to January 1, 2004) the plan would have been top-heavy for four additional years after the distribution. If the benefit due the key employee had not been distributed but retained in the plan, the plan would also be top-heavy for the year ending December 31, 2005.

When Are Two Companies One?

Chapter 10

This chapter discusses a key part of determining whether or not a qualified plan is discriminatory. It addresses the question, "Who is the employer?" The answer to that question also identifies the group of employees who must be considered in determining highly compensated employees (HCEs) and nonhighly compensated employees (NHCEs) (see Chapter 9). Although it seems rather basic, in many cases it is an extremely difficult question to answer. The initial response might be that the employer is sponsoring the qualified plan; however, in qualified retirement plans simple questions rarely have simple answers. The Internal Revenue Code (IRC) addresses this question in several sections. The *employer,* for purposes of nondiscrimination, is:

1. All corporations that are members of a controlled group of corporations
2. Partnerships, sole proprietors and others that are under common control, similar to item 1
3. All entities that are members of an affiliated service group
4. Any other entities that the secretary determines to be aggregated to avoid discrimination because of the use of separate organizations, employee leasing or other arrangements.

Once the employer is identified, all entities included in the definition of *employer* are considered to be one employer for purposes of nondiscrimination. This chapter analyzes the IRC rules, their application and how to avoid involuntary noncompliance and possible disqualification resulting from noncompliance.

CONTROLLED GROUP OF CORPORATIONS

There are three types of controlled groups of corporations: (1) parent-subsidiary, (2) brother-sister and (3) combined group.

A *parent-subsidiary-controlled group* is defined as one or more chains of corporations connected through stock ownership with a common parent corporation, if:

1. Stock with at least 80% of the total combined voting power of all classes of stock entitled to vote, or at least 80% of the total value of shares of all

classes of stock of each of the corporations, is owned by one or more of the other corporations.

2. The common parent corporation owns stock possessing at least 80% of the total combined voting power of all classes of stock entitled to vote or at least 80% of the total value of shares of all classes of stock of at least one of the other corporations.

This is quite a mouthful. The concept is best explained with an example.

Example 1: Power Marketing Corporation owns 90% of Atlas Printing Corporation. Because Power, the parent, owns 80% or more of Atlas, Power and Atlas are a parent-subsidiary-controlled group.

Example 2: Power Marketing Corporation owns 90% of Atlas Printing Corporation and Atlas Corporation owns 85% of Brittany Printing Corporation. Because Atlas and Brittany are controlled as a result of Atlas's 85% ownership of Brittany, then Power, which owns more than 80% of Atlas, is the parent and Power, Atlas and Brittany are a parent-subsidiary-controlled group.

Power Corporation owns➤   Atlas Corporation owns➤   Brittany Corporation

Example 3: Power Corporation owns 90% of Atlas Corporation and owns 85% of Brittany Corporation. Because Power owns at least 80% of each corporation, Power, Atlas and Brittany are a parent-subsidiary-controlled group.

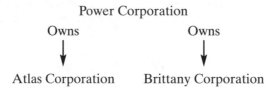

As you can see, there are many possible combinations of ownership. The key to proper identification of a parent-subsidiary is accurate and complete data, as is the key to any issue of identifying the employer sponsoring a qualified retirement plan. The concepts above also apply to partnerships and sole proprietorships.

BROTHER-SISTER-CONTROLLED GROUP

Another form of controlled entities due to ownership is the *brother-sister-controlled group*. This relationship is defined as:

Two or more corporations, if five or fewer persons who are individuals, estates or trusts own:

(a) At least 80% of the total combined voting power of all classes of stock entitled to vote, or at least 80% of the total value of shares of all classes of stock of each corporation (similar to the parent-subsidiary above)

(b) More than 50% of the total combined voting power of all classes of stock entitled to vote, or more than 50% of the total value of shares of all classes of stock of each corporation, taking into account the stock ownership of each such person only to the extent such stock ownership is identical with respect to each such corporation.

The five or fewer persons referred to above must be the same five or fewer persons in all entities.

Example 4: Ownership of Iron Casting Corporations and Reliable Machining Inc. is shared by the following individuals (all owners are non-related):

Name	Iron Casting	Reliable	Common
John	25%	15%	15%
Stanley	10	0	0
Susan	30	30	30
William	15	10	10
Carol	20	30	20
Michael	0	15	0

This example satisfies item (a) in the preceding definition of *brother-sister-controlled group* because John, Stanley, Susan, William and Carol own at least 80% of both Iron (100%) and Reliable Corporation (85%). Since Michael does not own any of the stock in Iron, he is not considered in determining the 80% requirement (only the same five or fewer owners). Identical ownership is based on the lowest common ownership of all companies in the controlled group for each owner. John owns 25% of Iron and 15% of Reliable, so the lowest common ownership is 15%, whereas Michael's lowest common ownership is zero. The common ownership in Iron and Reliable is 75%. Because the ownership of Iron Corporation and Reliable satisfies both items (a) and (b) in the definition of a brother-sister-controlled group above, Iron and Reliable are a brother-sister-controlled group.

Example 5: Assume the same nonrelated owners as in Example 4. Changing the stock holdings slightly also changes the result:

Name	Iron Casting	Reliable	Common
John	25%	15%	15%
Stanley	10	0	0
Susan	0	30	0
William	15	10	10
Carol	20	30	20
Michael	30	15	15

Here there are two groups of five owners in each corporation who own more than 80% of the stock; however, there is no common group of the same five owners who own more than 80% of the stock in *both* corporations.

Iron Casting   John, Stanley, Carol and Michael own 85%, but only 60% in Reliable.

                 John, William, Carol and Michael own 90%, but only 70% in Reliable.

Reliable   Susan, William, Carol and Michael own 85%, but only 65% in Iron.

                 John, Susan, William and Carol own 85%, but only 60% in Iron.

Because there is no common group of the same five or fewer owners that own 80% or more of the stock of both corporations, this is not a brother-sister-controlled group.

AFFILIATED SERVICE GROUPS

If a group of businesses is not a controlled group, the next question is whether the group is an affiliated service group.

An *affiliated service group* has the following complex definition:

A group consisting of a service organization (the first organization, FSO) and one or more of the following:

1. Any service organization (A Organization) that:
    (a) Is a shareholder or partner in the first organization
    (b) Regularly performs services for the first organization or is regularly associated with the first organization in performing services for third persons. An example of this may be a medical practice in which one corporation employs the doctors and the other employs the support staff, e.g., nurse, receptionist. These two organizations perform services for patients.
2. Any other organization (B Organization) if:
    (a) A significant portion of its business is the performance of services (for the first organization, for organizations described in item 1, or for both) of a type historically performed in that service field by employees, also illustrated by the example in 1(b) above
    (b) Ten percent or more of that organization's interests are held by persons who are HCEs of the first organization or an organization described in item 1.

An affiliated service group also includes a group consisting of:

1. An organization the principal business of which is performing, on a regular and continuing basis, management functions for one organization (or one organization and other organizations related to that one organization). This may be an executive of a company that incorporates and provides management services through his corporation to only the company he originally worked for.
2. The organization (and related organizations) for which such functions are so performed by the organization described in item 1.

The concept of affiliated service groups is a complex one. In this case I advise seeking counsel from an experienced Employee Retirement Income Security Act (ERISA) attorney.

To help with the analysis of whether a group of organizations is an affiliated service group, some of the related concepts are defined here in the order in which they first appear in the preceding definition of affiliated services group.

Service organization's principal business. A service organization's principal business is the performance of services if capital is not a material income-producing factor for the organization. This is a facts-and-circumstances determination based on whether there is a substantial investment in inventories, plant, machinery or other equipment. Generally, if the income of the business consists primarily of fees, commissions or other compensation for personal services of an individual, capital is not a material income-producing factor. Some fields are specifically identified as service organizations, including health, law, engineering, architecture, accounting, actuarial science, performing arts, consulting and insurance.

Regularly performs. Whether an organization regularly performs services for the first service organization (FSO) or is regularly associated with the FSO in performing services for third persons is also a facts-and-circumstances determination. A key factor in this determination is the amount of income the organization receives from the FSO or from third persons.

Significant portion of the business. An organization is a B organization if a significant portion of the business of the organization is the performance of services for the FSO, or for one or more A organizations, or for both. This test is also a facts-and-circumstances determination, although an organization will not be considered a B organization if less than 5% of its gross receipts is derived from providing services to the FSO, or one or more A organizations.

Historically performed. An organization is a B organization if it performs services for an FSO, or for one or more A organizations that are historically performed by employees of the FSO in that service field. A service is considered historically performed if it was not unusual for the services to be performed by employees of organizations in that service field. An example of a B organization is one that employs nurses who provide services to an FSO that employs physicians and treats patients.

Management functions. Because there is no regulatory guidance on management functions, the typical responsibilities of a manager, including supervision, hiring and terminating employees and establishing priorities, would be applied to this relationship. The basis for determining which groups are affiliated service groups and management function groups is illustrated in the following examples:

Example 6: John is an attorney and provides legal services to the general public as John Q. Attorney, Esq., P.C. His P.C. (professional corporation) is also a partner in Legal Services Group Inc. John regularly provides services to the public in association with Legal Services Group Inc. The law firm would be considered a first service organization. John's P.C. would be an A organization because it is a partner in the law firm, and it is regularly associated with the law firm in providing services to third persons. The law firm and John's P.C. are therefore an affiliated service group.

Example 7: Farley Communications is a service organization that is a shareholder in Greene Marketing Services, another service organization. Farley regularly provides services for Greene. Neither corporation is a professional service corporation. Because neither corporation is a *professional* service corporation, neither Farley nor Greene can be an FSO, so Farley and Greene would not be an affiliated service group as an FSO and an A organization.

Example 8: Mark Spooner, CPA, owns a one-third interest in an accounting firm. He also owns a one-third interest in a computer consulting firm. A significant portion of the business of the computer consulting firm consists of assisting clients of the accounting firm (third persons) to develop computer systems for their financial functions. Frequently, the clients of the accounting firm are referred to the consulting firm to provide the design and implementation of their computer systems. Approximately 20% of the income of the consulting firm is derived from clients of the accounting firm. Considering the accounting firm is an FSO and the consulting firm is a B organization and a significant portion of the business of the consulting firm is the performance of services for the accounting firm, the accounting firm and the consulting firm are an affiliated service group. Furthermore, the employees of the consulting firm are performing services that would historically be performed by employees of the accounting firm (if the accounting firm were also offering computer consulting services).

Example 9: The classic example of an affiliated service group is the medical professional who is employed by a P.C. and owns all the stock of the P.C. The P.C. or the medical professional owns some interest in a clinic that employs several nurses and support staff, to which the P.C. provides professional services. Considering the clinic is the FSO and the P.C. is an A organization, the two constitute an affiliated service group. Before the issuance of regulations, it was common for the P.C. to set up a rich pension plan, with no plan or only a token plan for the clinic employees, assuming the two were not a parent-subsidiary- or brother-sister-controlled group.

Example 10: John Jay is a sports star. Jeffrey, his manager, is incorporated under the name Best of the Best Inc. and spends 80% of his time providing management services to John Jay, including negotiating endorsement contracts, television appearances and contracts with his team. The remaining 20% of his time is spent servicing a few minor clients. In accordance with the preceding rules for management function groups, John Jay and Best of the Best Inc. would be considered a management function group.

OWNERSHIP AND OWNERSHIP ATTRIBUTION

In the determination of controlled entities, the ownership of those entities are determinative in great part. In addition to the obvious, i.e., the interest actually owned by each individual, consideration must be given to constructive ownership.

The guidelines for constructive ownership apply to three main groups, each with its own rules: parent-subsidiary controlled groups, brother-sister controlled groups and affiliated service groups.

Following are the constructive ownership rules applicable to parent-subsidiary-controlled groups:

1. Any stock owned by the corporation directly is considered toward the 80% requirement.
2. Any person who holds an option to acquire stock is assumed to own that stock.
3. Stock owned directly or indirectly by or for a partnership is assumed to be owned by any partner with a 5%-or-more interest in the partnership in proportion to his or her interest.
4. Stock owned directly or indirectly by or for an estate or trust shall be considered as owned by any beneficiary who has an actuarial interest of 5% or more in the stock in proportion to that actuarial interest. An actuarial interest is based on the likelihood that the beneficiary will receive the stock considering the provisions of the estate or trust and the beneficiary's life expectancy. For example, if the trust provides a 10% interest at the death of x, what is the likelihood that the beneficiary will survive x?
5. Stock owned directly or indirectly by a grantor trust is considered to be owned by the grantor.

In a brother-sister-controlled group all of the preceding ownership rules apply, plus:

1. Stock owned directly or indirectly by or for a corporation shall be considered as owned by any person who owns 5% or more in value of its stock in proportion to the value owned.
2. An individual shall be considered as owning stock in a corporation owned directly or indirectly by or for his or her spouse, except when each of the following conditions is satisfied for the taxable year:
   (a) The individual does not at any time during the year own directly any stock in that corporation.
   (b) The individual is neither director nor employee and does not participate in the management of that corporation at any time during the year.
   (c) Not more than 50% of the corporation's gross income for the year is derived from royalties, rents, dividends, interest and annuities.
   (d) The stock is not at any time during the year subject to conditions that substantially restrict or limit the spouse's right to dispose of the stock in favor of the individual or his or her children under the age of 21.
3. An individual is considered as owning stock owned directly or indirectly by or for his or her children who have not attained the age of 21; if the individual has not attained the age of 21, he or she is considered to own the stock owned directly or indirectly by or for his or her parents.
4. An individual who owns more than 50% of the total combined voting power of all classes of stock or more than 50% of the total value of shares of all classes of stock is considered as owning the stock directly or indirectly owned by or for his or her parents, grandparents, grandchildren and children who have attained the age of 21.

The ownership rules for affiliated service groups are based on the same rules used to determine ownership for purposes of identifying HCEs and key employees under the top-heavy rules (see Chapter 9). These rules provide generally that:

1. An individual is considered owning stock owned directly or indirectly by or for his or her spouse, children, grandchildren and parents.
2. Stock owned directly or indirectly by or for a partnership or estate is considered owned proportionally by its partners or beneficiaries.
3. Stock owned by or for a trust is considered owned by its beneficiaries in proportion to the actuarial interest of the beneficiaries.
4. Stock owned by a grantor trust is considered owned by the grantor.
5. If any person owns 50% or more of the value of a corporation directly or indirectly, that person is considered as owning the stock owned directly or indirectly by the corporation in proportion to the stock that person owns.
6. Stock owned directly or indirectly by or for a partner or beneficiary of an estate is considered owned by the partnership or estate.
7. Stock owned directly or indirectly by or for a beneficiary of a trust is considered owned by the trust unless the beneficiary has a contingent interest actuarially valued at 5% or less.
8. Stock owned directly or indirectly by or for any person considered to be the owner of a trust is considered owned by the trust.
9. If 50% or more of the value of the stock in a corporation is owned directly or indirectly by any person, that corporation is considered as owning the stock owned directly or indirectly by the person.
10. If any person has an option to acquire stock, that stock shall be considered as owned by that person.

On the positive side, there is no double attribution among family members. If a person owns stock and his or her spouse constructively owns that stock, that stock cannot be again attributed to the spouse's parents. A similar concept is true regarding stock attributed to partnerships, estates, trusts and corporations. This stock cannot be attributed back to others to make them constructive owners if, in the absence of the stock being attributed to the partnership, estate, trust or corporation, they would otherwise not be constructive owners. These rules apply equally to partnerships, sole proprietorships and other business entities.

The table briefly reviews the constructive ownership rules for parent-subsidiary-controlled groups, brother-sister-controlled groups and affiliated service groups. This area of the pension rules is also highly complex and should be reviewed by competent ERISA counsel.

This discussion merely covers the surface issues and applications. This is an interpretation that should be left to the experts. Considering that the identification of the employer drives several rules and regulations for qualified retirement plans, many of which affect continued qualification of the plan, an experienced practitioner should be sought to assist in the analysis.

As part of the discussion of who is the employer, a review is necessary covering some other related concepts, including leased employees, shared employees and qualified separate lines of business. Although these relationships do not necessarily deal with controlled groups and constructive ownership, they do affect the operation

Table

CONSTRUCTIVE OWNERSHIP RULES

	Parent-Subsidiary	Brother-Sister	Affiliated Service
Options	Holder of option owns stock.	Same	Same
Partnership to partner	Partner with interest equal to or more than 5% of the partnership owns any stock owned by partnership in proportion to the partner's interest.	Same	No minimum interest required
Partner to partnership	N/A	N/A	Partnership owns any stock owned by partner.
Estate to beneficiary	Beneficiary with actuarial interest equal to or more than 5% owns any stock owned by the estate in proportion to the beneficiary's actuarial interest.	Same	No minimum interest required
Beneficiary to estate	N/A	N/A	Estate owns any stock owned by the beneficiary.
Trust to beneficiary	Same as estate to beneficiary	Same	No minimum interest required
Beneficiary to trust	N/A	N/A	The trust owns any stock owned by the beneficiary unless the beneficiary's contingent interest is equal to or less than 5%.
Corporation to stockholder	N/A	Stock is deemed owned by shareholder holding value equal to or more than 5% in proportion to the shareholder's value.	Stock is deemed owned by a shareholder holding value equal to or more than 50% in proportion to the shareholder's value.
Stockholder to corporation	N/A	N/A	Stock is owned by the corporation if the stockholder holds value equal to or more than 50%.
Spouse	N/A	All stock is deemed owned unless not involved in business.	All stock is deemed owned by spouse.
Minor child to parent	N/A	Parent owns stock.	Same
Parent to minor child	N/A	Child owns stock.	Same
Parent, child, grandparent, grandchild	N/A	Senior generation owns junior generation if junior generation owns more than 50% of the stock.	No minimum ownership required

of all qualified plans, including nondiscrimination issues, based on the relationship between the employees and the employer.

LEASED EMPLOYEES

A *leased employee* is any person who is not an employee of the recipient (the entity for whom the leased employee provides services) and who provides services to the recipient if:

1. Such services are provided pursuant to an agreement between the recipient and any other person (the leasing organization)
2. That person has performed such services for the recipient on a substantially full-time basis for at least one year
3. Such services are performed under the primary direction or control of the recipient.

Substantially full-time basis is defined as the performance of services during any 12-month period for at least 1,500 hours, or performance of services during any 12-month period for a number of hours at least equal to 75% of the average number of hours that are customarily performed by an employee of that recipient in a particular position.

Leasing employees became a popular method of eliminating common law employees from qualified plans so that only the HCEs or owners of the sponsoring company would be eligible to participate in the retirement plan. The classic example was a medical practice that employed only one professional and leased all the other employees from a leasing organization, claiming those employees were employees of the leasing organization, not the medical practice. A very rich plan was adopted by the medical practice employing the professional and no plan was adopted for the rank-and-file employees. Regulations now prevent these types of arrangements.

If an employee is determined to be a leased employee under the preceding definition, that employee is treated as an employee of the recipient (the organization for whom the leased employee performs services). In that case the employee would be included, if eligible, in any qualified plan sponsored by the recipient and subject to the same rules and regulations as a common law employee would be.

As an alternative, the leasing organization may establish a safe harbor plan that would allow the leased employee to be treated as an employee of the leasing organization for purposes of retirement benefits. The safe harbor plan must:

1. Be a money purchase pension plan (see Chapter 4) with a nonintegrated employer contribution of at least 10%
2. Provide for full and immediate vesting
3. Have each employee of the leasing organization, other than those employees providing substantially all of their services for the leasing organization, immediately participate in the plan.

In addition, to satisfy the safe harbor rule, leased employees may not be more than 20% of the recipient's workforce. If the facts and circumstances indicate that the employees are actually employees of the recipient, the safe harbor plan does not satisfy the recipient's obligations to cover those employees in any plan it sponsors.

INDEPENDENT CONTRACTOR VS. EMPLOYEE STATUS

There are 20 factors used in determining independent contractor vs. employee status (see the following list). These factors have been developed based on an examination of cases and revenue rulings considering whether an individual is an employee. The degree of importance of each factor varies depending on the occupation and the factual context in which the services are performed.

1. *Instructions.* A worker required to comply with other persons' instructions about when, where and how he or she is to work is ordinarily an employee. This control factor is present if the person or persons for whom the services are performed have the right to require compliance with instructions.

2. *Training.* Training a worker by requiring an experienced employee to work with the worker, corresponding with the worker, requiring the worker to attend meetings or by using other methods indicates that the person or persons for whom the services are performed want the services performed in a particular method or manner.

3. *Integration.* Integration of the worker's services into the business operations generally shows that the worker is subject to direction and control. When the success or continuation of a business depends to an appreciable degree upon the performance of certain services, the workers who perform those services must necessarily be subject to a certain amount of control by the owner of the business.

4. *Services rendered personally.* If the services must be rendered personally, presumably the person or persons for whom the services are performed are interested in the methods used to accomplish the work as well as in the results.

5. *Hiring, supervising and paying assistants.* If the person or persons for whom the services are performed hire, supervise and pay assistants, that factor generally shows control over the workers on the job; however, if one worker hires, supervises and pays the other assistants pursuant to a contract under which the worker agrees to provide materials and labor and under which the worker is responsible only for the attainment of a result, this factor indicates independent contractor status.

6. *Continuing relationship.* A continuing relationship between the worker and the person or persons for whom the services are performed indicates that an employer-employee relationship exists. A continuing relationship may exist where work is performed at frequently recurring although irregular intervals.

7. *Set hours of work.* The establishment of set hours of work by the person or persons for whom the services are performed is a factor indicating control.

8. *Full-time required.* If the worker must devote substantially full time to the business of the person or persons for whom the services are performed, such person or persons have control over the amount of time the worker spends working and impliedly restrict the worker from doing other gainful work. An *independent contractor,* on the other hand, is free to work when and for whom he or she chooses.

9. *Doing work on employer's premises.* If the work is performed on the premises of the person or persons for whom the services are performed, that factor suggests control over the worker, especially if the work could be done elsewhere. Work done off the premises of the person or persons receiving the services, such as at the office of the worker, indicates some freedom from control. This fact by itself does not mean, however, that the worker is not an employee. The importance of this factor depends on the nature of the service involved and the extent to which an employer generally would require that employees perform such services on the employer's premises. Control over the place of work is indicated when the person or persons for whom the services are performed have the right to compel the worker to travel a designated route, to canvass a territory within a certain time or to work at specific places as required.

10. *Order or sequence set.* If a worker must perform services in the order or sequence set by the person or persons for whom the services are performed, that factor shows that the worker is not free to follow the worker's own pattern of work but must follow the established routines and schedules of the person or persons for whom the services are performed. Often, because of the nature of an occupation, the person or persons for whom the services are performed do not set the order of the services or set the order infrequently. It is sufficient to show control, however, if such person or persons retain the right to do so.

11. *Oral or written reports.* A requirement that the worker submit regular oral or written reports to the person or persons for whom the services are performed indicates a degree of control.

12. *Payment by hour, week or month.* Payment by the hour, week or month generally points to an employer-employee relationship, provided that this method of payment is not just a convenient way of paying a lump sum agreed upon as the cost of a job. Payment made by the job or on a straight commission generally indicates that the worker is an independent contractor.

13. *Payment of business or travel expenses.* If the person or persons for whom the services are performed ordinarily pay the worker's business or travel expenses, the worker is ordinarily an employee. An employer, to be able to control expenses, generally retains the right to regulate and direct the worker's business activities.

14. *Furnishing of tools and materials.* The fact that the person or persons for whom the services are performed furnish significant tools, materials and other equipment tends to show the existence of an employer-employee relationship.

15. *Significant investment.* If the worker invests in facilities that are used by the worker in performing services and the facilities are not typically maintained by employees (such as the maintenance of an office rented at fair value from an unrelated party), that factor tends to indicate that the worker is an independent contractor. On the other hand, lack of investment in facilities indicates dependence on the person or persons for whom the services are performed for such facilities and, accordingly, the existence

of an employer-employee relationship. Special scrutiny is required with respect to certain types of facilities, such as home offices.

16. *Realization of profit or loss.* A worker who can realize a profit or suffer a loss as a result of the worker's services is generally an independent contractor, but the worker who cannot is an employee. For example, if the worker is subject to a real risk of economic loss as a result of significant investments or a bona fide liability for expenses, such as salary payments to unrelated employees, that factor indicates that the worker is an independent contractor. The risk that a worker will not receive payment for his or her services is common to both independent contractors and employees and thus does not constitute a sufficient economic risk to support treatment as an independent contractor.

17. *Working for more than one firm at a time.* If a worker performs more than *de minimis* services for a multiple of unrelated persons or firms at the same time, that factor generally indicates that the worker is an independent contractor. A worker who performs services for more than one person may, however, be an employee of each of the persons, especially where such persons are part of the same service arrangement.

18. *Making service available to general public.* The fact that a worker makes his or her services available to the general public on a regular and consistent basis indicates an independent contractor relationship.

19. *Right to discharge.* The right to discharge a worker is a factor indicating that the worker is an employee and the person possessing the right is an employer. An employer exercises control through the threat of dismissal, which causes the worker to obey the employer's instructions. An independent contractor, on the other hand, cannot be fired as long as the independent contractor produces a result that meets the contract specifications.

20. *Right to terminate.* If the worker has the right to end his or her relationship with the person for whom the services are performed at any time he or she wishes without incurring liability, that factor indicates an employer-employee relationship.

These tests are only guidelines and are not meant to imply that the only issues to consider are those referred to in the revenue ruling. Some leasing organizations are cosponsoring safe harbor plans with the recipient organization taking the position that one of them is the common law employer and therefore the plan has a proper sponsor. This is still a developing area of pension law and should be considered carefully before taking a specific position.

On a more familiar note, Microsoft faced this very issue when it classified many of its workers as independent contractors. After being challenged and audited by the Internal Revenue Service (IRS), Microsoft moved some of its workers to a temporary agency. The employees who were moved to the temporary agency then sued to be included in the Microsoft retirement plans, taking the position that they were common law employees of Microsoft. After the case traveled through several court systems, it ended up in the Ninth Circuit Court of Appeals, which ruled that, in effect, Microsoft and the temporary agency were co-employers. The result is that both Microsoft and the temporary agency would treat the employees as any other common law employee for purposes of nondiscrimination.

Until Congress issues guidelines or the IRS issues regulations, this will be a gray area and therefore a dangerous one. If an employee is incorrectly classified as a leased employee or an independent contractor and excluded from the plan of the recipient, the plan would not satisfy the nondiscrimination rules listed previously. In addition, the plan would not be operated in accordance with its terms because it excluded an employee who was eligible to participate. Either of these noncompliance issues could cause the plan to be disqualified. To avoid this problem, some plans specifically exclude employees who are considered to be leased employees or independent contractors by the employer as a class even if they are later classified as common law employees.

SHARED EMPLOYEES

The next issue involves *shared employees.* A typical example of shared employees is a professional office in which several professionals work, each with independent practices, but share support staff, e.g., secretaries, receptionists, typists and nurses. In some cases each professional is responsible for and pays a proportional share of the expenses of the office and, in some cases, one of the professionals pays all the expenses and is then reimbursed by the others. Unfortunately, there is no current guidance on this arrangement. Shared employees are full-time employees of all employers sharing their services. This conclusion assumes that the shared employee works at least 1,000 hours when service for all employers is aggregated. These employees would be eligible participants in any plan sponsored by any of the employers assuming the employee satisfies the eligibility requirements, e.g., age 21 and one year of service. The contributions or benefits would be provided by each employer based on that employer's share of the employee's compensation.

Example 11: Consider the case of various employees working for Professionals A, B and C for the following salaries and percentages of time:

	Salary	Professional A	Professional B	Professional C
Secretary	$30,000	20%	50%	30%
Typist	25,000	30	35	35
Nurse 1	40,000	100		
Nurse 2	45,000		50	50

Based on this data, Nurse 1 is the exclusive employee of Professional A and is not a shared employee. All other employees are shared and would participate in each professional's retirement plan to the extent of the employer's share of their compensation. Assume all the employees are over age 21 and have been employed more than one year. Professional A sponsors a 10% money purchase plan; Professional B sponsors a profit-sharing plan and has made a 15% contribution for the current year; and Professional C sponsors a defined benefit plan providing a retirement benefit of 50% of compensation.

The results would be as follows:

	Salary	Professional A	Professional B	Professional C
Secretary	$30,000	$600 contribution ($30,000 × 20% × 10%)	$2,250 contribution ($30,000 × 50% × 15%)	$4,500 benefit/year ($30,000 × 30% × 50%)
Typist	$25,000	$750 contribution ($25,000 × 30% × 10%)	$1,313 contribution ($25,000 × 35% × 15%)	$4,375 benefit/year ($25,000 × 35% × 50%)
Nurse 1	$40,000	$4,000 contribution ($40,000 × 100% × 10%)		
Nurse 2	$45,000		$3,375 contribution ($45,000 × 50% × 15%)	$11,250 benefit/year ($45,000 × 50% × 50%)

QUALIFIED SEPARATE LINES OF BUSINESS

A *line of business* is defined as "a portion of an employer that is identified by the property or services it provides to customers of the employer." A *separate line of business (SLOB)* is "a line of business that is organized and operated separately from the remainder of the employer," based on objective criteria.

If an employer operates separate lines of business for bona fide business reasons and:
1. The line of business has at least 50 employees excluding:
   (a) Employees who have not completed six months of service
   (b) Employees who normally work less than 17½ hours per week
   (c) Employees who normally work during not more than six months during any year
   (d) Employees who have not attained age 21
   (e) Union employees.
2. The employer notifies the secretary that the line of business is being treated as separate for purposes of IRC Section 410(b).
3. The line of business meets guidelines prescribed by the secretary or the employer receives a determination from the secretary that the line of business may be treated as separate for purposes of IRC Section 410(b).

Then the separate line of business satisfying these three rules is a "qualified" SLOB, and the employer may apply the coverage rules and participation rules (see Chapter 9) separately to each qualifying line of business. (Generally, this provision applies only to larger employers because of the nature of the SLOB qualification requirements above.) An employer is treated as operating qualified separate lines of business only if all property and services provided by the employer to its customers are provided exclusively by qualified separate lines of business. This means that once the separate lines of business have been determined, no portion of the employer may remain that is not part of a qualified separate line of business of the employer.

Retirement Plans and Estate/Business Planning

Chapter 11

In Chapters 2 and 3, we discussed the rules and regulations for designing plan benefits and contributions. Although most of these rules appear to be limiting, they can be used to meet more focused goals of the plan sponsor. Chapter 1 discusses choosing the right plan and relates that choice to two extremes: designing a tax shelter for the owners and key employees or providing a true retirement plan as an employee benefit for all employees of the company. Creative plan design takes that choice a step further and expands on the goal, focusing on the owners and key employees. This chapter reviews several plan designs that, although illustrated for a specific group of employees, can be applied to any group with the same or a similar profile. Companies exhibiting certain characteristics are usually more suitable for the types of plan designs that are illustrated. These characteristics include:

1. Older and more highly compensated owners or key employees
2. A high proportion of highly compensated employees (HCEs) relative to the number of total eligible employees
3. Varied job responsibilities allowing for a larger number of job classifications
4. Multiple business locations allowing for additional classifications.

This chapter is structured in a case study format to emphasize a specific benefit of the plan design.

CASE 1: SENIOR/JUNIOR

This case study uses the following census data, including each employee's job description. See Table I.

Case 1 includes a senior owner and two junior owners. This scenario could apply to a family business or three nonrelated owners. This company has never had a retirement plan, and Steve has no retirement savings other than a small individual retirement account (IRA). The company, currently in an industry that has recovered, expects high profits for at least the next five to ten years. The goal is threefold: (1) to accumulate a large retirement account for Steve without excessive costs for the

Table I

DEFINED BENEFIT (DB) PLAN (CASE 1): GENERAL EMPLOYEE INFORMATION

	Past Service	Age	Compensation	Job Description	Stock-holder
Steve	24 yrs.	60	$205,000	President	55%
Jonathan	9 yrs.	45	125,000	VP	35
Robert	4 yrs.	35	100,000	Treasurer	10
Carol	3 yrs.	42	25,000	Secretary	
Helen	4 yrs.	31	40,000	Bookkeeper	
George	1 yr.	38	35,000	Bookkeeper	
Thomas	7 yrs.	29	28,000	Shipping Clerk	
Ralph	3 yrs.	27	30,000	Shipping Manager	
Donald	2 yrs.	25	18,000	Shipping Clerk	
Rachel	5 yrs.	45	50,000	Office Manager	

seven nonhighly compensated employees (NHCEs), (2) offer some benefits to the employees (because the labor market is tight) and (3) provide reasonably high benefits to Jonathan.

In a defined contribution (DC) plan (see Chapter 4), the maximum contribution would be $41,000 for Steve (for the year 2004), i.e., the lesser of 100% of compensation or $41,000. If that contribution is made for five years until Steve is ready to retire at age 65, assuming a 10% return on investment, the total account value would be $268,624. This is insufficient to support Steve's retirement. The only type of plan that would allow for larger contributions would be a defined benefit (DB) plan (see Chapter 6). See Table II.

Does this plan satisfy the threefold goal identified earlier? The accumulation for Steve is large at $1,134,540. At $28,449, the cost for the seven employees is high but, as a percentage of the total (12.62%), it is acceptable; and the employees and Jonathan do receive some retirement benefits. A basic DB plan would appear to satisfy all the employer's goals. This is where basic plan design ends and creative plan design begins.

Chapter 9 discusses the coverage test and the participation test. These rules allow a qualified retirement plan to exclude employees who would otherwise be eligi-

Table II

DB PLAN: SALARY, BENEFIT AND CONTRIBUTION INFORMATION

	Annual Salary	Monthly Salary	Monthly Benefit	Theoretical Contribution	Lump Sum at Retirement
Steve	$205,000	$17,083	$ 8,250*	$156,617	$1,134,540
Jonathan	125,000	10,417	10,417	30,125	1,432,500
Robert	100,000	8,333	8,333	10,218	1,145,954
				$196,960	
Carol	25,000	2,083	2,083	$ 4,598	286,454
Helen	40,000	3,333	3,333	2,972	458,400
George	35,000	2,917	2,917	4,575	401,146
Thomas	28,000	2,333	2,333	1,779	320,834
Ralph	30,000	2,500	2,500	1,633	343,800
Donald	18,000	1,500	1,500	841	206,280
Rachel	50,000	4,167	4,167	12,051	573,046
				$ 28,449	
				$225,409	
		HCE % of Total		87.38%	

*Steve's benefit maximum would normally be $13,750 per month (the lesser of 100% of compensation or $165,000 annually); however, that maximum must be reduced if the employee will participate in the plan for less than ten years. In Steve's case his participation is six years from age 60 to age 65 inclusive; therefore, his benefit is ($165,000 / 12 x 60%) = $8,250 per month.

ble by job description or some other business-related classification. Suppose the DB plan is redesigned to exclude Jonathan and Robert and all NHCEs except the shipping department (Thomas, Ralph and Donald). In addition, a class allocation profit-sharing plan is added.

Table III shows the redesigned DB plan after excluding several employees.

The first step is to determine whether this plan satisfies the coverage test of Internal Revenue Code Section 410(b), the 70% test (see Chapter 9).

Table III

DB PLAN: REDESIGNED

	Annual Salary	Monthly Salary	Monthly Benefit	Theoretical Contribution	Lump Sum at Retirement
Steve	$205,000	$17,083	$8,250	$156,617	$1,134,540
Jonathan	125,000	exclude by name		0	
Robert	100,000	exclude by name		0	
				$156,617	
Carol	25,000	exclude by job class		$ 0	
Helen	40,000	exclude by job class		0	
George	35,000	exclude by job class		0	
Thomas	28,000	2,333	2,333	1,779	320,834
Ralph	30,000	2,500	2,500	1,633	343,800
Donald	18,000	1,500	1,500	841	206,280
Rachel	50,000	exclude by job class		0	
				$ 4,254	
				$160,871	
		HCE % of Total		97.36%	

Total number of HCEs eligible:	3
Total number of HCEs participating:	1
HCE coverage percentage:	33.3%
Total number of NHCEs eligible:	7
Total number of NHCEs participating:	3
NHCE coverage percentage:	42.9%
Coverage ratio (NHCE % / HCE %):	128.8% (42.9% / 33.3%)
(= > 70% − The test is passed.)	

Eligible employees are those employees who have satisfied the statutory eligibility requirements of one year of service, age 21, nonunion and full-time employment (1,000 hours during the plan year). Because the coverage ratio is equal to or more than 70%, the plan passes the coverage test. The next step is to determine whether the plan satisfies the participation test of IRC Section 401(a)(26), which requires that the lesser of 40% of the "eligible employees" or 50 employees participate

Table IV

PROFIT-SHARING PLAN: SOME EMPLOYEES EXCLUDED

	Salary	Age	Employer Contribution	Percent of Total Contribution
Steve	$205,000	60	$16,000	33.3%
Jonathan	125,000	45	21,000	43.7
Robert	100,000	35	725	1.5
	$430,000		$37,725	78.5%
Carol	$ 25,000	42	$ 1,474	3.1%
Helen	40,000	31	2,359	4.9
George	35,000	38	2,064	4.3
Thomas	28,000	29	exclude by job class	
Ralph	30,000	27	1,500	3.1
Donald	18,000	25	exclude by job class	
Rachel	50,000	45	2,948	6.1
	226,000		10,345	21.5
	$656,000		$48,070	100.0%

in a DB plan. In this test all employees are considered: the HCEs and the NHCEs. Because there are four employees participating out of a total of ten, the 40% minimum participation is satisfied.

Next, the company will adopt a profit-sharing plan for Jonathan and the remaining employees. See Table IV.

This profit-sharing plan is a class allocation plan (see Chapter 4) that excludes the shipping clerks. The allocation classes and contributions are:

Class A	Steve	$16,000
Class B	Jonathan	16.8%
Class C	Robert	$ 725
Class D	Shipping manager	5.0%
Class E	All other employees	5.9%

Although the classes are defined in the plan document, the allocation to each class is determined annually. Again, the first step is to determine if the plan satisfies the coverage test.

Total number of HCEs eligible:	3
Total number of HCEs participating:	3
Coverage percentage:	100%
Total number of NHCEs eligible:	7
Total number of NHCEs participating:	5
Coverage percentage:	71.4%
Coverage ratio (NHCE % / HCE %):	71.4%
(= > 70% − **The test is passed.**)	

Because the coverage ratio is equal to or more than 70%, the plan passes the coverage test.

DC plans are not subject to the participation test under IRC Section 401(a)(26); therefore, the next step is to determine if the plan satisfies the nondiscrimination rules described and illustrated in Chapter 9. This is accomplished by projecting each participant's contribution to retirement and converting the accumulation to a lifetime income flow (a life annuity). That income for the NHCEs, as a percentage of the employee's compensation (the rate group), is compared to the income percentage of the HCEs. All rate groups pass the nondiscrimination test described in Chapter 9.

The last test is to determine whether the contributions to both plans are within the 25% deduction limit when combining a DB plan and a DC plan (see Chapter 3 for a full discussion on deductions). In the case of a combined DC/DB plan sponsored by the same employer, the deduction limit is the greater of the minimum funding requirement (see Chapter 6) for the DB plan or 25% of total compensation of all participants. The total compensation of all eligible employees is $656,000, so the 25% limit is $164,000. Only the compensation of eligible employees may be counted. If the company had excluded Jonathan from the profit-sharing plan by name, it would not be able to include his compensation in determining the deduction limit.

The total contribution to the DB plan is $160,871, and the contribution to the profit-sharing plan is $48,070, a total of $208,941—$44,941 in excess of the deduction limit. In this case, either the DB plan would have to be designed with lower benefits so that the contribution is $44,941 lower or the deduction would have to be carried over to the next year. As an alternative the class allocation profit-sharing plan could include a safe harbor 401(k) plan (see Chapter 5) allowing Steve to defer $16,000 and Jonathan to defer $13,000. This would reduce the excess contribution from $44,941 to $15,941 since salary deferrals in a 401(k) plan do not count toward deduction limits.

If the excess contribution is carried over, that amount would have to be contributed in the year following the year in which the deduction is taken to avoid an excise tax on the nondeductible contribution. So, if the plans are calendar-year plans and the first year is 2003, a total contribution of $164,000 could be made and deducted in 2003 and the balance of $44,941 (or $15,941) contributed in 2004 for the 2003 plan year and deducted in 2004 with the 2004 contribution again up to the deduction limit of 25% for that year.

Table V

	Original DB Plan	% Share	Redesigned DB Plan	Profit-Sharing Plan	Total	% Share
Steve	$156,617	69.48%	$156,617	$16,000	$172,617	82.62%
Jonathan	30,125	13.36	—	21,000	21,000	10.05
Robert	10,218	4.53	—	725	725	0.35
	$196,960	87.38%	$156,617	$37,725	$194,342	93.01%
Carol	$ 4,598	2.04%	—	$ 1,474	$ 1,474	0.71%
Helen	2,972	1.32	—	2,359	2,359	1.13
George	4,575	2.03	—	2,064	2,064	0.99
Thomas	1,779	0.79	1,779	—	1,779	0.85
Ralph	1,633	0.72	1,633	1,500	3,133	1.50
Donald	841	0.37	841	—	841	0.40
Rachel	12,051	5.35	—	2,948	2,948	1.41
	28,449	12.62	4,254	10,345	14,599	6.99
	$225,409	100.00%	$160,871	$48,070	$208,941	100.00%

Table V shows how the two-plan design satisfies the original goals compared to how the single plan (DB plan) satisfies them.

After the plan redesign, Steve will receive a larger benefit at age 65. Jonathan has a reduced contribution, and the cost for the rank-and-file employees has gone down $13,850. Because the main concern is Steve, the newly designed plans satisfy that goal. After Steve retires at age 65, the plans can be redesigned to favor Jonathan, who will be the senior partner at that time, and provide some benefits to Robert. The total savings between the original plan design and the two-plan combination of $16,468 ($225,409 minus $208,941) can be used either to fund a nonqualified deferred compensation plan for Steve (see Chapter 7), further adding to his benefit package, or to fund a buy-sell agreement among the three shareholders. An added advantage of the two-plan combination is the flexibility of the contribution to the profit-sharing plan rather than the fixed contribution to the DB plan alone.

What are the disadvantages of the newly designed two-plan combination? Doubtless the redesigned alternative is much more complex, and it may be difficult to explain to employees—in particular, why some employees are in one plan and other employees in another plan. On the other hand, it is difficult to explain to employees that, when they reach age 65 in 34 years, they will receive a retirement benefit of $3,333 per month. Instead of that, after only one year their current account balance is $2,359. Consider as well that younger employees accumulate much higher benefits in DC plans than in DB plans, a topic discussed in Chapter 6 as it relates to cash balance plans. Another consideration is that because it is the business owners who are funding the retirement benefit, the plan(s) should be designed to satisfy their goals while still providing their employees with a meaningful benefit.

CASE 2: TWO-PLAN EXAMPLE, DISPROPORTIONATE NUMBER OF HCEs

This two-plan approach also works well in a company that employs a disproportionate number of HCEs. Consider a small Wall Street firm with several highly paid traders, an executive placement firm or a small technology company with several highly paid programmers. The profile of that type of company may be unique. Without using specific benefit levels, a possible census could be as shown in Table VI.

Table VI

COMPANY WITH DISPROPORTIONATE NUMBER OF HCEs

		Salary
Job Class A	HCE 1	$500,000
	HCE 2	$385,000
Job Class B	HCE 3	$275,000
	HCE 4	$110,000
	HCE 5	$320,000
	HCE 6	$135,000
Job Class C	HCE 7	$100,000
	HCE 8	$ 90,000
	HCE 9	$ 95,000
Job Class D	NHCE 1	$ 25,000
	NHCE 2	$ 40,000
	NHCE 3	$ 65,000
	NHCE 4	$ 55,000

Assuming HCE 1 and HCE 2 are equal partners and all other HCEs are employees, how could a plan be designed to favor the two owners substantially? If the owners are relatively young, a DB plan may not give them a contribution of more than $41,000, so the only option is a DC plan. If only HCE 1 and HCE 2 are covered, how many NHCEs would have to be in the plan? Referring to the coverage test in the two-plan combination discussed previously:

Total number of HCEs eligible:	9
Total number of HCEs participating:	2
Coverage percentage:	22.2%
Total number of NHCEs eligible:	4
Total number of NHCEs participating:	1
Coverage percentage:	25%
Coverage ratio (NHCE % / HCE %):	112.6%

Using the coverage rules, HCE 1, HCE 2 and as few as one of the NHCEs could be included. Because there is no NHCE job class with one employee, the plan would have to include job class C or D. The NHCE could be chosen based on his or her value to the company, the cost to include the group or any other criterion defined by the owners as critical to the business.

If the owners are older and a DB plan is appropriate along with the profit-sharing plan, at least two of the NHCEs and four HCEs would have to be covered to satisfy the participation rule of IRC Section 401(a)(26), which requires at least 40% of the employees to participate. That would also satisfy the coverage rule.

Total number of HCEs eligible:	9
Total number of HCEs participating:	4
Coverage percentage:	44.4%
Total number of NHCEs eligible:	4
Total number of NHCEs participating:	2
Coverage percentage:	50%
Coverage ratio (NHCE % / HCE %):	112.6%

CASE 3: BUSINESS EMPLOYING ONLY OWNER AND SPOUSE

The Economic Growth and Tax Relief Reconciliation Act of 2001 (EGTRRA) increased the deduction limit for profit-sharing plans to 25% of compensation (formerly the limit was 15%). Salary deferrals in 401(k) plans do not count against this deduction limit. Another change in the act increased maximum contributions for a participant to the lesser of 100% of compensation or $41,000 (for 2004).

Coordinating those changes for a business that employs only the owner and spouse more than doubles their available contributions. The example illustrates the old and new rules for a sample plan of such a business.

Example: Following are the former deduction limits for a profit-sharing plan of a sample business employing only the owner and spouse:

Old Rules:

	Salary	Profit-Sharing Contribution
Owner	$205,000	$30,750
Spouse	41,000	6,150
Total deposit:		$36,900

The business in the example would gain a greater advantage under the new rules if it adopted a combination 401(k)/profit-sharing plan, because salary deferrals under the 401(k) plan would not count against the new deduction limit of 25% of compensation. Based on the same salaries, the deduction limit would be $61,500, but the maximum contribution limit would be $82,000 (i.e., the lesser of 100% of compensation or $41,000 for each participant). If an employer contribution of $82,000 is made for the plan year, only $61,500 would be deductible, causing an excise tax on the balance of the contribution that is not deductible. Under the new rules, the plan contribution limits are as follows:

	Salary	Employee Deferral	Profit-Sharing Contribution	Total
Owner	$205,000	$13,000	$28,000	$41,000
Spouse	41,000	13,000	28,000	41,000
Total deposit:				$82,000

If the owner has reached age 50 during the year, an additional $3,000 could be deferred as a catch-up contribution bringing the total contribution to $85,000. Since the contribution of the owner's spouse is already 100% of salary, no additional contribution could be made for the spouse.

The change in deduction limits for profit-sharing plans and the ability to make salary deferrals to a 401(k) plan without impacting the deduction limit also impacts the ability of a one-person, owner-only plan to maximize its contribution at a lower salary level. Without these two changes, it would be impossible to reach the $41,000 limit in a profit-sharing plan, since the salary limit is $205,000 and the deduction limit prior to the change is 15% resulting in a contribution of $30,750. Even if a money purchase plan is adopted bringing the total to 25% to maximize the contribution, the owner would need a salary of $164,000 to reach the $41,000 limit. Under the new rules, assuming the owner has reached age 50, the salary and contributions would be:

Salary:		$112,000
Employer Profit-Sharing Contribution:	$28,000	
Employee 401(k) Deferral:	16,000	
Total Contribution:	$44,000	

CASE 4: INSURED BUYOUT

John, age 58, and Alan, age 50, are equal shareholders in Custom Built Homes, Inc., a sub-Chapter S corporation. Their business has flourished in the last few years, and they have decided to have their attorney prepare a stockholders' agreement providing for the purchase of the stock from a stockholder who dies, becomes disabled or chooses to retire. They also have decided they will purchase insurance on each partner's life to fund the buyout in the event of death. Their accountant has valued their business at $1 million. Their insurance agent has suggested a variable universal life policy for each stockholder in the amount of $500,000. The premium for John will be $8,400 and for Alan $5,500. Custom Built Homes, Inc. also has had a profit-sharing plan in place for the past six years, and John and Alan each have account balances of $250,000. The contribution for the current year is $10,000 for each partner.

If John and Alan purchase the insurance in the traditional manner, i.e., paying the premiums personally, what is the true cost? Assume that each is in a 40% tax bracket. The total cost of the insurance, including the income tax, would be:

	Net Premium	Pretax Cost
John	$8,400	$14,000
Alan	$5,500	$ 9,167

John would have to earn income of $9,167 to be able to pay $3,667 in income taxes and use the remaining $5,500 for the premium on Alan's policy. Alan would need income of $14,000 to be able to pay $5,600 in taxes and the $8,400 premium on John's policy.

Alternatively, the insurance can be purchased by using John and Alan's profit-sharing account or contributions. The availability of life insurance in DC plans and its limitations is discussed in Chapter 2. With a limit of 25% of cumulative annual additions (employer contributions plus employee contributions plus forfeitures) for variable life insurance, the current year's contribution of $10,000 each would not be enough to allow for premiums of $8,400 and $5,500. In addition to the rules discussed in Chapter 2 regarding the limits on the purchase of life insurance, regulations also allow for the unlimited use of "seasoned" funds. This approach allows for the use of all vested funds that have remained in the plan for at least two years and all vested funds for a participant who has at least five years of plan participation. John and Alan would be able to pay the premiums from the accumulated account balances because those are "seasoned" funds. The advantage of this approach is to convert an after-tax payment to a pretax payment. Because each partner is charged with the "economic benefit" of the insurance as measured by the PS-58 costs or the insurance company's term rates (see Chapter 2), the pure death benefit is considered to be paid with after-tax dollars; therefore, the net insurance proceeds (total death benefit less cash surrender value) are income tax-free. That amount, the net amount at risk, can be distributed from the account balance of the surviving stockholder tax-free, allowing that stockholder to use the funds to purchase the stock of the deceased stockholder.

The disadvantage of this approach is a possible drag on the investment returns in the profit-sharing account. That potential loss would have to be compared to the future value of the additional taxes that would have to be paid on the premium if paid personally. For example:

	Insurance in Plan	Insurance Personally
Income	$23,167	$23,167
Taxes Due	0	9,267
Cash Available	$23,167	$13,900
Premium Due	13,900	13,900
Income Remaining	$ 9,267	$ 0
Tax Due @ 40%	3,707	0
Available to Invest	$ 5,560	$ 0

This analysis takes the position that $23,167 of personal income is necessary for individuals in a 40% tax bracket to pay a premium of $13,900 after paying $9,267 in income taxes. The alternative is to use $13,900 to pay the premium in the profit-sharing plan assuming a sufficient annual contribution. Because only $13,900 of the $23,167 is used to pay the premium, the remaining $9,267 of income is still available. That income is taxable in a 40% tax bracket; $5,560 remains after tax ($9,267 × [100% − 40%]). If the $5,560 is invested (in a taxable account), the value of that account would be compared to the reduction in value of the profit-sharing accounts.

This analysis is one of many possible approaches. The decision must be based on the facts of each case; for example, availability of funds to pay the premiums and future intention of the stockholders regarding exit strategies. There is no general rule that says one approach is better than another.

CASE 5: ZERO-TAXABLE INCOME

It is not unusual for professionals to accumulate significant investments during their most active years of employment. Investment income may produce a high level of passive taxable income in later years, but it is usually not necessary for living expenses. When the investment income is added to the professional service income, the taxes are astronomical. Using a DB plan, consider this planning device.

The professional's income is:

	Service	Investment
2001	$115,000	$175,000
2002	110,000	210,000
2003	75,000	185,000

For the year 2004, service income is expected to be $160,000 and investment income in excess of $150,000. If a DB plan is established in which benefits are based on historical compensation (see Chapters 2 and 6), 2001 through 2003 compensation can be used to determine benefits. This would be sufficient to provide an annual benefit as illustrated in Case 1 above of $99,000 ($8,250 monthly). The contribution to fund the benefit would be $156,617, resulting in close to zero-taxable service income for the year 2004. If the professional is a sole proprietor, the pension deduction eliminates the taxable income. If the professional is a corporation, no salary would be paid, and the corporation's profit would be eliminated by the pension deduction. If the professional is a sub-Chapter S corporation and the contribution is in excess of the profits, the loss would be carried over to the professional's personal tax return and could have the effect of sheltering some of the investment income.

CASE 6: HIGH CONCENTRATION OF HCEs

Some businesses have a high percentage of HCEs compared to NHCEs. Examples include some Wall Street firms specializing in venture capital, companies involved in mergers and acquisitions, boutique brokerage firms, executive placement firms and high-tech firms. Such companies find it difficult to provide significant benefits for the owners of the company without high costs for no-owner HCEs, because of their high compensation. In this situation a two-plan design usually satisfies the needs of the owners. Illustrations for this case study are based on the following census data for a plan year in 2004: a DB plan providing a benefit of 80.5% of high three-year-average compensation and retirement age of 65.

	Past Service	Age	Compensation	Job Description	Stockholder
John	24 yrs.	55	$460,000	President	55%
David	9 yrs.	45	425,000	VP	45
Scott	4 yrs.	35	250,000	Broker	
Ellen	3 yrs.	42	325,000	Broker	
Joel	4 yrs.	31	220,000	Broker	
Betty	1 yr.	38	235,000	Analyst	
Harold	7 yrs.	29	428,000	Trader	
Carol	3 yrs.	27	45,000	Secretary	
Sarah	2 yrs.	55	38,000	Bookkeeper	
Nancy	5 yrs.	45	35,000	Receptionist	

If the goal is to maximize the contribution for John and David, the first plan considered would be a DB plan with the following results.

	Monthly Benefit	Lump Sum at Retirement	Initial Plan Deposit	Percent Share	Redesigned Plan Deposit	Percent Share
John	$13,750	$1,890,900	$124,335	42.95%	$124,335	71.51%
David	13,750	1,890,900	40,619	14.03	40,619	23.36
Scott	13,750	1,890,900	17,011			
Ellen	13,750	1,890,900	30,844			
Joel	13,750	1,890,900	12,339			
Betty	13,750	1,890,900	21,815			
Harold	13,750	1,890,900	10,544			
			$257,507		$164,954	
Carol	3,019	415,173	$ 1,982		$ 1,982	
Sarah	2,549	350,538	23,049			
Nancy	2,348	322,897	6,936		6,936	
			$ 31,968		$ 8,918	
			$289,474		$173,872	

If the plan did not exclude the employees as illustrated above, less than 60% of the total contribution would be funding the benefits of the two owners. This is not an efficient use of cash flow if the purpose is to maximize benefit to the owners with "reasonable" costs for the remaining employees, both HCEs and NHCEs. If the DB plan is redesigned to include only John, David, Carol and Nancy, the plan satisfies the coverage test, the 70% test (see Chapter 9) and the participation test (see Chapter 9).

Coverage Test

HCEs covered:	2
Total HCEs:	7
Percentage covered:	28.6%
NHCEs covered:	2
Total NHCEs:	3
Percentage covered:	66.7%
Coverage test:	66.7% / 28.6% = 233.2%
	(Passes if ≥ 70%)

Participation Test

Total employees participating:	4
Total employees eligible:	10
Percentage participation:	40%
	(Passes if ≥ 40%)

Adding a second plan, a safe harbor 401(k) plan (see Chapter 5), creates these results.

	Defined Benefit Deposit	Safe Harbor Deferral	Safe Harbor Non-Elective	Total Deposit	Percent of Total
John	$124,335	$16,000	$6,150	$146,485	$58.72%
David	40,619	13,000	6,150	59,769	23.96
Scott	—		6,150	6,150	
Ellen	—		6,150	6,150	
Joel	—		6,150	6,150	
Betty	—		6,150	6,150	
Harold	—		6,150	6,150	
				$237,004	
Carol	1,982		1,350	$ 3,332	
Sarah	—		1,140	1,140	
Nancy	6,936		1,050	7,986	
				$ 12,458	
				$249,462	

The result of the two-plan combination is to allocate 82.68% of the contribution instead of 56.98%, as in the original plan design. Although the only contributions illustrated here are employer-funded, the nonowner employees may also make deferrals to the 401(k) plan at their discretion. The sum of all employer contributions would still be within the 25% maximum deduction limit. The total considered compensation (limited to $205,000 per employee) is $1,553,000; 25% of that compensation is $388,250; and the employer contribution in this example is only $220,462, excluding employee deferrals.

CASE 7: ADDING SIZZLE TO A TRADITIONAL PROFIT-SHARING PLAN

In many small businesses, a traditional profit-sharing plan is the plan of choice because of its simplicity and flexibility; however, as a small business grows, the cost for rank-and-file employees tends to expand quickly, diminishing the traditional profit-sharing plan's appeal to the company owners funding it. Using Table I from Chapter 4, the results for a traditional profit-sharing plan are as follows on page 180.

	Salary	Age	Employer Contribution	Percent of Total Contribution	Calculation of Allocation
John	$205,000	60	$41,000	44.47%	((205,000 / 461,000) × 92,200)
Stuart	100,000	55	20,000	21.69	((100,000 / 461,000) × 92,200)
	$305,000		$61,000	66.16%	
Carol	$ 25,000	44	$5,000	5.42%	((25,000 / 461,000) × 92,200)
David	35,000	38	7,000	7.59	((35,000 / 461,000) × 92,200)
Helen	28,000	29	5,600	6.07	((28,000 / 461,000) × 92,200)
Fred	18,000	25	3,600	3.90	((18,000 / 461,000) × 92,200)
Steve	50,000	45	10,000	10.85	((50,000 / 461,000) × 92,200)
	$156,000		$31,200	33.84	
	$461,000		$92,200	100.00%	

An alternative would be to convert the traditional profit-sharing plan to a traditional 401(k) profit-sharing plan, to keep the total flexibility of contributions. In addition, assume the participation by NHCEs is moderate and the discretionary match is dollar for dollar on the first 2% of employee deferrals.

	Employee Salary	Employee Deferral	Discretionary Employer Match	ADP Test Percentage	Profit-Sharing Contribution	Total Deposit	Percent of Total
John	$205,000	$13,000	$4,100	8.341%	$23,900	$41,000	52.58%
Stuart	100,000	2,925	2,000	4.925	11,659	16,583	21.27
			HCE Average	6.633%	$35,559	$57,583	73.85%
Carol	25,000	1,300	500	7.200%	$ 2,915	$ 4,715	
David	35,000	2,000	700	7.714	4,080	6,780	
Helen	28,000	—	—	0.000	3,264	3,264	
Fred	18,000	—	—	0.000	2,099	2,099	
Steve	50,000	3,125	1,000	8.251	5,829	9,955	
			NHCE Average	4.633%	18,187	26,813	
					$53,746	$84,396	

By converting the traditional profit-sharing plan to a combination 401(k) and profit-sharing plan, the company has increased the percentage of its contribution going to the two HCEs from 66.16% to 73.85%, decreased the dollar allocation to the two HCEs by only $3,417, reduced the total employer contribution by $14,230 and given the employees an opportunity to add to their retirement accounts. Use of a safe harbor 401(k) and a catch-up deferral for John would result in even better allocations.

If the company adds a safe harbor 401(k) plan instead of a traditional 401(k) plan, these are the results.

	Employee Salary	Employee Deferral	Safe Harbor Deposit	Profit-Sharing Contribution	Total Deposit	Percent of Total
John	$205,000	$16,000	$6,150	$21,850	$ 44,000	46.33%
Stuart	100,000	16,000	3,000	10,659	29,659	31.23
				$32,509	$ 73,659	77.56%
Carol	25,000	1,300	750	$ 2,665	$ 4,715	
David	35,000	2,000	1,050	3,730	6,780	
Helen	28,000	—	840	2,984	3,824	
Fred	18,000	—	540	1,919	2,459	
Steve	50,000	2,500	1,500	5,329	9,329	
				16,627	27,107	
				$49,136	$100,766	

This alternative has a higher allocation to the HCEs and it is a more equitable distribution among the HCEs.

Creative plan design is nothing more than using the rules and regulations to accomplish the goals of the plan sponsor. The more the practitioner knows about these rules and regulations, the more effective the plan designs can be. Each company has its own unique profile. Design creativity is the ability to match the profile to the appropriate combination of rules, resulting in the plan or plans that best satisfy the goals of the company.

Fiduciary Responsibility and Prohibited Transactions

Chapter 12

The *American Heritage Dictionary* defines a *fiduciary* as *a person who stands in a special relation of trust, confidence or responsibility in his obligations to others, as a company director or an agent of a principal.* In this definition, the phrase "in a special relation of trust" is the basis for fiduciary responsibility under the Employee Retirement Income Security Act of 1974 (ERISA). Under ERISA, ". . . every employee benefit plan shall be established and maintained pursuant to a written instrument. Such instrument shall provide for one or more named fiduciaries who jointly or severally shall have authority to control and manage the operation and administration of the plan."

ERISA adds:

For purposes of this title, the term *named fiduciary* means a fiduciary who is named in the plan instrument, or who, pursuant to a procedure specified in the plan, is identified as a fiduciary (A) by a person who is an employer or employee organization with respect to the plan or (B) by such an employer and such an employee organization acting jointly.

This chapter discusses the nature of fiduciary responsibility and associated transactions.

WHO IS A FIDUCIARY?

Other than being a named fiduciary, individuals or organizations may be considered a fiduciary as a result of their actions. A person is considered a fiduciary with respect to a qualified plan if he or she does one or more of the following:

1. Exercises any discretionary authority or discretionary control respecting management of the plan. An example of management control would be the determination of benefit eligibility in a disputed claim.
2. Exercises any authority or control respecting management or disposition of plan assets. An example of control regarding management of assets would be the ability of a trustee to withdraw plan assets, usually to pay benefits or direct investments, but because the authority exists, it can also be abused.

3. Renders investment advice for a fee or other compensation, direct or indirect, with respect to any monies or other property of such plan, or has any authority or responsibility to do so. If the ultimate authority to make the decision to purchase, invest in, or sell an asset is held by another individual or entity, the investment advice may influence the decision, but it does not constitute authority or control.

    Investment advice is rendered only if two requirements are met:
    (a) The person must advise on the value of securities or other property or make a recommendation to invest in, purchase, or sell the asset
    (b) The person must either directly or indirectly have discretionary authority or control over the purchase or sale of the asset, or render advice in accordance with an agreement that provides that the advice will be the primary basis for investment decisions and that the advice will be individualized for the plan.

4. Has any discretionary authority or discretionary responsibility in the administration of such plan. An example of administration of the plan would be the authority to determine which employees will be eligible to participate if the facts are not clear. This issue may occur in a class allocation profit-sharing plan (see Chapter 4) in determining which job class an employee falls into if his or her responsibilities do not clearly fit in one job class.

A fiduciary is held to high standards and is required to discharge its duties solely in the interest of the participants and beneficiaries of the plan and:

1. For the exclusive purpose of
    (a) Providing benefits to participants and their beneficiaries
    (b) Defraying reasonable expenses of administering the plan.

        This rule prohibits the return of plan assets to the employer-sponsor of the plan except in specific cases, e.g., a contribution made in error as determined by the Internal Revenue Service (IRS), contributions made conditioned on plan qualification, contributions made conditioned on deductibility and recovery of excess assets on termination of a defined benefit plan (see Chapter 15). Any loss to the plan caused by a breach of this duty must be made up by the fiduciary.

2. Do so with the care, skill, prudence and diligence under the circumstances then prevailing that a prudent person acting in a like capacity and familiar with such matters would use in the conduct of an enterprise of a like character and with like aims.

    The prudent man rule applies to both the result of the fiduciary's action and the action that created the result. In this context, both the investment performance and the process followed to reach that result are considered in determining whether the fiduciary acted prudently. For example, did the fiduciary consider the makeup of the investment portfolio, including diversification, the liquidity requirements and the overall return vs. its objective when choosing a specific investment?

3. By diversifying the investments of the plan to minimize the risk of large losses, unless under the circumstances it is clearly prudent not to do so. Diversification of plan assets should consider the purpose of the plan, e.g.,

to pay out lump sums or monthly retirement income at retirement; the amount of the plan assets; overall financial conditions; the type of investment (asset class); geographical distribution of investments; industry section distribution of plan assets; and dates of maturity, if applicable.

4. In accordance with the documents and instruments governing the plan insofar as they are consistent with the provisions of ERISA.

Investing in a high-risk asset is not necessarily imprudent by itself but must be judged as part of the overall investment plan and portfolio. Similarly, an investment in a highly conservative asset does not protect the fiduciary from liability. Consider a qualified plan in which a third-party administrator (TPA) calculates the contribution and determines each participant's share of the contribution, which employees are eligible and the amount that must be paid to terminated employees. Is this person or organization a fiduciary? According to ERISA, the answer is "no" because these are ministerial functions and do not fall under any of the activities or powers detailed in the preceding discussion. The contribution is calculated in accordance with the provisions of the plan document; the eligibility is determined based on information provided by the plan sponsor, i.e., date of birth, date of hire, compensation and the provisions in the plan document; and the amount to be paid and when it is to be paid to terminated participants is determined by the provisions in the plan document.

If the individual or organization also had the authority to validate whether the employee should collect benefits in a disputed claim, this person or organization *would* be a fiduciary because this person has discretionary control.

401(k) PLANS AND FIDUCIARY RESPONSIBILITY

With the growing popularity of 401(k) plans, in which employees' money is withheld as contributions to the qualified plan, the determination of fiduciary responsibility is particularly important.

A 1999 case in the Ninth Circuit was right on target. A plan sponsor engaged a TPA to provide services to the plan. After a few months, the TPA discovered discrepancies between the employee deferrals withheld from employees' paychecks and the amounts that were actually deposited to the plan. When the TPA suspected embezzlement by one of the trustees of the plan, it notified the trustees, including the one suspected of misappropriation of the funds, that failure to deposit the employee deferrals was a breach of the trustees' fiduciary duties and violated both IRS and Department of Labor (DOL) regulations. The TPA advised the trustees that they would have to disclose the discrepancy on the financial reports they had to prepare. The trustee suspected of the embezzlement assured the TPA that all shortages would be made up in accordance with a repayment schedule sent to the TPA.

The TPA agreed to the repayment schedule and advised the trustees that the following caveat would be placed on all participant account statements: "Contrary to the requirements of the Department of Labor and the Internal Revenue Service, a portion of the 401(k) benefits have not yet been received by the trust." The TPA also required that it be sent copies of all deposited checks and advised the trustees that if the repayment schedule were not adhered to, the TPA would resign. Accepting the agreement, the suspected trustee signed a letter agreeing to all these terms and deposited $35,000 of the funds due. After the trustee's later request to modify the repayment schedule and the TPA's refusal, and the subsequent discovery by the TPA of falsified financial data provided by the trustee, the TPA resigned without any further action or notification of the suspected embezzlement to the plan participants or any government agencies.

After the suspected trustee pleaded guilty to embezzling more than $450,000, the participants sued the TPA to recover the lost assets. The participants took the position that the TPA was a fiduciary because:

1. It exercised authority and control over the plan administration after its discovery of the embezzlement.
2. The TPA failed to take reasonable steps to warn the plan participants or governmental agencies of the embezzlement.
3. The TPA had a duty to report to the plan participants its suspicions regarding the breach of fiduciary duty.

The court ruled that the TPA was not a fiduciary because it was performing only ministerial duties and did not exercise any discretionary control over the plan. In addition, because the TPA was not a fiduciary it did not have a duty to report to the participants its suspicions regarding the possible embezzlement and had satisfied its duty as a nonfiduciary by placing the appropriate caveat on the participant's statements.

This case is of prime importance to any individual or organization involved in the administration of qualified plans, particularly 401(k) plans: accounting firms that prepare the financial reports, investment brokers that provide the funding vehicles and financial professionals that advise the plan sponsor. In this case, the TPA took all the right steps to protect itself and in the end prevailed. Even though the TPA won, it still had the expense of the legal fees to defend against the claims of the participants, the loss of time to prepare for the case and appear in court, and the added stress of impending significant financial liability if it lost the case. The lesson learned is to prepare for the worst and hope for the best.

INVESTMENT EDUCATION

In the same vein, the issue of potential fiduciary liability when an employer offers investment education to employees should be addressed. To encourage educational programs yet protect the employer from fiduciary liability, DOL issued an interpretive bulletin that sets forth safe harbor guidelines allowing employers to offer investment education without offering "investment advice" and exposing themselves to fiduciary liability. Under those guidelines, the employer may offer the following information:

1. *Plan information,* regarding the benefits of participating in the plan and increasing plan contributions, the effect of premature withdrawals, and the terms of the plan
2. *Investment alternatives,* information about alternative plan investments including investment objectives, risk and return characteristics, historical performance, and prospectuses
3. *General financial and investment information,* including basic concepts such as risk and return, dollar cost averaging, compound return, diversification, tax-deferred vs. taxable investments, the difference between various

asset classes, determination of risk tolerance, determination of retirement income needs and the effect of inflation on future income

4. *Asset allocation models,* for participants with various time periods until retirement

5. *Interactive investment materials,* including software to estimate future retirement income needs, questionnaires to identify an acceptable risk level and software to illustrate the effect of different asset allocations.

To encourage employers to provide investment education for plan participants, the Retirement Security Act of 2001 created a new exemption to the prohibited transaction rules of ERISA allowing financial institutions like brokers, banks and mutual fund companies, that administer defined contribution (DC) plans to provide investment advice to plan participants without causing the employer to be liable for that advice. The investment advisors would have to disclose the fees being charged to avoid any conflict of interest. The investment advice may only be provided by "fiduciary advisors," including registered investment advisors, banks, insurance companies or registered broker dealers. If this service is offered, the fiduciary that arranges for the service or the plan sponsor would not be required to monitor the investment advice offered by the advisor but is required to select the advisor prudently.

BREACH OF FIDUCIARY RESPONSIBILITY

ERISA indicates that:

Any person who is a fiduciary with respect to a plan who breaches any of the responsibilities, obligations, or duties imposed upon fiduciaries by this title shall be *personally liable* to make good to such plan any losses to the plan resulting from each such breach, and to restore to such plan any profits of such fiduciary which have been made through use of assets of the plan by the fiduciary, and shall be subject to such other equitable or remedial relief as the court may deem appropriate, including removal of such fiduciary [emphasis added].

As you can see, the position of fiduciary is taken quite seriously. If an improper investment is made by a fiduciary, the damages would be measured by the difference between a reasonable return on the investment and the actual return of the investment. A fiduciary may also be liable for the act of a cofiduciary.

To protect against the exposure to liability, the plan may purchase insurance for itself or for the fiduciaries to pass to an insurer the risk of loss caused by a breach of fiduciary duties. In addition, the fiduciary or the employer may purchase the insurance. Generally all fiduciaries and individuals who handle qualified plan assets must be bonded. The amount of the bond is determined at the beginning of each plan year and may not be less than 10% of the plan assets (but not less than $1,000) and not more than $500,000, although the Secretary of Labor may require a bond in excess of $500,000 (but not in excess of 10% of plan assets) depending on the facts and circumstances. The bond must protect the plan against loss caused by fraud or dishonesty on the part of a fiduciary or plan official. On Schedule H, Part IV(e), of the Form 5500, the question is asked, "Was the plan covered by a fidelity bond?" If this question is not answered or is answered in the negative, or if the amount of the bond is not within the preceding guidelines, the plan may be flagged for audit. If a fiduciary breaches his or her duty, a participant, beneficiary of the plan, the secretary of labor, or other fiduciaries may sue for any loss caused by the fiduciary breach.

A fiduciary may assign its responsibility to manage the investments of the plan by appointing an investment manager. This would eliminate its responsibility with respect to those assets, and generally the fiduciary would not be responsible for the acts of the investment manager; however, the fiduciary that appointed the investment manager may still be responsible for the acts of the investment manager unless the fiduciary had complied with the prudent man rule in selecting the investment manager. The fiduciary appointing the investment manager also has the responsibility of monitoring the performance of the investment manager. Generally, nonfiduciaries cannot be held liable for losses to a plan under DOL rules regarding fiduciary liability. This longstanding position may be changing because of two cases decided in the Supreme Court in 2000. One case in particular involves a qualified retirement plan.

> **Example 1:** Harris Trust was the trustee of the Ameritech Pension Trust. Salomon Smith Barney provided broker/dealer services to the Ameritech Pension Trust in the sale of interests in several motel properties to the trust for almost $21 million. At a later date, Harris Trust determined that the motel properties were almost worthless. Harris Trust brought a suit against Salomon Smith Barney under ERISA Section 502(a)(3), which allows for civil actions to obtain "other equitable relief." The case revolved on the question of whether Harris Trust could sue Salomon Smith Barney because Salomon was not a fiduciary to the plan and only fiduciaries could be sued under ERISA. The Supreme Court reached a different conclusion based on the exact language of ERISA Section 502(a)(3), which it interpreted to mean that the plaintiffs were limited to "participants, beneficiaries, or fiduciaries." The limiting language was not whom the plaintiff could sue. Furthermore, the court relied on ERISA Section 502(l), which imposes penalties for breach of responsibility by a fiduciary or by "any other person" who participates knowingly in that breach of action. This led the court to believe that penalties could be imposed against nonfiduciaries as well as fiduciaries. The court concluded Salomon Smith Barney had to take back the motel chain and return the funds it received to the plan.

CORRECTION OF FIDUCIARY BREACH

Chapter 14 discusses a variety of voluntary correction programs offered by IRS to deal with errors that occur in the operation of qualified plans. On March 14, 2000, DOL announced a similar program to deal with fiduciary breaches: the Voluntary Fiduciary Correction (VFC) Program. This program lists several specific types of fiduciary breaches that may be corrected and sets out the required method of correction. Any party that may be liable for a fiduciary violation may apply under the VFC Program. The violation must be completely corrected before filing as provided for in the guidelines of the VFC Program. The primary advantage of the VFC Program is the reduction of potential risk and the elimination of civil penalties levied on the fiduciary. Unlike IRS voluntary compliance programs, the VFC Program does not require the payment of any fee or sanction.

The only transactions that may be submitted for correction under the VFC Program are:

1. Delinquent participant contributions to a pension plan
2. Loans at fair market interest rate to a "party in interest"
3. Loans at below-market interest rate to a party in interest
4. Loans at below-market interest rate to a person who is not a party in interest
5. Loans at below-market interest rate because of a delay in perfecting the plan's security interest
6. Purchases of assets by a plan from a party in interest
7. Sales of assets by a plan to a party in interest
8. Sales and leasebacks of real property to the employer
9. Purchases of assets by a plan from a person who is not a party in interest at other than fair market value
10. Sales of assets by a plan to a person who is not a party in interest at other than fair market value
11. Payments of benefits by a DC plan based on incorrect valuation of assets
12. Payments by a plan of duplicative, excessive or unnecessary compensation
13. Payments of dual compensation to a plan fiduciary.

PROHIBITED TRANSACTIONS

The following transactions are prohibited under ERISA:

1. Sale or exchange, or leasing, of any property between the plan and a *party in interest* (defined below)
2. Lending of money or other extension of credit between the plan and a party in interest
3. Furnishing of goods, services or facilities between the plan and a party in interest
4. Transfer to, or use by or for the benefit of, a party in interest, of any assets of the plan
5. Acquisition, on behalf of the plan, of any employer security (other than an ESOP, see Chapter 4) or employer real property.

A fiduciary with respect to the plan cannot:

1. Deal with the assets of the plan in his or her own interest or for his or her own account
2. In his or her individual or in any other capacity act in any transaction involving the plan on behalf of a party (or represent a party) whose interests are adverse to the interests of the plan or the interests of its participants or beneficiaries; or
3. Receive any consideration for his or her own personal account from any party dealing with the plan in connection with a transaction involving the assets of the plan.

These excerpts from ERISA define a *prohibited transaction*. Essentially, any transaction prompted by a fiduciary that involves a party in interest is a prohibited transaction.

PARTY IN INTEREST/
DISQUALIFIED PERSON DEFINED

1. Any fiduciary
2. A person providing services to the plan, e.g., TPA, investment advisor
3. An employer, any of whose employees are covered by the plan
4. An employee organization, any of whose members are covered by the plan, e.g., a union
5. An owner of the company sponsoring the plan, direct or indirect, of 50% or more of:
   (a) The combined voting power of all classes of stock entitled to vote or the total value of shares of all classes of stock of a corporation
   (b) The capital interest or the profit interest of a partnership, or
   (c) The beneficial interest of a trust or unincorporated enterprise that is an employer or employee organization described in items 3 or 4.
6. A relative of any individual described in items 1, 2, 3 or 5
7. A corporation, partnership, trust or estate of which (or in which) 50% or more of:
   (a) The combined voting power of all classes of stock entitled to vote or the total value of shares of all classes of stock of that corporation
   (b) The capital interest or profits interest of that partnership, or
   (c) The beneficial interest of that trust or estate is owned directly or indirectly, or held by persons described in items 1, 2, 3, 4 or 5.
8. An employee, officer, director (or an individual having powers or responsibilities similar to those of officers or directors), of a 10%-or-more shareholder directly or indirectly, of a person described in items 2, 3, 4, 5 or 6, or of the employee benefit plan; or
9. A 10%-or-more (directly or indirectly in capital or profits) partner or joint venturer or a person described in items 2, 3, 4, 5 or 6.

From a practical approach, a *party in interest* is anyone who has a relationship with the plan either directly or indirectly. The parallel provisions in the Internal Revenue Code refer to *disqualified persons* rather than a party in interest.

EXCISE TAX LEVIED ON A PROHIBITED TRANSACTION

A party in interest or disqualified person who enters into a prohibited transaction is subject to a two-tier excise tax. The first level of the tax is 15% and is automatic, i.e., it is levied even if the violation is inadvertent or even prudent or beneficial to the plan. The second-tier tax is 100% of the amount involved and is assessed if the prohibited transaction is not corrected between the date the transaction occurs and 90 days after the date of the mailing of a notice of deficiency for the first-tier tax. It is interesting to note that both DOL and IRS have jurisdiction in this area. Generally, DOL determines whether a transaction is a prohibited transaction and IRS levies the penalty. Originally, the first-tier tax was 5%. This was amended to 10% in the Small Business Job Protection Act of 1996 and later to 15% in the Tax Relief Act of 1997.

A unique concept relating to prohibited transactions is the *amount involved*. This is defined as:

1. The amount of money and the fair market value of property given by the disqualified person, or
2. The amount of money and the fair market value of property received by the disqualified person.

In most cases, the amount involved is obvious. In the sale of a piece of property for $50,000, the amount involved is $50,000. In a lease of property for an annual rental of $15,000, the amount involved is $15,000. In a prohibited transaction that involves a loan, the amount involved is not so obvious. The value of the property—the loan—given by or received by the disqualified person is based on the value of the use of the money being loaned, i.e., the interest. A loan in the amount of $100,000 is issued and then determined to be a prohibited transaction at an interest rate of 12%; the amount involved is the annual interest charge of $12,000, not the amount of the loan.

The amount of the excise tax on an outstanding loan escalates at an increasing rate based on the assumption that a new prohibited transaction occurs each year the loan is outstanding.

Example 2: Consider the case of a loan outstanding for five years made by the plan to the employer:

Loan amount:	$100,000
Annual interest rate:	12%
Date issued:	January 1, 2000
Period outstanding:	5 years

Calculation of excise tax:

First prohibited transaction occurs on January 1, 2000:
$100,000 \times 12\% \times 5$ years $\times 15\%$ = $9,000

Second prohibited transaction occurs on January 1, 2001:
$100,000 \times 12\% \times 4$ years $\times 15\%$ = $7,200

Third prohibited transaction occurs on January 1, 2002:
$100,000 \times 12\% \times 3$ years $\times 15\%$ = $5,400

Fourth prohibited transaction occurs on January 1, 2003:
$100,000 \times 12\% \times 2$ years $\times 15\%$ = $3,600

Fifth prohibited transaction occurs on January 1, 2004:
$100,000 \times 12\% \times 1$ year $\times 15\%$ = $1,800

Total excise tax due: = $27,000

Loans to plan participants are not prohibited transactions if made in accordance with current regulations (see Chapter 8).

Correction of a prohibited transaction usually involves placing the plan in a financial position no worse than it would have been in if the disqualified person were acting under the highest fiduciary standards. Generally, this requires rescinding the transaction although the prohibited transaction can "self-correct" if the property transferred to the plan substantially appreciates in value. In any case, correction of the prohibited transaction does not eliminate the penalty taxes, as illustrated previously.

A prohibited transaction must be reported on Form 5500, and the excise tax must be remitted with Form 5330. If the prohibited transaction is disclosed, a three-year statute of limitations applies; otherwise a six-year statute of limitations applies. If neither Form 5500 nor 5330 is filed, or fraudulent information is filed there is no statute of limitations.

From time to time, a practitioner might be contacted by a client who presents a scenario similar to the following:

> **Example 3:** An opportunity just came up to invest in a new company that is not yet publicly traded; however, the minimum investment is $100,000. Steve, a business owner, can put together only $50,000 right now, but he does not want to miss out. He manages the investments in his retirement plan. Can the plan invest the other $50,000?

Even assuming the investment would be prudent within the strict interpretation of prudence, the answer is still no. A disqualified person and the plan may invest in the same asset only if the following requirements are satisfied:
1. The interest of the plan and the disqualified person are exactly the same with respect to risk
2. The disqualified person is able to make the investment independent of the plan's investment.

In Example 3, Steve needs the plan's $50,000 to be able to invest his $50,000 in order to satisfy the minimum investment requirement of $100,000, so he does not satisfy requirement 2.

APPLICATION FOR EXEMPTION TO PROHIBITED TRANSACTION RULES

Both IRS and DOL have established procedures that would allow a disqualified person to apply for an exemption to the prohibited transaction rules for a specific transaction. An exemption may be granted if it is administratively feasible; is in the best interest of the plan, its participants, and its beneficiaries; and is protective of the rights of participants and beneficiaries. If an application is to be submitted, adequate notice must be given to interested persons (participants and beneficiaries) and an opportunity to comment on the application and the pending application must be published in the *Federal Register.*

CLASS EXEMPTIONS

In addition to individual exemptions that apply only to the applicant, e.g., participant loans, a class exemption may be requested. If granted, such an exemption would apply to any party entering into that approved transaction. Some of the more common class exemptions fall within the following classes:

Purchase and sale of life insurance by the plan or participant. A plan may acquire an insurance policy from a participant insuring that participant's life or a participant may acquire an insurance policy on his or her life from the plan. (Prohibited Transaction Exemption 92-5, 92-6)

Insurance agents and brokers. Insurance agents and brokers, pension consultants, insurance companies, investment companies, and investment company principal underwriters who are parties in interest may invest plan assets in insurance contracts or mutual fund shares or receive sales commissions subject to certain requirements. (Prohibited Transaction Exemption 77-9)

Insurance company general accounts. These transact business with parties related to employee benefit plans for which the insurer is a fiduciary. (Prohibited Transaction Exemption 95-60)

Guaranteed contract separate accounts. Transactions between a guaranteed contract separate account and a party in interest are allowable if they are not part of an arrangement by which a plan has acquired an interest in the separate account. (Prohibited Transaction Exemption 81-82)

Investment advisory firms. These may continue to invest the assets of employee benefit plans that they advise in open-end mutual funds that they manage. (Prohibited Transaction Exemption 77-4)

Qualified professional asset managers. A general exemption allows plans managed by qualified professional asset managers such as banks, insurance companies, or regulated investment advisors to engage in a wide variety of party-in-interest transactions with entities associated with the plan if certain conditions are met. (Prohibited Transaction Exemption 84-14)

STATUTORY EXEMPTIONS

In addition to individual and class exemptions to the prohibited transaction rules, several transactions are exempt by statute, including:

1. Loans to participants or beneficiaries if the loan is available to all participants and beneficiaries on a reasonably equivalent basis; the loan does not discriminate in favor of highly compensated employees; the loan is made in accordance with specific plan provisions; the loan bears a reasonable rate of interest; and the loan is adequately secured (see Chapter 8 for a full discussion of participant loans)
2. A plan's contracting or making reasonable arrangements with a party in interest, including a fiduciary, for office space or legal, accounting, or other services necessary for the establishment or operation of the plan
3. A loan made by a disqualified person to an ESOP (see Chapter 4)
4. The investment of plan funds in deposits that bear a reasonable rate of interest in a bank (or similar financial institution) supervised by federal or a state government, even if the bank is a fiduciary of the plan or other party in interest
5. The purchase of life insurance, health insurance, or other annuity contracts with one or more insurers that are qualified to do business in a state if the plan pays no more than adequate consideration
6. Ancillary services by a bank or similar financial institution to a plan for which it acts as a fiduciary

7. Allowing the plan to exercise the privilege to convert employer securities if the plan receives no less than adequate consideration
8. Any transaction between a plan and a common trust fund or pooled investment fund maintained by a bank
9. Receipt by a disqualified person of (a) any benefit to which he or she may be entitled as a participant or beneficiary of the plan and (b) compensation for services rendered or reimbursement of expenses.

The issue of fiduciary responsibility and prohibited transactions is extremely sensitive. This discussion of these topics should make it clear that the rules and regulations governing proper conduct are strictly interpreted and costly if violated. This is not an area that can be managed without experienced professional assistance. Plan fiduciaries should seek counsel with a specialty in ERISA matters if a violation is suspected or a transaction contemplated.

USE OF PLAN ASSETS TO PAY PLAN EXPENSES

Section 403(c) of ERISA provides that plan assets may be used to "defray reasonable expenses of administering the plan." In the absence of that statement, such a transaction would be a prohibited transaction. DOL has taken the position that some expenses are *settlor functions,* which include the establishment, amendment and termination of a plan. These expenses must be paid entirely by the plan sponsor and not from plan assets. DOL also takes the position that certain other expenses relating to maintaining the qualified status of a retirement plan, such as nondiscrimination testing, determination letter applications and amendments required to maintain plan qualification should be shared by the employer and plan. The basis for this position is that both plan participants and the plan sponsor benefit from these actions. This latter position has been a point of contention between DOL and the pension community. Recently DOL issued new guidance on the issue, changing its opinion that expenses necessary to maintain plan qualification can be paid with plan assets.

Under the new guidance, both settlor expenses and nonsettlor expenses are identified as follows:

1. *Settlor expenses* (may not be paid from plan assets):
   (a) Plan design studies and projections of the financial impact of a plan change
   (b) The cost of activities prior to a plan change, e.g., union negotiations, benefit studies and actuarial analyses
   (c) Analyzing options for compliance with changes required by law
   (d) A plan amendment for the spin-off of plan assets in a corporate transaction, e.g., merger or acquisition
   (e) A plan amendment to establish an early retirement window program
   (f) A plan amendment to add a participant loan program
   (g) Expenses to comply with a Financial Accounting Standards Board (FASB) statement.
2. *Nonsettlor expenses* (may be paid from plan assets without sharing the cost with the plan sponsor):
   (a) The cost of plan administrative functions, e.g., calculating benefits
   (b) Plan amendments to comply with tax law changes

(c) The cost of applying for an IRS determination letter

(d) The cost of nondiscrimination testing for an ongoing plan

(e) The cost of complying with disclosure requirements, e.g., distributing a summary plan description and summary annual report

(f) The cost of communicating plan information, e.g., notice requirements

(g) In a corporate merger or acquisition, the cost of determining the amount of plan assets to be transferred

(h) The cost to communicate information on an early retirement window program or a participant loan program

(i) Start-up fees and administration fees associated with outsourcing plan administration.

More recent guidance from DOL has indicated that expenses attributable to plan administration, e.g., investment management fees, can be charged to terminated employees' accounts in proportion to the value of their accounts, and can be paid by the employer for the portion attributable to active employees.

The issue of fiduciary responsibility is particularly important in the operation of 401(k) plans in which the participants direct their individual investment choices. Enter ERISA Section 404(c), which states in part:

In the case of a pension plan which provides for individual accounts and permits a participant or beneficiary to exercise control over assets in his account, if a participant or beneficiary exercise control over the assets in his account (as determined under regulations of the Secretary)—

(A) such participant or beneficiary shall not be deemed to be a fiduciary by reason of such exercise, and

(B) no person who is otherwise a fiduciary shall be liable under this part for any loss, or by reason of any breach, which results from such participant's or beneficiary's exercise of control.

Initially, this appears to relieve the employer from responsibility if the employee's account suffers a severe loss as a result of poor investments. A closer look brings the focus to the last part of paragraph (B), which states, ". . . which results from such participant's or beneficiary's exercise of control." In a self-directed 401(k) plan employees choose which funds to invest in, their exercise of control, but the employer decides which funds to offer the employees. ERISA Section 404(c) relieves the employer from fiduciary responsibility and liability with respect to the employee's choice of which funds to invest in, but not the employer's choice of which funds to offer. This limited relief is usually not worth the excessive administrative cost that would be incurred to comply with ERISA Section 404(c) unless the employer is large enough to monitor compliance internally in its own human resource department.

Generally, an ERISA Section 404(c) plan provides that participants may exercise control over the assets in their account and must have an opportunity to choose from a broad range of investment alternatives. The exercise of control includes the ability to give investment instructions to be carried out as directed by the employee based on sufficient investment information provided to them by the plan to make an informed decision regarding their investment alternatives. Sufficient investment information means that an identified plan fiduciary (usually a representative of the employer) provides the participant with:

1. An explanation that the plan is intended to qualify under ERISA Section 404(c) relieving the fiduciaries of any liability with respect to investment directions given by the participant
2. A description of the investment alternatives available under the plan, including the investment objective, risk and return characteristics, and information relating to the type and diversification of assets within each alternative
3. Identification of any designated investment managers
4. An explanation about how the participants are to give their investment instructions and any limitations on those instructions, e.g., transfers between two accounts
5. A description of any transaction fees and expenses chargeable to the participant's account balance as a result of purchase or sale of the investment
6. The name, address and phone number of the plan fiduciary responsible for providing the above information
7. If the plan allows for the purchase of employer securities, a description of the procedures established to provide for the confidentiality of the transaction; holding and sale of the securities; exercise of voting and tender rights by participants; and the name, address and phone number of the plan fiduciary responsible for monitoring compliance with these procedures
8. A copy of the most recent prospectus for any investment alternatives subject to the Securities Act of 1933
9. Any materials relating to voting, tender or similar rights incidental to holding a specific investment to the extent that those rights are passed through to the participant.

In addition, the participant must be provided with:

1. A description of the annual operating expenses of each investment alternative to the extent the rate of return is reduced
2. Copies of any prospectuses, financial statements and reports with respect to the investment alternatives
3. A list of the assets constituting the portfolio of each investment alternative
4. Information concerning the value of shares or units for each investment alternative, in addition to the past and current investment performance of each alternative, net of expenses.

BROAD RANGE OF INVESTMENT ALTERNATIVES

The regulations under ERISA Section 404(c) define specifically what constitutes a broad range of investment alternatives. The participant must have a reasonable opportunity to:

1. Materially affect the return in his or her individual account and the degree of risk
2. Choose from at least three investment alternatives:
    (a) Each of which is diversified
    (b) Each of which has materially different risk and return characteristics
    (c) That allow the participant, by choosing among them, to create a portfolio with risk and return characteristics that are appropriate for that participant

(d) Each of which, through diversification, tends to minimize the overall risk of the participant's portfolio

3. Diversify the investments so as to minimize the risk of large losses.

Assume the employer is willing to expend the time and money to comply with all the preceding requirements, either internally or through a third party. The fiduciary protection gained applies only to the employee's choice from among the investments offered. It does not protect the fiduciary (employer) from claims arising out of the choices offered to the employees. If the employer's intention is to maintain an ERISA Section 404(c) plan, the employer should also monitor the investments being offered for performance, management and expenses, to satisfy its fiduciary responsibility with respect to offering those investments to its employees. In the absence of the proper exercise of the employer's fiduciary duty, it can be held personally liable.

For most plan sponsors, compliance with ERISA Section 404(c) is impractical to say the least and for larger companies the protection is limited relative to the cost of compliance.

REMITTANCE OF EMPLOYEE DEFERRALS IN 401(k) PLANS

Fiduciary duty also applies to the processing of employee contributions. In the past, there have been articles in various newspapers regarding the security of these deposits. Are the funds protected from unscrupulous employers? One of the most well-known cases of employer misconduct is the embezzlement of more than $1.5 million from the Emergi-Lite Incorporated 401(k) plan *(United States v. Moore)*. In this case, both DOL and the Federal Bureau of Investigation were involved and pursued criminal prosecution. To prevent mishandling of employee contributions, DOL issued final regulations indicating when employee contributions must be deposited in the plan.

In all qualified plans, assets can be treated as qualified plan assets, including favorable taxation, only if they are held in a qualified tax-exempt trust under IRC Section 501(a). For purposes of employer-funded plans, the tax deduction depends on the contribution being deposited into that trust by a specific date (see Chapter 3). For employee contributions, the qualified status of the plan can depend on the timely deposit of those contributions. One of the requirements to maintain the qualified status of a plan is "under the trust instrument it is impossible, at any time prior to the satisfaction of all liabilities with respect to employees and their beneficiaries under the trust, for any part of the corpus or income to be (within the taxable year of thereafter) used for, or diverted to, purposes *other than for the exclusive benefit of his employees or their beneficiaries."* [Emphasis added.] Retaining funds in the employer's business account because of delayed remittance would be considered diversion for purposes other than the exclusive benefit of employees and beneficiaries.

Although the interpretation of "reasonably be segregated" is subject to the facts and circumstances for each employer, it is not an open-ended guideline:

Maximum time period for pension benefit plans. (1) Except as provided in paragraph (b)(2) of this section, with respect to an employee pension benefit plan as defined in Section 3(2) of ERISA, in no event shall the date determined pursuant to paragraph (a) of this section occur later than the 15th business day of the month following the month in which the participant contribution amounts are received by the employer (in the case of amounts that a participant or beneficiary pays to an employer) or the 15th business day of the month following the month in which such amounts would otherwise have been payable to the participant in cash (in the case of amounts withheld by an employer from a participant's wages).

The key in these guidelines is that the maximum periods are not safe harbors. DOL regulations offer an example where a small employer, at a single payroll location, issues a check for the employee's deferrals within two days of the date the employees are paid. The example concludes, "In view of the relatively small number of employees and the fact that they are paid from a single location, the employer could reasonably be expected to transmit participant contributions to the trust within two days after the employee's wages are paid." Unfortunately, the example does not quantify the size of the employer. If the small employer is consistent with DOL regulations on reporting, this example would apply to any employer with fewer than 100 employees.

The Form 5500 Schedule H asks the following question in Section IV: "Did the employer fail to transmit to the plan any participant contributions within the maximum time period described in 29 CFR 2510.3-102?" This question refers to the preceding statement in the definition of plan assets, which requires remittance by the earliest date on which such contributions can reasonably be segregated from the employer's general assets. An answer of "yes" to this question would most likely be an audit flag for both IRS and DOL.

With the popularity of 401(k) plans and the concern for security of the plan's assets as evidenced by the Emergi-Lite case, DOL and IRS are tightening the rules regarding the transmittal of employee deferrals and the safety of plan assets, particularly in small plans (those with fewer than 100 employees). DOL has taken the position in recent investigations that deferrals under a 401(k) plan of a small employer should be contributed to the trust within seven days of the payroll date from which the deferral is withheld. If, in fact, this position is taken, and on audit the employer was operating under the assumption that 15 days was acceptable, DOL would consider this a breach of fiduciary duty. In that case, the employer would be responsible for all investment gains that were lost because of the lateness of deposits for all open years (six years under ERISA Section 413).

One of the purposes of ERISA is to provide benefit security, which is addressed in part in ERISA Section 103, the annual reporting requirements. Although the annual reporting guidelines do not reference any specific plan size, ERISA Section 104(a)(2)(A) allows for simplified reporting for small plans. Generally all plans must file an annual report (Form 5500 and attachments; see Chapter 13) and engage an independent qualified public accountant to examine the books and records of the plan and offer an opinion about the accuracy of those books and records. Although small plans file an abbreviated Form 5500, the requirement for an independent audit is waived. With the huge amount of employee deposits in 401(k) plans and the potential for misuse of those assets, DOL has been reconsidering that waiver. Rather than subject small plans to a costly additional administrative process, DOL offered an alternative solution in regulations recently issued. Under these new rules, small plans would still be exempt from the audit requirements if at least 95% of the plan assets were held as *qualifying plan assets*. This term is defined in the proposed regulations as:

1. Qualifying employer securities as described in ERISA Section 407(d)(1)
2. Any loan meeting the requirements of ERISA Section 408(b)(1)
3. Any assets held by the following institutions
   (a) A bank or similar financial institution defined in DOL Regulations Section 2550.408b-4(c)
   (b) An insurance company qualified to do business under the laws of the state
   (c) An organization registered as a broker/dealer under the Securities and Exchange Act of 1934
   (d) Any organization authorized to act as a trustee for individual retirement accounts under IRC Section 408
4. Shares issued by an investment company registered under the Investment Company Act of 1940 (mutual funds)
5. Investment and annuity contracts issued by any insurance company qualified to do business under the laws of the state
6. In an individual account plan (DC plan), any assets over which the participant or beneficiary exercises control and for which the participant or beneficiary receives, at least annually, a statement from a regulated financial institution (listed in preceding items 3 and 5), describing the assets held or issued by the financial institution and the amount.

Qualifying plan assets do not include nonpublicly traded assets, e.g., some limited partnerships, real estate and collectibles.

If the plan has less than 95% of the assets in a regulated financial institution and chooses to avoid the audit requirements, a fidelity bond must be secured for the plan fiduciaries equal to the assets that are not held in the regulated financial institutions. The plan sponsor will have to notify participants in the summary plan description (see Chapter 2) of their right to request and review copies of the asset statements from the financial institutions, a copy of any fidelity bond that must be secured and the right to notify DOL if the required information is not provided.

Ongoing Administration of Retirement Plans

Chapter **13**

Accountants and tax attorneys always wonder why it takes so long for pension administration firms to provide tax practitioners with the year-end contribution so they can complete the clients' tax returns. Financial professionals who sell products such as investments or insurance probably wonder why it takes the administration firms so long to provide their clients with benefits or contribution data so they can place investments or insurance for the additional benefits or contributions. Financial planners wonder why it takes the administration firms so long to provide their clients with the year-end contribution so they can update their clients' personal financial plan for the year. This chapter reviews the various steps necessary to provide the benefit and contribution information to clients and their advisors and the roadblocks that slow down or hinder that process.

THE ADMINISTRATION PROCESS

The administration process for a generic plan using a calendar year as its plan year attempts to follow a logical progression. Early in January, following the end of the prior plan year, the plan administrator (third-party administrator or TPA) sends a letter to the client, usually copying the tax professional, requesting certain information: company information, e.g., officers and stockholders; financial information about the plan assets, including gains and losses, income, contributions, distributions and description of plan assets; and employee information, including dates of birth, hire and termination, hours worked, compensation and, in some plans, job description (see class allocation plan in Chapter 4 and estate and business planning in Chapter 11). For calendar-year plans, this information is usually sent in May or later because the tax professional who assists the client in providing the information is busy with tax return preparation before May. When the TPA receives the data, it is logged in and passed on to the plan administrator assigned to process that plan. The administrator does a preliminary review of the data for completeness and files it for processing based on the date received.

The first roadblock in this process is the delay in receiving data and a high percentage of plans using calendar-year reporting. In some TPA companies, approximately 65% of plans report on the calendar year. More than half of these plans report to TPAs in May or later (Form 5500 is due July 31 for a calendar-year plan), usually requiring TPAs to file extensions for many of the calendar-year plans. Usually the flow of data received comes to a halt from May through August, making matters worse after the summer months when, in addition to fiscal-year plans, the remainder of the calendar-year plans are received. Most TPA firms have a "crunch": around March 15, corporate tax returns due; April 15, noncorporate tax returns due; July 31, Form 5500 due for calendar-year plans; August 15, noncorporate tax returns on extension due; September 15, corporate tax returns on extension due; and October 15, Form 5500 due for calendar-year plans on extension.

When the administrator is ready to process the plan data, all new or changed information is entered in the database (e.g., salaries, new employees). Then the assets are reconciled, and the contribution is calculated and communicated to clients and their accountants or tax attorneys. Here is the next roadblock—inconsistent data and assets that do not balance based on the transactions reported to the administrator for the plan year. This process can be compared to a bank reconciliation that does not balance. Beginning with the value of assets at the end of the prior year and adjusting for all transactions during the year, the result should agree with the value of the assets at the end of the current year. After all discrepancies are resolved, the plan is reviewed for any payouts to terminated participants for the year being reported, and required distribution forms are prepared. Then a plan valuation report including benefit statements for all participants is prepared. When clients make the contribution and communicate it to the administrator, Form 5500 and attachments are prepared and sent to clients for signature and remittance to the Internal Revenue Service (IRS), and the valuation report sent to the plan sponsor.

COMMON DATA FAULTS

When the administrator is ready to process the plan, the procedures followed depend on the type of plan, i.e., defined contribution (DC) or defined benefit (DB), although some procedures are common to all plans. Regardless of the type of plan, the first step is to review the employee census data for accuracy, consistency and detailed completeness. The items to look for would be:

1. Hire dates and dates of birth that seem illogical, e.g., March 4, 1996, as a date of birth for a plan year ending December 31, 2000. This could be the employee's date of hire or it could be a typographical error.
2. The date of hire or date of birth listed for an employee that is included in the prior year's data is different.
3. An employee is listed on the prior year's data but is not listed on the current year's data. Many employers leave out an employee who terminated during the year even though that employee may be eligible for additional benefits in the year of termination and may have a vested benefit to be paid out.
4. An employee is listed with a date of hire in a year before the current year but is not listed on the prior year's data. Some employers assume that an employee is part time if he or she does not work seven or eight hours a day,

five or more days per week. If a part-time employee increases his or her hours to full time, the employer then includes that employee on the census data. As discussed, full-time employment for pension purposes is 1,000 hours during the year (see Chapter 2).

5. If the plan is based on a class allocation or excludes employees by job class (see Chapters 4 and 9), the job classes are excluded on the census form, or in some cases an employee's job class has changed from the prior year. If the employees have been misclassified in a prior year, the issue can be very serious and the plan can be disqualified if it fails nondiscrimination testing (see Chapter 9).

6. If an employee is listed as terminated, both the date of termination and the hours worked must be listed. This is necessary to determine whether the employee is entitled to additional benefits for the year, additional vesting and, if one is due, the timing of the distribution to the terminated employee.

7. Two or more employees have the same last name. It must be determined whether they are related and, if so, how. This affects the determination of highly compensated employees (HCEs) for nondiscrimination testing purposes (see Chapter 9) and the identification of the employer for purposes of determining whether it belongs to a controlled group of employers (see Chapter 10). In some cases, employees with different names are related, e.g., a married daughter. These relationships must also be identified.

8. The employer participates in a union. The union members, including the owners if they are union members, must be identified because many plans exclude union members.

9. The total number of employees on the census data should seem reasonable for this employer. Many employers automatically exclude employees they consider part time who may be eligible. This could result in disqualification because of discrimination if the coverage rule is not satisfied (see Chapter 9) or because of failure to follow the plan document if the employees should have been included based on the eligibility requirements.

10. Salaries are consistent with the definition of *compensation* in the plan. If the plan document excludes overtime, that should be broken out on the census data (see Chapter 2).

11. Salaries are for the period defined in the plan document, e.g., plan year or calendar year.

12. Salaries are the amount actually paid for the year, not the employees' "rate of pay as of the end of the year."

13. If the employer sponsors a cafeteria plan, each employee's deferrals to the cafeteria plan are reported to determine his or her taxable compensation for deduction purposes (see Chapter 3).

14. All employees of a controlled group of companies are identified (see Chapter 10).

A *cafeteria plan* is a welfare benefit plan under Internal Revenue Code Section 125 that allows participating employees to defer a portion of their compensation before income and Social Security tax to be used to reimburse the employees for certain out-of-pocket medical expenses, e.g., coinsurance payments, deductibles on health insurance plans and eyeglasses.

These are only some of the issues that must be reviewed before the plan administrator can proceed with the administration for the year. Unique plan designs, e.g., multiple plans, may require more extensive review of the census data (see Chapter 11). Once the census data has been reviewed and is determined to be accurate and complete, the next step is to review the financial data.

For all plans other than 401(k) plans, contributions are usually made annually. At the end of the plan year, an asset reconciliation must be prepared, taking into consideration all gains, losses and income earned by the pension trust account. In addition, all transactions must be analyzed and factored into the reconciliation. Typical trust account activities would include:

1. Sale of an asset and determination of realized gains or losses
2. Purchase of new investment, e.g., a mutual fund
3. Receipt of dividends or interest
4. Issuance of a new participant loan
5. Receipt of payments toward an outstanding participant loan
6. Hardship distribution
7. Receipt of contributions and determination of the plan year to which the contribution applies
8. Payout to terminated participants
9. Payment of trust expenses, e.g., investment management fees
10. Receipt of a rollover from a new participant who has received a distribution from a prior employer
11. Unrealized gains or losses on trust investments.

Based on the preceding activity and the determination of any unrealized gains or losses, a "balance sheet" must be prepared to reconcile the actual financial activity with the actual assets as of the end of the plan year. Any discrepancy must be identified and corrected. In many cases, the information reported to the TPA at year-end has no detail but indicates only the total assets as of the end of the year. Because the reporting to IRS must include a detailed analysis, this would not be sufficient (see later discussion of Form 5500 and attachments). The process of asset reconciliation is even more sensitive in a DC plan than in a DB plan because the employee's account balance determines his or her benefit. If the assets are incorrectly valued, an employee may be underpaid or overpaid at termination depending on the valuation error. If the employee who was paid out happens to be a highly compensated employee (HCE) and the payout was based on an incorrectly inflated value, the plan is in violation of the nondiscrimination rules. This whole process becomes even more involved in a 401(k) plan because there are now multiple contributions each time an employee makes a deferral or repays a loan. To allocate gains and losses correctly, every transaction must be date-stamped unless each employee has his or her own individual account.

Other plan asset issues that must be resolved before plan administration can be completed include:

1. If a plan invests in nonpublicly traded assets, an outside appraisal must be prepared each year, e.g., a private placement in a limited partnership.
2. If the plan is subject to a financial audit (more than 100 participants), the Form 5500 filing with IRS and Department of Labor (DOL) cannot be completed until the audit is complete.

3. There are transactions that are not in accordance with regulations, e.g., a loan to an employee in excess of the allowable limit.
4. There are prohibited transactions, e.g., a loan to the company sponsoring the plan.

If the plan is a DB plan and the assets are incorrectly valued and reported to the TPA, the deduction may be overstated or understated. If the plan assets are undervalued, resulting in a contribution that is overstated, a portion of the contribution would be nondeductible and subject to a 10% excise tax. If the plan assets are overvalued and the contribution is understated, the shortfall would be considered a funding deficiency and subject to a 10% penalty and possibly a 100% penalty if not corrected in a timely manner (see Chapter 6). These types of defects are usually identified at the time of an IRS audit, typically a random audit.

PLAN REPORT/FORM 5500 ANNUAL FILING

Once the employee data and financial data are complete and accurate, the administrator inputs the data to the computer program being used to generate the year-end report and produces the plan valuation. This includes the status of each employee, e.g., active, terminated and excluded; calculation of each employee's contribution to a pension plan (target benefit, DB and money purchase); allocation of the contribution to each employee for a profit-sharing plan; preparation of participant statements showing the account balance for a DC plan or the retirement benefits for a DB plan; vested benefits; payouts to terminated participants; actuarial data for a DB plan and the summary annual report (SAR) that provides employees with the financial information for the plan, including contributions, expenses, benefits paid, investment income, gains, losses and the value of plan assets.

The next step is for the valuation to be reviewed for accuracy and completeness and the preparation of related documents, including distribution forms for terminated participants, notification to plan sponsors of contributions due, enrollment forms for new participants in a 401(k) plan, Form 5500 and attachments for IRS and Form PBGC-1 for DB plans. In addition, for a DB plan, an enrolled actuary must sign the Schedule B, Actuarial Information, certifying that the plan is properly funded.

SMALL AND LARGE PLANS

Beginning in the 1999 plan year, i.e., plan years that begin in 1999, the entire Form 5500 package was redesigned. Filing requirements are based on whether the plan is a *small plan,* covering fewer than 100 participants as of the beginning of the plan year or a *large plan,* covering 100 or more participants as of the beginning of the plan year. The table on page 206 summarizes the forms and attachments that must be filed by small and large plans.

Some of the more common errors and audit flags should be avoided. For example, Form 5500-EZ must be filed if plan assets exceed $100,000 at the end of the plan year. This filing alternative is available only to a business owner and spouse or partners in a business and their spouses. In the year in which at least one rank-and-file employee becomes a participant, the EZ form may no longer be used. Until the

Table
FORMS AND ATTACHMENTS TO BE FILED BY SMALL AND LARGE PLANS

Form Attachment	Small Plan	Large Plan
Form 5500	Yes	Yes
Form 5500-EZ (see comments below) If no common law employees, only owners and their spouses participating	Yes/If eligible	No
Schedule A—Insurance information If the plan invests in products offered by an insurance company, e.g., life insurance, annuities, etc.	Yes	Yes
Schedule B—Actuarial information Only for DB plans other than 412(i) (see Chapter 6)	Yes DB plan only	Yes DB plan only
Schedule D—Direct filing entity If plan trust assets invested in common/ collective trusts, pooled separate accounts, master trust investment accounts or 103-12 investment entity	Yes/If applies	Yes/If applies
Schedule E—ESOP information Only for an employee stock ownership plan (see Chapter 4)	Yes/If applies	Yes/If applies
Schedule G—Defaulted obligations To report defaulted or uncollectible fixed income or loan obligations, leases in default or uncollectible or nonexempt (party in interest) transactions	No	Yes/If applies
Schedule H—Financial information Balance sheet and contribution information	No	Yes
Audit by independent accountant Only for large plans	No	Yes
Schedule I—Financial information Balance sheet and contribution information	Yes	No
Schedule P—Fiduciary information Begins clock on statute of limitations	Yes	Yes
Schedule R—Retirement plan information Report on plan distributions, funding and amendments that increase benefits in a DB plan	Yes/If applies	Yes/If applies
Schedule SSA—Separated vested participants Only if the plan is holding vested benefits of terminated employees past the year in which the benefit would normally be paid out	Yes/If applies	Yes/If applies
Schedule T—Coverage information To report information regarding the minimum coverage requirements of IRC §410(b)	Yes/If applies	Yes/If applies

year-end that assets are in excess of $100,000, no filing is required. IRS refers to these plans as *one-person plans*. To qualify as a one-person plan, the plan must:

a. Meet the IRC Section 410(b) minimum coverage requirements without being combined with any other plan that covers other employees of the same employer (see Chapter 9)

b. Not cover a business that is a member of an affiliated service group, controlled group of corporations or a group of businesses under common control (see Chapter 10)

c. Not cover a business that leases employees (see Chapter 10).

If the business hires an employee who later becomes eligible, the plan must then file Form 5500 and attachments.

FORM 5500 LINE ITEMS OF INTEREST

On Form 5500, question 1b asks for a three-digit plan number. If this is the first and only plan ever sponsored by the employer, the number is 001. The employer is identified by its employer identification number (EIN). In many cases, small employers periodically adopt the prototype plans of banks, brokerage companies and insurance companies, without terminating the plans previously adopted, to change their investments. Each time a new plan is adopted, whether or not the old plan is terminated, a new sequential plan number must be assigned and a separate Form 5500 filed as applicable.

Question 3a asks for the plan administrator. This question refers to the Employee Retirement Income Security Act of 1974 (ERISA) definition of *plan administrator,* not the third-party administrator (see Chapter 12).

Question 7a asks for active participants. This includes all eligible employees and terminated employees who have not been paid out by the end of the plan year. In a 401(k) plan, an employee who chooses not to make a deferral and therefore has no assets in the plan is still considered an active employee. Therefore, the number of active employees does not necessarily agree with the number in question 7g: number of participants with account balances (in a DC plan).

The next item of interest on Form 5500 is found in question 8a. This question asks for information on pension benefits based on a group of codes found in the instructions to Form 5500. The following three Codes should be considered closely:

1. 2F—ERISA Section 404(c) plan. This plan, or any part of it, is intended to meet the conditions of 29 CFR Section 2550.404c-1.

2. 2G—Total participant-directed account plan. Participants have the opportunity to direct the investment of all the assets allocated to their individual accounts, regardless of whether the plan is intended to comply with 29 CFR Section 2550.404c-1.

3. 2H—Partial participant-directed account plan. Participants have the opportunity to direct the investment of a portion of the assets allocated to their individual accounts, regardless of whether the plan is intended to comply with 29 CFR Section 2550.404c-1.

Chapter 12 discusses ERISA Section 404(c) plans at length (item #1 above). Many plan sponsors believe that if they offer the appropriate number of investment choices, they are in compliance with ERISA Section 404(c). If this question is answered incorrectly, to indicate that the plan does have an ERISA Section 404(c) provision (2F), the Employee Benefits Security Administration has advised that it would consider this to be a misrepresentation and therefore a fiduciary breach (see Chapter 12). Unless the plan is in total compliance with the rules of ERISA Section 404(c), Code 2G or 2H, not 2F, should be included as appropriate.

FORM 5500 ATTACHMENTS

Schedule A. Schedule A, Insurance Information, must be filed for each insurance company that is providing benefits for the plan. If one insurance company is providing life insurance and another is providing annuity contracts, two Schedules A must be filed.

Schedule B. For a DB plan, Schedule B, Actuarial Information, can be completed only by a licensed enrolled actuary.

Schedules H and I. Schedules H and I, Financial Information, ask three questions that may trigger an audit. Question 4a asks, "Did the employer fail to transmit to the plan any participant contributions within the maximum time period described in 29 CFR 2510.3-102?" This question refers to the remittance of employee deferrals in 401(k) plans. Chapter 12 discusses at length DOL requirements for remittance of employee deferrals and the extent of public awareness of this issue. An answer of "No" to this question almost guarantees an audit, possibly by IRS and DOL. Question 4e asks if the plan is covered by a fidelity bond that protects the plan from misappropriation of funds by fiduciaries. Again, an answer of "No" can prompt an IRS audit. Question 4g asks if the plan held assets whose value could not be determined on an established public marketplace and, if so, whether those assets were properly appraised.

Because the value of the participant's account balance, or the extent of the funding of a participant's benefit in a DB plan, depends on the proper valuation of assets such as real estate, collectibles and private placements, this is also a concern of IRS and DOL. In addition, to some extent, it is a concern of the Pension Benefit Guaranty Corporation (PBGC) because that federal organization is responsible for guaranteeing some of the benefits in a DB plan (see Chapter 6). Assets that were not appraised are another potential audit flag.

Other items on the Form 5500 package that may trigger an audit include a large number of terminated participants with less than 100% vesting; a large portion of the assets listed as "Other Assets," i.e., probably nonpublicly traded assets; a large distribution from the plan; a low percentage of participants relative to the total number of employees; a large percentage of loans as a percent of total assets; an underfunded DB plan (a funding deficiency); the date of most recent amendment prior to 1993, i.e., plan was not amended for the Tax Reform Act of 1986; and a large percentage of plan assets in any one investment.

Schedule P. Schedule P, Annual Return of Fiduciary, must be filed to trigger the three-year statute of limitations. If this form is not filed, there is no statute of limitations on the plan filing. Once a plan year is closed because of the statute of limitations, it cannot be reopened for audit unless a fraudulent act is under investigation.

Schedule R. On Schedule R, question 6, parts a and b, asks about the required contribution and the actual contribution. This question applies only to pension plans, i.e., money purchase, target benefit, cash balance and DB, subject to the minimum funding requirements. If the amounts in 6a and 6b are not the same, there is either a funding deficiency or a nondeductible contribution, both of which are subject to penalties. Because the question asks how much has been *contributed* for the plan year, the filing cannot be completed and remitted until the total required contribution has been made.

FORM 5500 DEADLINE
VOLUNTARY COMPLIANCE PROGRAM
PBGC FORMS

The entire Form 5500 package is due by the end of the seventh month after the end of the plan year. An extension of two and one-half months can be granted by filing a request for extension on Form 5558. Although IRS will not send back an approved copy of the form, a copy should be attached to the Form 5500 submission. In addition, a corporate extension would be valid in place of the extension granted in response to the filing of Form 5558, although it would be for one month less than the Form 5500 extension. A calendar-year plan sponsored by a calendar-year taxpayer would have its business tax return due by March 15 or by September 15 on extension. The Form 5500 filing would be due by July 31 or by October 15 if an extension is requested on Form 5558. If the plan fails to file the appropriate forms by the due date, a penalty of up to $1,100 per day may be levied for incomplete forms and $25 per day up to $15,000 for not filing.

DOL and IRS have announced a joint effort to identify 5500 nonfilers. The joint project will match various databases including qualified plan deductions on tax returns, determination letter applications and e-fast (electronic filing). If employers are found on these databases but have not filed 5500 forms, IRS will send letters requesting an explanation. To avoid the onerous penalties, nonfilers should take advantage of DOL's Delinquent Filer Voluntary Compliance Program (DFVCP). Under this program, the maximum DOL penalties are $750 for a small plan (less than 100 participants) and $2,000 for a large plan. In addition, IRS will waive its penalties. For multiple-year failures, the cap is $1,500 for small plans and $4,000 for large plans. Before taking advantage of this program, be sure to engage competent ERISA counsel.

In addition to the Form 5500 package, a DB plan must file Form PBGC-1 with the PBGC and, if applicable, a Schedule A (not the same Schedule A as attached to Form 5500). If the plan sponsor is a professional service employer, e.g., a medical practice, with 25 or fewer participants, the PBGC filings are not required. Once the number of participants exceeds 25, the plan must file with the PBGC every year thereafter regardless of the participant count. The PBGC-1 form is for calculation of the premium due based on $19 per participant. If the plan's vested benefits are not fully funded, there is an additional premium due based on the extent of underfunding. The PBGC forms must be filed by nine and one-half months after *the first day of the plan year for which the premium payment applies,* not nine and one-half months after the end of the plan year. The PBGC also has the authority to levy penalties for late filing of up to $1,100 per day, although the penalty is generally between $25 and $50 per day. In addition, interest will be charged on the late premium payments.

RETIREMENT PLAN AUDITS

Generally, plan audits are random and focus on specific compliance issues. Periodically sponsors of qualified plans should conduct a self-audit to uncover defects and take advantage of the many voluntary correction programs developed by IRS (see Chapter 14).

IRS includes in its examination letter a list of documents and information being requested. The request may be for all items that apply, depending on the type of plan or only limited items. Depending on the size of the plan, some items checked may not apply, e.g., an investment committee in item 2 below for a small plan would not apply, but the financial reports would. In all cases, the audit should be handled by a pension professional who is experienced in this field, generally the TPA that is providing the administrative services for the plan. In addition, it is advisable to have the audit conducted at the office of the TPA rather than at the employer's place of business.

Documents and information requests include:

1. Copies of the plan, the trust, amendments and the determination letter
2. The trustee's or administrator's (not the TPA's) reports; trust administrative committee and investment committee minutes; investment analyses; certified audits; and other financial reports, such as receipt and disbursement statements, income and expense statements, and balance sheets
3. Copy of Form 5500 or 5500-C Annual Return/Report or Employee Benefit Plan, for the prior year, the year under examination and the succeeding year. Copies of all schedules, such as Schedules A, B and SSA, as applicable
4. Copies of Form 5500 or 5500-C for any other deferred pension plans
5. The payroll records that were used to decide the employees' eligibility to take part in the plan. Also copies of the Form 940, Employer's Annual Federal Unemployment Tax Return; Form 941, Employer's Quarterly Federal Tax Return; and Form W-2, Wage and Tax Statements
6. Complete census data for all employees as of the valuation date (includes employees of all entities considered to be a controlled group)
7. Copies of Form 1120, U.S. Corporation Income Tax Return (Form 990, 1040 or 1065) and canceled checks verifying contribution
8. Evidence of fidelity bond for all people handling trust funds
9. Copies of the following items: the summary plan description, summary annual reports required under Title 1, Section 104, of ERISA
10. Supporting documents for plan assets and liabilities (i.e., monthly investment statements for the entire year)
11. Copies of Forms W-2P, Statement for Recipients of Periodic Annuities, Pensions, Retired Pay, IRA Payments; Form 1099R, Statement for Recipients of Periodic Annuities, Pensions, Retired Pay; and statements required under IRC Section 6057(e) (participant benefit statement), given to those who terminate participation
12. Copy of Form 5330, Return of Initial Excise Taxes Related to minimum funding deficiencies (if applicable)
13. Worksheets A and B used with Form 5500 or 5500-C to figure the deduc-

tion for contributions made on behalf of common law employees and self-employed people (to illustrate the calculation of compensation used to determine the contribution or benefit for a self-employed participant or partner in a partnership)

14. A schedule using the forms in Revenue Ruling 70-200, to show that the plan meets the classification test under IRC Section 410(b)(1)(B) (the coverage test)

15. Complete actuarial report for the year(s) under examination and the preceding four years

16. Funding standard account (pension plans only)

17. A detailed demonstration of the present value of accrued benefits for individual participant (DB plans only)

18. A detailed demonstration of IRC Section 412(m) quarterly contribution determination (DB plans only).

As you can see, the list of requested information is quite extensive and in many cases involves technical issues. Please see the second case scenario in the Introduction.

SARBANES-OXLEY ACT (SOX)

The well-known debacle caused by the failure of Enron has caused Congress to sit up and take notice. Unfortunately, in my opinion, what Congress has created is too little too late. The Enron retirement plan was largely invested in the stock of Enron. As Enron was imploding, a blackout period prohibiting trading was imposed on the stock held by the retirement plan. When it was all over, Enron had lost approximately 80% of its value. The SOX Act was signed into law on July 30, 2002 to prevent a recurrence. In fact, two notices were actually provided to the employees of Enron before the blackout period. In any case, the SOX Act provides very strict rules in the event of a blackout period in any DC plan allowing for employee direction of the investments. A blackout period is defined as *any period of more than three consecutive business days during which the plan administrator suspends, restricts or limits, temporarily, the ability of the participants or beneficiaries to (1) direct or diversify account assets, (2) obtain plan loans or (3) obtain plan distributions.* In the event of such a blackout, the plan administrator must provide a notice at least 30 days before the blackout period begins, regardless of whether the assets are invested in the stock of the plan sponsor.

On its surface, this seems like a reasonable requirement. The difficulty arises when interpreting what constitutes a blackout period. Let's consider some common circumstances that may come under these rules:

Plan termination—When a plan is being terminated, distributions to terminated participants are generally suspended until the termination is complete. This suspension would fall under item 3 in the above definition of a *blackout period.*

Change of investment provider in a 401(k) plan—Generally when the plan administrator changes investment providers, there is a period, usually more than three business days, during which the funds are frozen so the assets can be transferred to a new investment provider, e.g., Prudential to Charles Schwab. This falls under item 1. In addition to freezing the assets, the availability of loans would most likely be suspended during the transition (item 2).

If the required notice is not provided, the penalties are severe. The civil penalty is $100 per participant per day without limit. The criminal penalty, i.e., willful violation, is ten years in prison and/or a $100,000 fine. The effective date of the SOX Act is January 26, 2003.

Correcting Errors and Oversights

Chapter 14

The rules and regulations governing qualified retirement plans are, to say the least, complex. With this complexity comes the increased possibility of noncompliance, even for the professionals and certainly for the employer.

The introduction brushes the surface of scenarios involving involuntary noncompliance in the hypothetical telephone conversations. At one time, this type of noncompliance would result in disqualification of the plan by the Internal Revenue Service (IRS) retroactive to the occurrence of the plan defect. In the worst case, the assets of the plan would be taxed to the participants and subject to the 10% premature distribution tax if the employee has not yet attained the age of 59½. The plan sponsor would lose all the pension deductions taken and owe back taxes, interest and penalties.

Furthermore, if an employee rolls over a distribution from a disqualified plan to a conduit individual retirement account (IRA), the rollover would be nonqualified and subject to a 6% excise tax each year it remains in the IRA. If the rollover is made to another qualified plan, it is treated as after-tax employee contributions.

To the extent the plan assets are taxed to the participants in a plan that maintains separate accounts, i.e., a defined contribution (DC) plan, the employer may deduct those contributions. In an unallocated account plan, i.e., a defined benefit (DB) plan (see Chapter 6), the employer loses its deduction entirely. This is still a draconian result. The Tax Reform Act of 1986 relaxed these adverse results under certain circumstances by limiting the taxation of benefits to highly compensated employees (HCEs) only if the defect was caused by noncompliance with IRC Section 410(b) (coverage rules, see Chapter 9), 401(a)(26) (participation rules, see Chapter 9) or 401(a)(4) (nondiscrimination rules, see Chapter 9). Disqualifications for noncompliance with other Code sections would probably cause all participants to be taxed.

SELF-CORRECTION OF DEFECTS

The regulations under IRC Section 401(a)(4) were adopted in 1991 and later amended in 1993, including the introduction of self-correction methods. The concept of self-correction was further advanced under related regulations by allowing for corrective amendments for limited plan defects. These regulations allowed plan amendments to correct the minimum coverage requirements of IRC Section 410(b), the nondiscrimination in contribution and benefit amount requirements, and the nondiscriminatory plan amendment requirement (see Chapter 9). To qualify, the amendment must be adopted and implemented on or before the 15th day of the tenth month following the plan year in which the defect occurs.

Because the pension community voiced its strong support for the concept of voluntary compliance, the IRS continued to expand the correction options available. In 1998, Revenue Procedure 98-22 consolidated several voluntary compliance programs that the IRS had introduced in prior years, including the Administrative Policy Regarding Self-Correction (APRSC), the Voluntary Compliance Resolution Program (VCR), the Walk-In Closing Agreement Program (Walk-In CAP) and the Audit Closing Agreement Program (Audit CAP); and it illustrated a number of acceptable standardized correction methods. The consolidated program, including all the individual programs, was called the Employee Plans Compliance Resolution System (EPCRS). The IRS later issued Revenue Procedure 99-13, which applied the EPCRS to 403(b) plans (tax-sheltered annuities, see Chapter 7). Previously, defects in 403(b) plans were corrected through the Tax-Sheltered Annuity Voluntary Correction Program (TVC), introduced in 1995.

To make it easier for plan sponsors and their advisors to correct defects and be confident that the correction was acceptable to the IRS, Revenue Procedure 99-31 offered several sanctioned correction mechanisms that would be acceptable to the IRS. Revenue Procedure 2000-16 significantly enhanced the self-correction concept and, in January 2001, the EPCRS was updated and consolidated in Revenue Procedure 2001-17. A further expansion and update was introduced by IRS in 2002 with Revenue Procedure 2002-47.

EMPLOYEE PLANS COMPLIANCE
RESOLUTION SYSTEM (EPCRS)

The concept of EPCRS is based on several principles:
1. Practices and procedures should be established by plan sponsors to ensure that plans operate in accordance with the appropriate rules and regulations (i.e., procedures to avoid noncompliance, e.g., maintaining accurate records).
2. Plan documents should be kept updated to satisfy all qualification requirements. This is usually a cause for concern when the document is provided free of charge without the services of a third-party administrator (TPA) by a financial institution that is managing the investments or offering some other product (see Chapter 2).
3. Voluntary corrections of any plan defects or noncompliance should be made in a timely manner. This implies that the plan sponsor should be proactive in correcting defects rather than waiting for an audit to uncover those defects.
4. There should be minimal fees for voluntary corrections approved by the IRS in order to promote the use of the EPCRS program.

5. Sanctions imposed by the IRS should be reasonable, relative to the nature, extent and severity of the violation.
6. EPCRS should be administered consistently, i.e., treat the same defect consistently in applying correction methods, sanctions, etc.

These principles appear to have been followed, considering the continued expansion of the EPCRS program by the IRS. The basis of EPCRS includes self-correction of both significant and insignificant failures with no fee or sanction; voluntary correction of certain failures with IRS approval before audit with a limited fee; and correction after a defect is uncovered through audit with reasonable fees based on the severity of the defect.

THE EPCRS PROGRAMS

Each program within EPCRS focuses on a different type of defect or circumstance.

1. Administrative Policy Regarding Self-Correction (APRSC) includes provisions to self-correct *insignificant* operational failures in plans of all sizes without a fee or sanction and the ability to correct significant operational failures without fee or sanction if the plan has a favorable letter of determination, which must include the most recent required amendments. In addition, the plan must have established administrative procedures in place to promote compliance, e.g., an administrative checklist. This program was renamed the Self-Correction Program (SCP).
2. Voluntary Corrections Program (VCP) allows plan sponsors to pay a limited fee and receive IRS approval for corrections as long as the plan is not under examination. This program has several subparts.
   (a) *Voluntary Correction of Operational Failures (VCO)* corrects operational failures in plans with a favorable letter of determination.
   (b) *Voluntary Correction of Operational Failures Standardized (VCS)* corrects limited operational failures using standardized correction methods.
   (c) *Voluntary Correction of Tax-Sheltered Annuity Failures (VCT)* corrects failures in 403(b) plans.
   (d) *Anonymous Submission Procedure* submits corrections without divulging the name of the plan sponsor until an acceptable agreement is reached with the IRS.
   (e) *Voluntary Correction of Group Failures (VCGroup)* allows certain organizations, such as master and prototype sponsors or third-party administrators, to receive a compliance statement for correcting failures that affect more than one plan sponsor. An example of this may be a defect in the plan document that the master or prototype sponsors are providing for employers that has been adopted by several employers.
   (f) *Voluntary Correction of SEP Failures (VCSEP)* permits small employers to self-correct insignificant SEP failures.
3. Audit CAP allows the correction of failures identified on audit that cannot be corrected by SCP or VCP above.

As long as defects covered in this self-correction system are corrected in compliance with the preceding programs, the plan will continue to enjoy its qualified status.

KEY DEFINITIONS

To differentiate between the various EPCRS programs, certain terms must be defined because the nature of the defect determines the correction program to be used. The key definitions are listed here.

1. *Qualification failure* is any failure that adversely affects the qualification of a plan, including:

    (a) Plan document failure—a plan provision or absence of a plan provision that violates the requirements of IRC Section 401(a) or 403(a), or that is not an operational failure or a demographic failure, e.g., failure to amend a plan to reflect new qualification requirements

    (b) Operational failure—failure to follow the plan provisions, e.g., including an employee in the plan who has not satisfied the eligibility requirements

    (c) Demographic failure—a failure to satisfy the provisions of IRC Section 401(a)(4), 401(a)(26) or 410(b) that is not an operational failure, e.g., noncompliance with the coverage requirements (see Chapter 9).

2. *Excess amount* is:

    (a) An overpayment

    (b) An employee contribution returned to satisfy IRC Section 415 (maximum annual additions)

    (c) An elective deferral in excess of the maximum under IRC Section 402(g) that is distributed ($13,000 for the year 2004)

    (d) An excess contribution or excess aggregate contribution that is distributed to satisfy IRC Section 401(k) or 401(m), e.g., excess matching contributions

    (e) Any amount required to be distributed to maintain the qualified status of the plan, e.g., a refund to satisfy the actual deferral percentage (ADP) test in a traditional 401(k) plan (see Chapter 5).

3. *Maximum payment amount* is the amount that is approximately equal to the income tax the IRS could collect upon plan disqualification, including the tax on trust income, tax caused by the loss of deductions of prior contributions plus interest and penalties, and tax on a participant's accounts or benefits.

4. *Overpayment* is a distribution to an employee or beneficiary that exceeds his or her benefit under the terms of the plan because of noncompliance with the plan terms as they relate to maximum compensation ($205,000 for the year 2004), IRC Section 401(m) maximum after-tax employee contribution subject to the actual contribution percentage (ACP) test (see Chapter 5), forfeiture of excess matching contributions or maximum annual additions (the lesser of $41,000 or 100% of compensation for the year 2004).

5. *Under examination* means a plan that is under an Employee Plans Examinations (audit) or a plan sponsor that is under an Exempt Organization Examinations. A plan is also considered to be under examination if the

plan sponsor or its representative has received notification of an impending examination. Once a plan is under examination, defects that are uncovered must be corrected through Audit CAP.

6. *Egregious failures* are defined by example in a plan that has consistently and improperly covered only HCEs or, if in a DC plan, the contribution for an HCE is several times greater than the maximum contribution allowable.

Under the EPCRS program, a plan defect must be corrected for all years in which the defect has occurred, including years closed by the statute of limitations.

CORRECTION METHODS

Generally, corrections under the EPCRS program must restore the plan to the position it would have been in had the defect not occurred. This includes all current participants, terminated participants and beneficiaries. Although there are several methods set forth as correction mechanisms acceptable to the IRS, other methods are permitted if the correction is reasonable and appropriate. This determination is based on the facts and circumstances of the specific plan.

WHAT IS AN INSIGNIFICANT FAILURE?

Insignificance of a failure is determined by factors such as the following:
1. Whether other failures have occurred during the period being examined
2. The percentage of plan assets and contributions involved in the failure
3. The number of years the failure occurred
4. The percentage of participants affected
5. The number of participants who were affected relative to the number of participants who could have been affected
6. Whether correction was made within a reasonable time after the failure was discovered
7. The cause of the failure, e.g., erroneous data.

Example 1: Alliance Manufacturing Corporation adopted a profit-sharing plan in 1994. In 2003, of the 250 participants, 50 were limited by IRC Section 415(c) maximum annual additions equal to the lesser of 100% of compensation or $40,000. On audit, in the year 2004, it was discovered that three of those employees still exceeded the IRC Section 415(c) limit, with excess contributions of $4,550 out of a total contribution in 2003 of $3.5 million. Because the number of participants affected by the failure relative to the number that could have been affected was small and the amount of the contribution involved in the failure relative to the total contribution for the year was insignificant, the failure can be corrected under APRSC/SCP.

Example 2: Same facts as in Example 1; however, the failure occurred in 2001, 2002 and 2003, and the affected participants were different each year. According to the IRS, this, too, is an insignificant failure and the multiple occurrences do not make it a significant failure.

Example 3: In this case, 18 of the 50 employees whose benefits were limited by IRC Section 415(c) exceeded the maximum limitation in 2003. The amount of the excess contribution ranged from $1,000 to $9,000 and totaled $150,000. Since the number of participants affected and the amount of money involved were considered significant by IRS, this section of the SCP program could not be used to correct the failure.

Example 4: Stryker Manufacturing Inc. maintains a 10% money purchase plan. During an audit for the 2003 plan year, it was discovered that the data entry for six employees' salaries out of a total of 40 was erroneously overstated, causing excess allocations to those employees. Because the number of participants who were affected relative to the number who could have been affected is small and the failure was caused by minor data errors, SCP would be available to correct this defect.

VOLUNTARY CORRECTIONS PROGRAM

The Voluntary Corrections Program (VCP) provides for a wide variety of self-correction mechanisms through several subparts, including:
* Voluntary Correction of Operational Failures (VCO)
  The VCO program is available for operational failures that cannot be corrected under SCP for plans that have a favorable letter of determination. This is not a self-correction program, but requires IRS approval. Upon submission to the IRS with the appropriate fee, the application will be reviewed only with respect to the failures identified by the plan sponsor or those uncovered by the IRS in processing the VCO application.
* Voluntary Correction of Operational Failures Standardized (VCS)
  Certain operational failures can be corrected using the Voluntary Correction of Operational Failures Standardized program. Use of the VCS program limits the number of failures to two in any VCS application and allows only for the specific correction methods as defined in IRS Revenue Procedures. Similar to VCP submission, the VCS program will also result in the IRS issuing a compliance statement. The specific failures that can be corrected under this program include failure to provide the top-heavy minimum benefit (see Chapter 9); failure to satisfy the ADP, ACP, or multiple use test in a 401(k) plan (see Chapter 5); failure to distribute excess deferrals in a 401(k) plan to correct the ADP test (see Chapter 5); exclusion of an eligible employee from participation for one or more plan years; failure to pay the minimum distribution required (see Chapter 8); failure to obtain participant or spousal consent for a distribution (see Chapter 8); and failure to satisfy the Section 415 limits (the lesser of $41,000 or 100% of compensation for the year 2004) in a DC plan.
* Voluntary Correction of Tax-Sheltered Annuity Failures (VCT)
  A separate correction program for 403(b) plans (see Chapter 7)
* Anonymous Submission Procedure and Voluntary Correction of Group Failures (VCGroup)

The IRS has established an anonymous submission procedure that permits submission of a qualified plan for correction under VCP without initially identifying the plan or the plan sponsor. A VCGroup submission is subject to the same procedures as any VCP submission, except that the eligible organization is responsible for performing the procedural obligations imposed on the plan sponsor.

- Voluntary Correction of SEP Failures (VCSEP)

A VCP submission for a SEP plan is required to be made under the VCSEP procedure, which follows the same procedures as the general VCP procedures discussed previously. A SEP plan is not eligible for VCO or VCS but is eligible for the anonymous submission procedure.

VCP may be used only to correct failures identified by the plan sponsor or failures identified by the IRS in processing the VCP application. A submission is made to the IRS under the various rules of VCP and, if agreement is reached, the IRS will send the plan sponsor an unsigned compliance statement specifying the corrective action required. Within 30 calendar days of the date the compliance statement is sent, a plan sponsor must sign the compliance statement and return it and any compliance fee required to be paid at the time that the compliance statement is signed. The IRS will then issue a signed copy of the compliance statement to the plan sponsor. If the plan sponsor does not send the IRS the signed compliance statement with the appropriate fee within 30 calendar days, the plan may be referred to Employee Plans Examinations for examination consideration.

The compliance statement issued for a VCP submission addresses the failures identified; the terms of correction, including any revision of administrative procedures to avoid future failures; and the time period within which proposed corrections must be implemented, including any changes in administrative procedures. The compliance statement also provides that the IRS will not treat the plan as failing to satisfy the applicable requirements of the Internal Revenue Code on account of the failures described in the compliance statement if the conditions of the compliance statement are satisfied. The compliance statement is conditioned on there being no misstatement or omission of material facts in connection with the submission and the implementation of the specific corrections and satisfaction of any other conditions in the compliance statement. If, during review of the application, the IRS discovers other defects outside the scope of the application, the plan may be forwarded to Employee Plans Examinations for possible audit.

VCP FEES

The table on page 220 shows the compliance fees for applications under VCP. The table contains a graduated range of fees based on the size of the plan and the number of participants. Each range includes a minimum amount, a maximum amount and a presumptive amount. In each case, the minimum amount is the applicable VCO fee. Generally, the compliance fee will be at or near the presumptive amount in each range; however, the fee may be a higher or lower amount within the range, depending on the factors considered.

Table

Participants	Fee Range	Presumptive Amount
10 or fewer	VCO fee* to $ 4,000	$ 2,000
11 to 50	VCO fee* to $ 8,000	$ 4,000
51 to 100	VCO fee* to $12,000	$ 6,000
101 to 300	VCO fee* to $16,000	$ 8,000
301 to 1,000	VCO fee* to $30,000	$15,000
Over 1,000	VCO fee* to $70,000	$35,000

*Refers to the VCO compliance fee that would apply if the plan had been submitted under VCO.

FACTORS CONSIDERED IN DETERMINING THE FEE

Whether the compliance fee should be equal to, greater than or less than the presumptive amount depends on factors relating to the nature, extent and severity of the failure. These factors include:

1. Whether the failure is a failure to satisfy the requirements of IRC Section 401(a)(4) (nondiscrimination), 401(a)(26) (participation) or 410(b) (coverage)
2. Whether the plan has both operational and plan document failures
3. The period over which the violation occurred (for example, the time that has elapsed since the end of the applicable remedial amendment period (see Chapter 2))
4. The extent to which the plan has accepted transferred assets and the extent to which the failures relate to the transferred assets and occurred before the transfer
5. Whether the plan has a favorable determination letter.

Unless VCS is applicable, the VCO compliance fee depends on the assets of the plan and the number of plan participants. The compliance fee for a VCGroup submission is based on the number of plans to which the compliance statement is applicable. The initial fee is $10,000. With some minor adjustments, the applicable VCSEP compliance fee is the same as the fee for VCP discussed previously.

When all else fails or the IRS uncovers a defect before the plan sponsor does, there is Audit CAP. In the event the IRS and the plan sponsor cannot reach an agreement under Audit CAP, the plan will be disqualified. If the plan is disqualified retroactively, the consequences are effective only for taxable years that are still open, i.e., for which the statute of limitations has not expired. The statute of limitations ends three years after the later of the date the plan sponsor files the annual return with the trust statement Schedule P attached or the last day allowed for filing the annual returns. The procedures for Audit CAP are similar to those for VCP; however, in the case of Audit CAP, a sanction must be paid that is a negotiated amount and that is generally a percentage of the maximum payment amount (see previous definitions). The actual amount of the sanction depends on the nature, extent and severity of the failures.

DELINQUENT FILER VOLUNTARY COMPLIANCE PROGRAM

In 1995, the Department of Labor (DOL) established a voluntary compliance program for plan sponsors that had not filed the required annual forms with the IRS (see Chapter 13). To participate in the program, the plan sponsor must file the missing forms with the appropriate penalty. The advantage of the program is a reduced limit on the penalties. For a small plan (of fewer than 100 participants) that is less than 12 months late in filing the required forms (disregarding extensions), the penalty is $50 per day with a maximum of $1,000 and, for a large plan (of 100 or more participants), a maximum of $2,500. For a filing that is more than one year past due (disregarding extensions), the maximum is $2,000 for a small plan and $5,000 for a large plan. Before the availability of the program, the penalty could be up to $1,000 per day. This program is not available if the plan sponsor has already been notified by the DOL that the form was not timely filed or was filed with incomplete information, and that a civil penalty will be assessed.

The End of the Line— Plan Termination

Chapter 15

Plan terminations—What can employers do when all else fails, and how do they do it? The company has adopted a retirement plan it hopes provides attractive benefits for its employees and offers the employer some appealing tax benefits. The plan has been operating for several years but now must be terminated because of a business reversal, the owner's retirement, the sale of the business or some other equally compelling reason.

The complexity of the termination process is dependent on whether the plan sponsor files with the Internal Revenue Service (IRS) for an approval letter and on the type of plan being terminated—a defined contribution (DC) plan or a defined benefit (DB) plan. If the sponsor applies to IRS, the determination letter received confirms that the plan termination will not adversely affect the qualified status of the plan, i.e., the plan sponsor, and that the employee participants will not lose any of their tax benefits.

Because a DB plan is promising retirement benefits that may or may not be properly funded, the procedure is much more complex than for a DC plan, where each participant has an account balance representing the actual assets in the plan. Also, in some cases, DB plans have excess assets that may revert to the plan sponsor at plan termination. The rules under the Employee Retirement Income Security Act of 1974 (ERISA) and the Internal Revenue Code (IRC) and Treasury regulations for terminating DB plans in part protect participants from plan terminations designed to allow the plan sponsor to recapture excess assets that were originally meant to provide plan benefits.

PLAN QUALIFICATION CONSIDERATIONS

In all cases, when a qualified retirement plan is terminated, the plan must be amended to meet the qualification requirements that are in effect at the time of termination. Ongoing plans have until the end of the remedial amendment period to make the necessary amendments (see Chapter 2). In addition, when a plan is terminated, all participants become 100% vested in their accrued benefits, regardless of their service credits for vesting. *Accrued benefit* is defined as the benefit earned as of the date of termination under a DB plan (see Chapter 6) in the form of an annual benefit beginning at normal retirement age or the balance of a participant's account in a DC plan. Partial terminations, discussed later in the chapter, are also required to provide 100% vesting with respect to the terminating employees.

Plans not subject to minimum funding standards, including profit-sharing and stock bonus plans, are also required to provide 100% vesting in the case of a complete discontinuance of contributions (see Chapters 4 and 6). Although a determination of complete discontinuance of contributions is based on the facts and circumstances, the following factors should be considered:

1. Whether the employer may be calling an actual discontinuance of contributions a suspension in order to avoid the requirement of full vesting
2. Whether contributions are recurring and substantial. Even though the employer is making some contributions, a complete discontinuance may exist if the amounts are not substantial enough to indicate the employer's intent to maintain the plan. In one case, an employer did not make contributions for five consecutive years because it did not have profits or accumulated earnings. This was not considered to be a discontinuance of contributions, as long as contributions resumed when the employer did have profits.
3. Whether there is any reasonable probability that the lack of contributions will continue indefinitely.

Even though an employer discontinues contributions and the 100% vesting rule applies, the plan does not have to be formally terminated. Instead, the plan can be maintained and distributions made to employees in accordance with the plan provisions. This is called a "wasting trust" and is considered a qualified tax-exempt trust.

One of the requirements for a retirement plan to be qualified is that it is intended to be permanent. If IRS determines that a plan was not intended to be permanent because it terminates within a few years of adoption, the plan can be disqualified retroactively. The determination of permanence is based on the facts and circumstances involved. A plan terminated because of a business necessity, e.g., ongoing losses caused by a business depression, would still be considered to have had the intent of being permanent at the time it was adopted. Furthermore, a plan must satisfy the vesting (discussed previously) and nondiscrimination rules on termination (see Chapter 9). Failure to satisfy these rules could result in plan disqualification, causing disallowance of employer deductions for prior contributions, assessment of taxes on plan investment earnings and assessment of taxes on employees for contributions that would have been included in their income if the plan had not been a qualified plan.

PARTIAL PLAN TERMINATION

The only absolute guideline is that a partial termination is something less than a plan termination. Unfortunately, a partial plan termination is based on the ever-present facts and circumstances. In some cases, a partial termination occurs when a group of employees is excluded from coverage through plan amendment, e.g., a *class* (specific job or geographical location) of employees is excluded from coverage that was not excluded before. In some cases, the discharge of a significant number of employees or a significant percentage of the total workforce could be considered a partial termination. In a partial termination, 100% vesting is required only for the employees affected by the partial termination.

Although there are no hard guidelines for determining whether a plan has had a partial termination, the courts have indicated some by various case rulings. They have taken the position in some cases that a partial termination has occurred if a "significant percentage" of employees have been excluded from coverage:

1. A court ruled that a partial termination had occurred when 95 out of 165 participants (57.6%) were discharged because one division of the employer was dissolved, regardless of whether the discharge was caused by adverse economic conditions.

2. In another case, 12 out of 15 employees who refused to transfer to the employer's new business location were discharged, causing the plan to have a partial termination.

3. Other cases have indicated that 34%, 51%, 70.6% and 80% were considered significant percentages.

4. In one case, the exclusion of 15% of the participants did not constitute a partial termination, and the same court noted that 34% was the lowest percentage that would be considered significant.

If an employee leaves voluntarily, absent a significant corporate event causing that voluntary termination, a partial termination is not triggered. To further confuse matters, the courts differ on which employees are to be considered when calculating the number or percentage of terminated employees. On remand from the Supreme Court, the Seventh Circuit held that only nonvested plan participants can be counted in determining whether a partial termination has occurred. Yet, the original determination by the Seventh Circuit held that both vested and nonvested participants should be counted.

TERMINATION OF DC PLAN

If the plan sponsor will be filing for a favorable letter of determination to IRS for the termination, the plan participants and beneficiaries must be notified. For a DC plan subject to minimum funding standards, i.e., money purchase or target benefit plans (see Chapter 4), a notice must be sent to participants and beneficiaries that the plan is being amended to reduce future contributions significantly (an ERISA Section 204(h) notice). This notice must be provided before the employee's entitlement to the current year's contribution, generally before 1,000 hours of service during the plan year, to avoid the otherwise required current year's contribution.

If the plan sponsor is a corporation, a corporate resolution should be adopted by the board of directors to terminate the plan. If the plan sponsor is not incorporated, a company resolution should be prepared and signed by the sole proprietor or partners. The resolution should also state that all future contributions will be discontinued. If legislation has been passed since the last time the plan document was prepared or restated, an amendment must be adopted to bring the plan into compliance with the current qualification rules. The plan sponsor must then determine whether the termination will be submitted to IRS for approval. Although filing is voluntary, it does assure the employer and the employees that the termination will not adversely affect the qualified status of the plan and that all plan benefits will retain their tax-favored status. The following must be submitted if the termination is to be filed with IRS:

1. Form 5310, Application for Determination for Terminating Plan
2. Schedule Q, Nondiscrimination Requirements
3. Form 6088, Distributable Benefits From Employee Pension Benefit Plans
4. Form 8717, User Fee for Employee Plan Determination Letter Request (currently $225).

If a third party, e.g., a third-party administrator, is to submit the termination package to IRS, a Form 2848, Power of Attorney, must also be included.

In addition to the required forms, the following information must also be included with the filing:

1. A copy of the plan document
2. A copy of all amendments made since the last determination letter
3. A statement explaining how the amendments affect or change this plan or any other plan maintained by the employer
4. Copies of all records of all actions taken to terminate the plan
5. A copy of the plan's latest determination letter, opinion letter or notification letter.

The termination process with IRS can take four to eight months, sometimes longer. While this process is going on, the plan sponsor must still file the annual Form 5500 and continue to do so until the last one is filed for the year in which all the assets in the plan are distributed. That filing would be marked "final."

Once the favorable determination letter is received from IRS, or after proper notice to employees as indicated above if an application to IRS has not been filed, a formal notice must be prepared for each participant, including:

1. A participant election form with spousal consent (If the participant is married and elects to receive the benefits in a form other than a joint and survivor (J&S) annuity, or joint and survivor annuity with a beneficiary other than the participant's spouse, the spouse must consent to the election in writing; see Chapter 8.)
2. A notice of rollover treatment explaining distribution options and tax treatment to the participants
3. A notice of tax withholding
4. A form W-4P withholding election
5. A notice on direct plan rollovers advising participants of the procedure to follow for a direct rollover
6. A notice on tax treatment for lump-sum distributions.

For the plan year in which all the assets are distributed to participants, i.e., there are no assets left in the plan trust, a final Form 5500 must be filed notifying IRS that the plan has been completely terminated. Sometimes the distribution of plan assets cannot be completed if an employee entitled to a distribution cannot be located.

The fiduciary responsibility provisions of Title I of ERISA do not offer specific guidance about what steps fiduciaries of a plan must take to locate missing participants. The Department of Labor (DOL) considers this question to be factual in nature and it therefore must be resolved by each plan fiduciary by applying ERISA's general fiduciary responsibility provisions to each plan's particular facts and circumstances. Each plan must adopt a procedure for locating missing participants in a manner expected to satisfy fiduciary obligations under Title I of ERISA. Appropriate steps that could be considered in locating a missing participant would be sending mailings to the participant's last known address, using newspaper advertisements and using a professional locator service.

If a participant cannot be located after making reasonable efforts to locate him or her, the plan administrator can request that IRS forward a letter from the plan administrator (or from a commercial locator service acting as an authorized agent) to the missing participant if IRS has the person's current address. IRS will also inform the missing participant that his or her address has not been disclosed and that IRS has no interest in the matter other than forwarding the letter. IRS has two programs of this type; one for less than 50 participants and the other for more than 49 participants. For the smaller group, there is no charge. The plan administrator should submit a written request including the Social Security numbers of the participants with the letter to be sent to the disclosure officer at the IRS district office nearest the plan. The hoped-for result is that the participants contact the plan administrator. For groups of more than 49 participants, a request for assistance will be processed according to Project 753 Computerized Mailout Program. For any plan participating in this program, IRS charges the plan a flat fee of $1,750 plus 1¢ per address search and 50¢ per letter forwarded. Requests for this program should be mailed to: Internal Revenue Service, Director, Office of Disclosure (CP:EX:D), 1111 Constitution Avenue, N.W., Room 1603, Washington, DC 20224.

Another aid in locating missing participants is provided by the Social Security Administration (SSA). Given a participant's Social Security number, the SSA will forward a notice from the administrator to the participant's last address in the SSA records. A fee of $3 for each forwarded letter must be included in the request and mailed to: Department of Health and Human Services, Social Security Administration, Office of Central Records Operations, Division of Certification and Coverage, 300 North Greene Street, Baltimore, MD 21201.

The Department of Labor (DOL) has taken the position that plan fiduciaries, after following the appropriate procedures they have established for locating a "lost" participant, can distribute the participant's benefits to an interest-bearing federally insured bank account opened in the participant's name if this manner of distribution is permitted under the terms of the plan and if the participant has an unconditional right to withdraw funds from the account. As a practical matter, the financial institution may be reluctant to open an account without the account owner's signature.

In addition to the preceding programs, the Pension Benefit Guaranty Corporation (see Chapter 6) has established a database called the Pension Search Directory. Once people find their names on the directory, they can provide additional details to PBGC for verification. The database can be found at www.pbgc.gov/search or from the Communications and Public Affairs Department, 1200 K Street, N.W., Room 240, Washington, DC 20005-4026.

TERMINATION OF DB PLANS

DB plans can be terminated voluntarily by the plan sponsor or involuntarily by the PBGC, a nonprofit corporation within DOL that insures participants and beneficiaries against the loss of benefits. The form of voluntary termination depends on whether the plan is properly funded. If the assets are sufficient to fund the accrued benefits (see Chapter 6), the plan is terminated in a standard termination. If the assets are insufficient, a distress termination is the only alternative but it is available only if:

1. The employer is in a liquidation proceeding under bankruptcy law.
2. The employer is in a reorganization proceeding under bankruptcy law.
3. The employer proves to the PBGC that plan termination is necessary to pay debts or to avoid burdensome costs.

An involuntary termination would be initiated by PBGC to protect the interests of plan participants.

Example 1: The concept of underfunded and overfunded DB plans is illustrated using the following example:

	Age	Retirement Age	Monthly Benefit	Accrued Benefit	Reserve	Present Value of Accrued Benefit
Steve	62	65	$8,000	$4,000	$1,100,132	$ 475,168
Michael	57	65	8,750	4,000	1,203,300	372,306
						$ 847,474
Sarah	44	65	2,188	1,292	300,894	$ 63,766
John	40	65	3,063	1,206	421,224	48,965
Ralph	31	65	2,450	1,929	336,924	50,491
Scott	27	65	1,575	1,085	216,594	23,367
Randy	47	65	4,375	3,445	601,650	196,829
						$ 383,418
						$1,230,892

The value of each participant's benefit as of the end of the plan year (December 31, 2004) is the present value of the accrued benefit (see Chapter 6). Here are the steps to calculate Steve's value:

1. (Accrued benefit / monthly benefit) × reserve at retirement
2. Step 1 / [(1 + i) ^ (retirement age − current age)]

The steps are shown in numeric form, as follows:

1. ($4,000 / $8,000) × $1,100,132 = $550,066
2. $ 550,066 / (1 + .05) ^ (65 − 62) = $475,168

At the end of the third plan year, December 31, 2004, assume the assets in the plan amount to $801,231. If the employer chooses to terminate this plan, it could only consider a distress termination since the assets are not sufficient to pay all the participants the value of their accrued benefits. To be eligible for a standard termination, the employer would have to make up the difference between the present value of the accrued benefits and the actual plan assets.

Before filing a standard termination notice with PBGC, the employer can make a commitment to contribute any additional amount necessary to fund all liabilities. This commitment must be made to the plan in writing and signed by the employer. As an alternative, an individual who owns 50% or more of the plan sponsor may waive receipt of all or a portion of his or her benefits until the assets are sufficient to fund the plan liabilities. The election must be in writing and the owner's spouse must consent if the plan otherwise requires spousal consent for distributions in a form other than a joint and survivor annuity (see Chapter 8). The contribution necessary to fund the remaining liabilities of $429,661 may not be totally deductible in the year it was contributed but it may have to be amortized over up to ten years. Contributions necessary to fund benefits guaranteed by PBGC (discussed later in this chapter) are fully deductible.

Example 1 clearly illustrates one of the dangers of improperly designed DB plans. Plans that provide for benefits based on past service will generally be underfunded in the early years. As time goes by, the plan's benefit liabilities will become closer to the actual assets and will eliminate the underfunding. Many employers that adopt DB plans do not understand that the contributions are funding future benefits at retirement age and may not be consistent with the rate that benefits are earned during the years before retirement age, i.e., contributions do not represent the value of benefits earned each year.

Example 2: Consider the following DB plan at the end of the first year:

	Age	Retirement Age	Monthly Benefit	Accrued Benefit	Reserve	Present Value of Accrued Benefit
Steve	60	65	$8,000	$1,333	$1,100,132	$ 143,664
Michael	55	65	8,333	1,333	1,145,954	112,564
						$256,228
Sarah	42	65	2,083	833	286,454	$ 37,305
John	38	65	2,917	583	401,146	21,489
Ralph	29	65	2,333	1,333	320,834	31,658
Scott	25	65	1,500	750	206,280	14,651
Randy	45	65	4,167	1,333	573,046	69,105
						$174,207
						$430,435

The contribution for the first plan year to fund these benefits is $246,414. If the plan were to terminate at the end of the first plan year, the assets would be short $184,021 ($430,435 − $246,414). Even though the value of benefits earned as of the end of the first plan year was $430,435, the contribution is calculated to fund the retirement benefit over future service, not the benefit earned during the plan year. This discrepancy is partially caused by the period over which the benefits are earned as noted previously, i.e., credit for past service.

It is also possible that a DB plan can be overfunded. In that case, the assets are in excess of the present value of accrued benefits. The implications of overfunded DB plans are discussed later in this chapter.

DB STANDARD TERMINATION

To begin a voluntary standard termination, a notice of intent to terminate must be given to *affected parties* at least 60 days, but no more than 90 days, before the termination date set forth in the notice. The 60-day time limit will not be extended by the PBGC. If it is missed, the termination date has to be changed, which could require additional plan contributions if additional benefits were earned between the original termination date and the new termination date.

Affected parties, with respect to a plan, means:
1. Each participant in the plan
2. Each beneficiary under the plan who is a beneficiary of a deceased participant or who is an alternate payee under an applicable qualified domestic relations order
3. Each employee organization representing participants in the plan
4. The corporation, except that, in connection with any notice required to be provided to the affected party, if an affected party has designated, in writing, a person to receive such notice on behalf of the affected party, any reference to the affected party shall be construed to refer to such person.

The notice of intent to terminate must include the following information:
1. The name and plan number of the plan
2. The name and employer identification number of each contributing employer
3. The name, address and telephone number of the person to contact by an affected party with questions concerning the termination
4. A statement that the plan administrator intends to terminate the plan in a standard termination by a specific date and that the affected party will be notified if the date is changed or the termination does not occur
5. A statement that plan assets must be sufficient to terminate the plan in a standard termination
6. A statement, if applicable, that:
   (a) Benefit accruals will stop on the termination date but continue if the plan is not terminated.
   (b) A plan amendment has been adopted terminating benefit accruals in

accordance with ERISA Section 204(h) as of the termination date or some other date, regardless of whether the plan is terminated.

    (c) Benefit accruals terminated as of some date before the notice of intent to terminate was issued.

7. A statement that each affected party entitled to benefits will receive written notification regarding the plan benefits

8. A statement explaining how an affected party can obtain the most recent summary plan description

9. A statement to participants receiving monthly benefits, if applicable, either informing them that their monthly benefits will not be affected by the termination or explaining how their benefits will be affected

10. A statement that the PBGC will not guarantee a participant's or beneficiary's benefits after plan assets have been distributed in satisfaction of those benefits.

Although it is not required to adopt an amendment to stop benefit accruals in the termination process, it is recommended to avoid additional benefit costs because of benefits that would be earned after the termination date if the termination is nullified for noncompliance with the termination requirements listed previously.

If the plan sponsor is a corporation, a corporate resolution should be adopted by the board of directors to terminate the plan. If the plan sponsor is not incorporated, a company resolution should be prepared and signed by the sole proprietor or partners. The resolution should also state that all future benefit accruals will be discontinued. If legislation has been passed since the last time the plan document was prepared or restated, an amendment must be adopted to bring the plan into compliance with the current qualification rules. The plan sponsor must then determine whether the termination will be submitted to IRS for approval. Although this is a voluntary filing, it does assure the employer and the employees that the termination will not adversely affect the qualified status of the plan and all plan benefits will retain their tax-favored status. If the plan is submitted to IRS for a determination letter on plan termination, the participants and beneficiaries of the plan must be notified.

After the notice of intent to terminate is provided to participants, the plan administrator files a standard termination notice with PBGC no later than 180 days after the proposed termination date as set forth in the notice of intent to terminate. This is done on PBGC Form 500, Standard Termination Notice, Single Employer Plan Termination with Schedule EA-S and Standard Termination Certification of Sufficiency. The Form EA-S must be certified by an enrolled actuary that the assets are sufficient to pay all benefits.

If the termination notice is not filed on time, PBGC will issue a notice of noncompliance. A new termination date will have to be chosen and the process started over again. Because the 180-day period ends when the PBGC receives the notice, the plan sponsor should send the notice certified mail with a return receipt requested.

The ERISA plan administrator (usually the employer) must provide a notice of plan benefits to the participants and beneficiaries no later than the day on which the standard termination notice is filed with PBGC. The notice of plan benefits must include:

1. The name of the plan
2. The name and employer identification number of the contributing sponsors
3. The plan number
4. The name, address and telephone number of the person to contact to answer questions regarding the participant's or beneficiary's benefits
5. The proposed termination date
6. A statement that the amount of the plan benefits is an estimate and that benefits actually paid may be more or less than the estimate
7. The data on which benefits have been based, to the extent applicable, including:
   (a) Participant's age at retirement
   (b) The age of the participant's spouse
   (c) Participant's length of service
   (d) The participant's actual or estimated Social Security benefit and, if estimated, the earnings history used for the estimate.

PBGC has 60 days to issue a notice of noncompliance if it determines that assets are not sufficient to pay all benefits or if the procedural requirements for the termination are not followed. A notice of noncompliance nullifies the termination proceedings and returns the plan to active status, i.e., an ongoing plan.

If a notice of noncompliance is not issued, the plan assets must be distributed by the later of 180 days after the end of the PBGC 60-day review period or 120 days after receipt of a favorable determination letter, usually later than the prior deadline, from IRS if the termination was filed with IRS. To take advantage of the later date, IRS submission must be made by the time the standard termination notice was filed with the PBGC. Within 30 days after the assets are distributed, the plan administrator must file PBGC Form 501, Post-Distribution Certification for Standard Terminations, that the participants have received all of their benefits.

The formality in terminating a DB plan is much broader than in terminating a DC plan. Missing a deadline can add significant administrative and plan funding costs to the termination process.

OVERFUNDED DB PLANS

In a standard termination, the assets could exceed the benefits due the participants because of above-average investment performance or accelerated funding. The excess assets must be allocated in a nondiscriminatory manner or revert to the employer. If the assets are to be reallocated to the participants, the method used would be to amend the plan so the present value of the amended accrued benefits is equal to the total plan assets.

Example 3: The Wiley Manufacturing Company Plan provides a level retirement benefit for all participants of 10% of salary per year of service up to ten years. At the end of the third year, Wiley chooses to terminate the plan with the following benefits:

	Age	Retirement Age	Salary	Monthly Benefit	Reserve at Retirement	Accrued Benefit	Accrued Benefit	PV Excess Assets
Harold	54	65	$100,000	$8,333	$1,146,000	$2,500	$232,697	$28,138
Jonathan	37	65	35,000	2,917	401,100	875	35,534	4,297
Arthur	28	65	28,000	2,333	320,880	700	18,324	2,216
Debbie	24	65	18,000	1,500	206,280	450	9,691	1,172
							63,549	7,685
							$296,247	$35,823

In the Wiley Plan, allocating excess assets based on the present value of the accrued benefit provides a nondiscriminatory result. Each participant's increase in the present value of the accrued benefit is 12.092% ($28,138 / $232,697 = 12.092%). Some DB plan designs do not provide benefits equally to all plan participants, e.g., a DB plan integrated with Social Security (see Chapter 6) would provide a higher benefit as a percentage of compensation for higher paid participants than lower paid participants. In that case, the excess assets cannot be allocated based on the present value of the accrued benefit but must be allocated in some other nondiscriminatory manner.

ASSET REVERSION TO THE EMPLOYER

The other alternative for the disposition of excess assets is to return the assets to the plan sponsor. Generally, the excess assets that are returned to the plan sponsor are subject to a 50% excise tax in addition to income taxes at the plan sponsor's tax bracket. If the employer establishes a *qualified replacement plan* or increases the benefits in the DB plan, the excise tax on any remaining reversion is reduced to 20%.

A *qualified replacement plan* is a qualified plan established or maintained by the employer in connection with a qualified plan termination that meets the following requirements:

1. At least 95% of the active participants in the terminated plan who remain employees of the employer after the termination are active participants in the replacement plan.
2. Exactly 25% of the excess assets must be transferred to the replacement plan.
3. If the replacement plan is a DC plan, the amounts must be allocated to the participants in the year transferred or, if the amounts are in excess of statutory limits, must be held in a suspense account and credited to the participants over no more than seven years.

If, instead, benefits in the DB plan are increased to reduce the excise tax, at least 20% of the excess assets must be used to increase the accrued benefits to the participants of the terminating plan in a nondiscriminatory manner.

This two-level excise tax rate structure has several purposes. First, it is designed to recapture the tax benefits for the employer of tax-deferred earnings and tax-deductible contributions made during the life of the plan that are not being used to provide benefits to the participants. Second, it is intended to encourage the plan sponsor either to maintain a qualified plan after terminating the DB plan or to provide benefit increases before terminating the plan. If a qualified replacement plan terminates before the suspense account has been allocated to participants, the suspense account must be allocated to participants as of the termination date. If a portion of the suspense account referred to in item 3 cannot be allocated to any participants when the qualified replacement plan terminates, the portion remaining is treated as a reversion to the employer and is included in the employer's gross income subject to the 50% excise tax on reversions. This may occur if all the participants are at their IRC Section 415 limit, i.e., the lesser of 100% of compensation or $41,000 (for the year 2004).

In one case, 100% of the excess assets from a terminated DB plan were transferred to a qualified replacement plan; only the minimum 25% of the surplus required to be transferred to qualify for the 20% excise tax rate was exempt from the excise tax. The remaining 75% of the excess assets was subject to the 20% excise tax, although none of the excess assets transferred to the qualified replacement plan was included in the taxable income of the employer sponsoring the plan.

DB DISTRESS TERMINATION

For a DB plan to file voluntarily as a distress termination, PBGC must determine that one of the following requirements is met:
1. The plan sponsor has filed for a liquidation in bankruptcy.
2. The plan sponsor has filed for reorganization.
3. The plan sponsor cannot continue in business.
4. The costs to continue the plan would be unreasonably burdensome.

Before terminating the plan in a distress termination, the plan administrator must:
1. Provide a notice of intent to terminate to each affected party at least 60 days and no more than 90 days before the proposed termination date
2. File a distress termination notice with PBGC on PBGC Form 601, Distress Termination Notice Single Employer Plan Termination, including a Schedule EA-D, Distress Termination Enrolled Actuary Certification, no later than 120 days after the proposed termination date
3. Confirm that PBGC has determined that the plan sponsor has satisfied at least one of the four preceding requirements.

PBGC-GUARANTEED BENEFITS

One of the primary responsibilities of PBGC is to guarantee benefits, up to certain limits, in DB plans that do not have sufficient assets to pay benefits. For plans terminating in 2003, PBGC guarantees a benefit of up to $3,664.77 per month (payable only in the form of an annuity). This amount is adjusted annually based on formulas in ERISA and PBGC regulations. For the benefit to be guaranteed:
1. The benefit must be nonforfeitable. A benefit that becomes nonforfeitable only because of plan termination is not considered nonforfeitable for this

purpose, i.e., the plan's vesting schedule determines the extent of the non-forfeitable benefit for this purpose.

2. The benefit is a *pension benefit*. A pension benefit is a benefit payable as an annuity to a participant who permanently leaves or has permanently left covered employment or a surviving beneficiary, and is paid in payments that, by themselves or in combination with Social Security, Railroad Retirement or workers' compensation benefits, provide a substantially level income to the recipient.

3. The participant must be entitled to the benefit. A participant or his or her surviving beneficiary is entitled to a benefit if, under the provisions of a plan:

    (a) The benefit was in pay status on the date of the termination of the plan.

    (b) A benefit payable at normal retirement age is an optional form of payment, e.g., a J&S annuity, and the participant elected the optional form of benefit before the termination date of the plan.

    (c) Except for a benefit described in paragraph (b), before the termination date, the participant had satisfied the conditions of the plan necessary to establish the right to receive the benefit.

    (d) Absent an election by the participant, the benefit would be payable upon retirement.

    (e) In the case of a benefit that returns all or a portion of a participant's accumulated mandatory employee contributions upon death, the participant (or beneficiary) had satisfied the conditions of the plan necessary to establish the right to the benefit other than death or designation of a beneficiary.

If none of the conditions set forth in preceding items (a) to (e) is met, PBGC will determine whether the participant is entitled to a benefit on the basis of the provisions of the plan and the circumstances of the case.

PBGC does not guarantee lump-sum payments but will guarantee an alternate payment method, e.g., a life annuity, that is the equivalent of the lump-sum payment (the actuarial equivalent, see Chapter 6).

Upon submission to PBGC, if it is determined that the plan assets are sufficient to pay PBGC-guaranteed benefits, or more, but not benefit liabilities (the present value of accrued benefits, assuming they are higher than guaranteed benefits), PBGC will issue a notice allowing the plan to terminate.

If the plan assets are not sufficient to pay guaranteed benefits, PBGC will issue a notice of inability to determine sufficiency and advise the plan administrator that the plan will continue to operate under the limitations of a plan in distress termination.

DB PLANS INVOLUNTARY TERMINATION

In addition to the voluntary termination procedures, PBGC may initiate an involuntary termination in the U.S. district court if:

1. The loss to PBGC will increase unreasonably if the plan is not terminated.
2. The plan has not met the minimum funding standards (see Chapter 6).

3. The plan is deficient in paying the tax for failure to meet the minimum funding standards (see Chapter 6).
4. The plan will not be able to pay benefits when due.
5. A distribution is made to a substantial owner of $10,000 or more, for a reason other than death, so that, after the distribution, the vested benefits of the other participants are not totally funded.

If the plan is terminated under PBGC involuntary proceedings, the employees can recover benefits in excess of those provided under PBGC insurance from the employer. Once proceedings are initiated by PBGC, an application will be made to the U.S. district court to appoint a trustee to administer the plan pending the issuance of a court decree to terminate the plan. In some cases, PBGC may be appointed as trustee. Once the trustee is appointed, a notice regarding the termination must be given to interested parties, including:

1. The plan administrator
2. Participants and beneficiaries
3. The employer
4. Employers in multiemployer plans that may be subject to withdrawal liability
5. Employers that have an obligation to contribute under a multiemployer plan
6. Employee organizations that represent plan participants of employers in preceding items 3, 4 and 5.

When a plan is terminated in a distress termination or involuntarily by PBGC, the employer is liable to PBGC for the total amount of the unfunded benefit liabilities of all participants and beneficiaries plus interest. Generally, this amount is due to PBGC as of the termination date. In some cases, PBGC will arrange for special payment terms. If PBGC determines that the liability exceeds 30% of the collective net worth of the entity subject to the liability, PBGC will prescribe reasonable terms for payment of the portion of the liability that exceeds 30% of the collective net worth of the entity liable.

Taxation of Plan Distributions

Chapter 16

Other chapters discuss how to accumulate retirement savings, the types of plans that are available, the possible hazards and cures and when the money ultimately has to be distributed. This chapter addresses how the distributions are taxed. Benefits under any qualified plan are taxed only when "actually distributed" to the employee or beneficiary and are not taxed if only "made available" or "constructively received."

Constructively received applies to income credited to the participant's account or otherwise made unconditionally available (vested) to the employee. Income is not constructively received if the taxpayer's control of this receipt is subject to substantial limitations or restrictions, e.g., no in-service distributions in pension plans (see Chapter 8).

Although benefits are credited to the taxpayer's account in a qualified retirement plan, particularly in a defined contribution (DC) plan, control of the account is subject to substantial limitations. In most plans, distributions may not be made until retirement, death, disability, attainment of age 59½ or termination of service, although profit-sharing plans may allow for in-service distributions (see Chapter 8). Even though upon attainment of age 59½, the limitations and restrictions are removed and the account may be considered constructively received, taxation does not occur until the account is actually distributed.

The taxation of distributions from qualified plans also depends on the form and timing of the distribution. Some plans, such as defined benefit (DB) plans, may pay benefits in the form of an annuity, whereas DC plans generally pay benefits in the form of a lump-sum distribution. Although DB plans for larger employers, typically more than 100 employees, generally pay benefits in the form of an annuity, the smaller plans usually pay benefits in a lump sum, i.e., the present value of the accrued benefit (see Chapter 6).

Periodic payments, i.e., annuity payments, are taxable in the year received. If the taxpayer has an after-tax investment in the account, part of each payment would be received tax-free as a return of basis, e.g., after-tax employee contributions.

Lump-sum distributions are fully taxable in the year received unless eligible for special tax treatment (forward averaging, discussed later in this chapter) or rolled over to another eligible qualified plan or individual retirement account (IRA). All qualified plans are required to allow participants to elect a direct transfer (trustee to trustee) of their benefits to another eligible retirement plan: a DC plan or an IRA.

A *lump-sum distribution* is a payment of the balance within one tax year of the participant (generally calendar year) to the credit of the participant (the total value of the benefit) that becomes payable as a result of death, attainment of age 59½, separation from service or disability. Even though the distribution of an annuity contract represents the lump sum at the time of distribution, it is taxable when payments begin, not when the annuity contract is distributed. Some plans allow for *in-kind* distributions, i.e., distributions of underlying investments such as stocks or shares in a mutual fund. To avoid difficult administration issues, this option is not recommended. When property is distributed, the fair market value of the property is the amount taxed. The exception to this rule is the distribution of employer stock. In that case, the net unrealized appreciation is taxed not at distribution but rather when the stock is later sold, e.g., in an employee stock ownership plan (ESOP) (see Chapter 4). In this context, net unrealized appreciation is the excess of the market value of a security at the time of distribution over the cost or other basis to the qualified retirement plan trust.

If, for example, the employee's account held 500 shares of the stock of the company sponsoring the plan, with a total cost basis of $5,000 to the plan, and a value at the time of distribution of $6,000, the $1,000 of net unrealized appreciation would not be taxed until the stock was sold. (Also see Chapter 4 for the treatment of stock distributed to a terminated participant in an ESOP.) If the stock is part of a lump-sum distribution as defined previously, the employee has the option of including the net unrealized appreciation in his or her taxable income rather than of deferring the tax until the stock is sold. This option could be chosen if the employee's tax bracket in the year of distribution was lower than the expected tax bracket in the year the stock was sold.

TAXATION OF ANNUITY PAYMENTS

When an annuity contract is distributed to an employee, it is generally not considered a taxable distribution unless the annuity contract is surrendered for its cash surrender value. If the employee has no basis in the annuity contract, the full amount of each payment is includable in income in the year paid to the employee. If the employee has basis in the contract, e.g., after-tax employee contributions, a part of each annuity payment is received tax-free as a return of basis. The concept of "basis in the contract" also applies to a DC account balance. The exclusion ratio, the percentage of each payment that is tax-free, is determined by the following formula:

$$\frac{\text{Investment in the annuity contract}}{\text{Expected return}}$$

The exclusion ratio is applied to each annuity payment received to determine the tax-free portion of each payment until the entire basis is recovered. *Investment in the annuity contract (basis)* is the total amount of premiums or other consideration the employee paid with after-tax dollars, less any amounts received tax-free before the *annuity starting date. Expected return* is the amount the employee expects to receive based on actuarial tables if a life contingent distribution is being made, e.g., an annuity paid for life, or based on the length of the installment payment, e.g., 20 years if a life contingent payment is not being made. *Annuity starting date* is the first day of the first period, e.g., monthly, for which an amount is received as an annuity payment under the annuity contract.

The investment in the contract includes employee contributions (after tax), repayment of a defaulted loan previously taxed as a deemed distribution, cumulative insurance costs taxed to the employee (PS-58 costs, see Chapter 4) and excess contributions to a 401(k) plan (see Chapter 5).

If the annuity provides for lifetime payments, so the expected return depends on the life expectancy of the annuitant (or annuitants), the expected return is computed using tables prescribed by the Internal Revenue Service (IRS). Table I is used to calculate the expected return if the annuity starting date is after November 18, 1996, but before January 1, 1998.

Table I

**ANTICIPATED PAYMENTS:
ANNUITY STARTING DATE
BEGINNING AFTER 11/18/96
BUT BEFORE 1/1/98**

Age as of Annuity Starting Date	Anticipated Payments
Age 55 or less	360
Age 56 to 60	310
Age 61 to 65	260
Age 66 to 70	210
More than 70	160

Table I is used whether the annuity distributions are based on a single life or on joint lives. For annuity payments beginning after 1997, the anticipated number of payments is determined based on the combined ages of the annuitants if payments are being made over joint lives. Table I is used if the payments are based on one individual's life expectancy. In the case of a joint life distribution, Table II is used.

Table II

ANTICIPATED PAYMENTS:
ANNUITY STARTING DATE
BEGINNING AFTER 1997
(JOINT LIFE EXPECTANCIES)

Combined Age as of Annuity Starting Date	Anticipated Payments
Not more than 110	410
More than 110 up to 120	360
More than 120 up to 130	310
More than 130 up to 140	260
More than 140	210

Whether the annuity payments to each annuitant are the same, e.g., 100% joint and survivor annuity (J&S), or different, e.g., a 50% J&S annuity, the same table is used. Following are sample expected return calculations using Tables I and II.

Example 1: For a single individual age 60, with $32,000 total after-tax employee contributions and a monthly annuity payment of $1,200, the expected return would be calculated as follows:

Age of annuitant:	60
After-tax employee contributions (basis, investment in the contract):	$ 32,000
Monthly annuity payment:	$ 1,200
Anticipated payments (from Table I):	310
Tax-free return of basis ($32,000 / 310):	$ 103.23
Taxable portion of payment ($1,200 − $103.23):	$1,096.77

Example 2: In the case of a joint life distribution where each annuitant receives the same annuity amount, the calculation would be as follows:

Age of annuitant:	60
Age of second annuitant:	58
After-tax employee contributions (basis, investment in the contract):	$ 64,000
Monthly annuity payment:	$ 2,100
Anticipated payments (from Table II):	360
Tax-free return of basis ($64,000 / 360):	$ 177.78
Taxable portion of payment ($2,100 − $177.78):	$1,922.22

Example 3: Where the joint life payments are unequal amounts, the calculation would be as follows:

Age of annuitant:	60
Age of second annuitant:	58
After-tax employee contributions (basis) (investment in the contract):	$ 64,000
Monthly 50% joint life annuity payment:	$ 2,100
Monthly survivor life annuity payment:	$ 1,050
Anticipated payments (from Table II):	360
Tax-free return of basis ($64,000 / 360):	$ 177.78
Taxable portion of payment during joint life payments ($2,100 − $177.78):	$1,922.22
Taxable portion of payment during survivor life payments ($1,050 − $177.78):	$ 872.22

In all cases, once the investment in the contract is recovered, the remaining payments are fully taxable. In Examples 1, 2 and 3, once the anticipated number of payments is reached, i.e., the basis is fully recovered, any subsequent payments are fully taxable.

LUMP-SUM DISTRIBUTIONS

To be considered a lump-sum distribution eligible for special tax treatment, distributions must satisfy the following guidelines:

1. The distribution must consist of the entire amount *(balance to the credit)* in an employee's account. If an employer maintains multiple plans, similar plans must be aggregated in determining whether the balance to the credit of the employee's account has been distributed. Generally, all pension plans must be treated as a single plan, all profit-sharing plans must be treated as a single plan and all stock bonus plans must be treated as a single plan.

2. The distribution must be made upon the occurrence of death, attainment of age 59½, separation from service (not applicable to self-employed) or disability.

3. The distribution must be received by the employee within one taxable year of the employee. The amount of the lump sum is determined as of the date the distribution is made. Any benefits credited to the employee's account after that date and distributed in the same tax year may be considered to be part of the initial lump-sum distribution but are not required to be considered part of that initial distribution.

   There are some exceptions to the one-year rule. In one case, IRS ruled that distributions from a terminating profit-sharing plan, delayed for several years because of litigation, was a lump-sum distribution. In another case, funds that were withheld from distribution under a court order and distributed in a later year did not prevent the remaining funds currently distributed from being treated as a lump-sum distribution.

4. A minimum of five years of service is required with the employer.

For the special tax treatment to be available:

1. The distribution must satisfy the definition of *lump-sum distribution.*

2. The employee must not have previously elected special lump-sum tax treatment for a distribution made after 1986 from the same employer's retirement plans.

3. The employee must be a plan participant in at least five full tax years before the tax year of the distribution.

4. The employee must make the election for special tax treatment.

The election must cover all lump-sum distributions received during that tax year from all plans of the employer. The election is made by filing Form 4972 with the employee's tax return for the year of distribution. If a lump-sum distribution is made from both a profit-sharing plan and a money purchase plan of the same employer, the employee may not treat one as a lump-sum distribution for purposes of special tax treatment and roll over the other to an IRA rollover account.

For employees born before 1936, there are two types of special tax treatment available for lump-sum distributions: the ten-year averaging method and the 20% flat tax method available for the pre-1974 portion of the distribution. A lump-sum distribution is first divided into two parts to determine the amount subject to each type of special tax treatment. The pre-1974 portion is calculated as follows: (number of months of participation before 1974 / total months of participation) × distribution.

The remaining portion of the distribution is considered post-1973. In determining the number of months, any part of a calendar year of pre-1974 participation is considered as 12 months, and any part of a month of post-1973 participation is considered one month. The number of months of total participation begins with the first month the employee becomes a participant and ends with the earlier of the month he or she receives the lump-sum distribution, the month he or she separates from service of the employer (if not a self-employed individual), the month of death or, for a self-employed individual, the month he or she becomes disabled.

Example 4: The special tax treatment of a lump-sum distribution to an employee born before 1936 is illustrated as follows:

Date of participation:	October 1, 1970
Date of retirement:	February 15, 2000
Taxable lump-sum distribution:	$350,000
Pre-1974 participation:	48 months
October 1, 1970 to December 31, 1970:	12 months
January 1, 1971 to December 31, 1973:	36 months
Total participation:	362 months
October 1, 1970 to December 31, 1970:	12 months
January 1, 1971 to December 31, 1999:	348 months
January 1, 2000 to February 15, 2000:	2 months

Distribution subject to capital gains at 20%:

$(48 / 362) \times (\$350{,}000) = \$46{,}408.81$

Tax due: $\$46{,}408.81 \times 20\% =$ $ 9,281.76

Distribution subject to ordinary income:

$(314 / 362) \times (\$350{,}000) = \$303{,}591.15$

Tax due under ten-year averaging:

Tax due on $30,359.12 ($303,591.15 / 10) = $6,755.10

Ten times tax: $67,551.00

          Total tax due: **$76, 832.76**

Table III is used to determine the tax for ten-year averaging.

Table III

TAX RATE FOR LUMP-SUM DISTRIBUTION USING TEN-YEAR AVERAGING

Adjusted Total Taxable Amount

Over	But Not Over	Initial Separate Tax	Of Amount Over
$ 0	$ 1,190	11%	$ 0
1,190	2,270	$ 130.90+12%	1,190
2,270	4,530	260.50+14%	2,270
4,530	6,690	576.90+15%	4,530
6,690	9,170	900.90+16%	6,690
9,170	11,440	1,297.70+18%	9,170
11,440	13,710	1,706.30+20%	11,440
13,710	17,160	2,160.30+23%	13,710
17,160	22,880	2,953.80+26%	17,160
22,880	28,600	4,441.00+30%	22,880
28,600	34,320	6,157.00+34%	28,600
34,320	42,300	8,101.80+38%	34,320
42,300	57,190	11,134.20+42%	42,300
57,190	85,790	17,388.00+48%	57,190
85,790	—	31,116.00+50%	85,790

ROLLOVERS OF LUMP-SUM DISTRIBUTIONS

A lump-sum distribution from a qualified plan may be rolled over tax-free, in part or in total, to an eligible retirement plan within 60 days of the employee's receipt of the distribution. An *eligible retirement plan* is:

1. An individual retirement account described in Internal Revenue Code (IRC) Section 408(a)
2. An individual retirement annuity described in IRC Section 408(b)
3. A qualified trust (qualified retirement plan)
4. An annuity plan described in IRC Section 403(a)

5. An eligible deferred compensation plan described in IRC Section 457(b) that is maintained by an eligible employer described in IRC Section 457(e)(1)(A) (see Chapter 7)
6. An annuity contract described in IRC Section 403(b) (see Chapter 7).

Regarding the 60-day rule, IRS is generally not authorized to grant any extension. In one case, rollover treatment was denied to an employee who deposited a pension distribution in a money market account he thought was an IRA. In another case, rollover treatment was denied to an employee who transferred a pension distribution to a trustee that was not qualified as an IRA trustee. In some cases, IRS will offer relief for a procedural defect if the rollover rules have been substantially followed. In a tax court case, the rollover deadline was extended because of the failure of the trustee's brokerage firm to record the transfer correctly. If the distribution is not rolled over within the 60 days, the distribution is taxed in the year it is distributed, not the year in which the 60 days expire.

Generally, taxable distributions are eligible for rollover except:
1. Any distribution that is one of a series of substantially equal periodic payments (annuity payments) made at least annually over:
   a. The life of the employee or joint lives of the employee and his or her beneficiary
   b. The life expectancy of the employee or joint life expectancy of the employee and his or her beneficiary
   c. A specified period of at least ten years.
2. Required minimum distributions (see Chapter 8)
3. Portions of distributions not included in gross income, e.g., return of an employee's after-tax contributions
4. Return of 401(k) elective deferrals that caused an excess in the maximum allowable annual addition under IRC Section 415, the lesser of 100% of compensation or $41,000 for the year 2004 (see Chapter 5)
5. Corrective distributions of 401(k) plan excess deferrals (limited to the lesser of 100% of compensation or $13,000 for the year 2004) including income allocable to the corrections (see Chapter 5)
6. Corrective distributions of excess 401(k) contributions and aggregate contributions (total of salary deferrals and any matching contributions) including income allocable to the corrections (see Chapter 5)
7. Dividends paid on employer securities held by an ESOP
8. The cost of life insurance coverage, i.e., PS-58 costs (see Chapter 2)
9. Loans that are treated as distributions because they do not meet IRS requirements or because they are in default (see Chapter 8)
10. Hardship distributions made after 1998 are not eligible for rollover treatment. This rule was changed by IRS Restructuring and Reform Act of 1998 to make hardship distributions ineligible for rollover treatment; however, under a transition rule, a 401(k) plan can allow hardship distributions made before January 1, 2000 to be treated as eligible rollover distributions.

TAX CONSIDERATIONS

Once a distribution from a qualified plan is rolled over to an IRA, distributions are taxed in accordance with the IRA distribution rules under IRC Section 408(d). This results in the loss of capital gains treatment, ten-year averaging and the exclusion for net unrealized appreciation on employer securities. If the IRA is a conduit IRA, i.e., it holds only assets that were rolled over from a qualified retirement plan, the assets may, at a later date, be rolled back into another qualified retirement plan in which the account owner participates, thereby recapturing capital gains treatment, ten-year averaging and the exclusion for net unrealized appreciation on employer securities if they apply.

In the case of a rollover, the account is physically distributed to the employee, who then deposits the distribution into an eligible retirement plan, usually an IRA, within the allowable 60-day period. Additionally, the employee has the option of making a *direct rollover,* i.e., a plan-to-plan transfer. All qualified plans are required to provide a direct rollover option. If an employee chooses not to use the direct rollover option, the distribution, even though it is later rolled over tax-free to an IRA account, is subject to 20% withholding tax. Because the amount withheld is not rolled over, it is subject to income tax.

> **Example 5:** Assume the following for Michael, a participant in his employer's profit-sharing plan:
>
> | | |
> |---|---|
> | Total account balance to be distributed: | $300,000 |
> | Tax withheld at 20%: | $ 60,000 |
> | Actual distribution rolled over to IRA: | $240,000 |
>
> Michael will be taxed on $60,000 unless he can make up the $60,000 with other funds so the total amount rolled over would be $300,000. When his tax return is filed for the year of distribution, the $60,000 withheld would be refunded if a total of $300,000 was rolled over, assuming all other income taxes were paid through payroll withholding, because the entire $300,000 was rolled over and is not taxable.

In a direct rollover there is no withholding because the funds are transferred directly from the trustee of the current qualified plan to the trustee or custodian of the eligible retirement plan.

WITHHOLDING RULES

Federal income tax withholding is applied to the taxable portion of any pension, profit-sharing or stock bonus plan distribution that is not rolled over through a direct rollover. The determination of the amount to be withheld is based on the percentage method under IRC Section 3402(b), the wage bracket method under IRC Section 3402(c) on periodic payments, or on a flat 20% on any distribution that is eligible for rollover treatment but is not directly transferred to an eligible retirement plan. Taxes withheld are reported on Form 1099-R. If the distribution includes employer securities and cash, the amount withheld, even if otherwise in excess of the cash amount, is limited to the cash distributed (employer securities would not have to be liquidated if there were not enough cash to pay the total withholding amount). This is not true if any property other than employer securities is distributed with cash. In that case, the plan administrator must either sell enough property to pay the withholding taxes or collect the shortfall from the employee. If a distribution is less than $200, withholding is not required.

Withholding applies to distributions made in the form of periodic payments as if the payments were wages subject to the employee's withholding certificate (number of exemptions). If the employee has not filed a withholding certificate, the plan administrator can withhold based on a married individual with three exemptions. Even though the withholding is applied as if the distribution were wages, the amount of the withholding is calculated separately from any amounts actually paid as wages. For a nonperiodic payment, i.e., a lump-sum payment, a flat rate of 20% is withheld on any distribution eligible for rollover but not transferred directly to an eligible retirement plan. Employees who receive periodic payments or nonperiodic payments that are not eligible for rollover treatment, e.g., required minimum distributions (see Chapter 8), may elect not to have withholding apply to the distribution. In the event the employee does not make an election, 10% withholding would apply.

It is generally the responsibility of the Employee Retirement Income Security Act (ERISA) plan administrator, usually the employer, to withhold taxes. The responsibility can be shifted to the payer of the distribution if the plan administrator advises the payer in writing to withhold the taxes and provides the payer with all the required information necessary to compute the amount of the withholding.

The payer of periodic payments, e.g., an insurance company, must also advise the recipient of the withholding rules, including the employee's right not to apply the withholding rules to distributions that are not eligible for rollover treatment. Each year the employee must be given notice of his or her right to make, renew or revoke the withholding election.

The taxes withheld must be remitted under the same procedures that apply to W-2 wage withholding, including monthly or semiweekly payments submitted with a Federal Tax Deposit Form 8109. Form 945, Annual Return of Withheld Federal Income Tax, is used to remit nonpayroll taxes withheld, i.e., on pensions, annuities, IRAs and other deferred income. State withholding is unique to each state.

Index

A

Accrued benefit, 224
Actual contribution percentage test (ACP test), 40, 79
Actual deferral percentage test (ADP test), 76
Adopting resolution, 25
Affected parties, 230
Affiliated service groups, 152-154
Age Discrimination in Employment Act, 101
Age-weighted profit-sharing plans, 3, 45
Annual additions limit, 3
Attribution, 12
Audits, 26, 42, 205

B

Back loading, 64
Beneficiary designation, 124
Blackout period, 211
Break in service (BIS), 43

C

Cafeteria plan, 203
Class allocation, 49
Compensation
    participant's compensation, 32
Compliance, 11
Contribution allocation
    age-weighted profit-sharing plan, 7, 46-48
    class allocation plan, 49
    cross-tested profit-sharing plan, 8
    defined benefit plan, 8
    money purchase plan, 60
    process, 5
    profit-sharing plan integrated with Social Security, 5
    target benefit plan, 60
    traditional profit-sharing plan, 4
Contributions
    definition, 40
    flexibility, 36
    permanent, 40
    timing, 29
    waiver, 36
Controlled groups, 149-152
Cross-testing, 137, 139

D

Defined benefit plans, 2
  basic plan design features, 91-96
  cash balance plans, 99
  distress termination, 234
  flexibility of contributions, 96
  fractional rule, 95
  overfunded plans, 232
  Pension Benefit Guaranty Corporation (PBGC), 97, 234-236
  qualified preretirement survivor annuity (QPSA), 95
Defined contribution plans
  asset valuation, 42-43
  audit, 41
  contributions, 40, 43
  definition, 39
  distribution, 40
  distribution from ESOPs, 55
  see also individual account plans
  types, 39, 43-64
Definitely determinable benefits, 58
Delinquent Filer Voluntary Compliance Program (DFVCP), 109, 209, 221
Department of Labor, 101
Deposits
  fixed, 1
  flexible, 1
Determination date, 143
Direct rollover, 246
Distributions
  calendar year, 124
  early distributions, 122-123
  hardship distributions, 120-122
  mandatory distributions, 123-124

E

Economic Growth and Tax Relief Reconciliation Act of 2001 (EGTRRA), 20, 27, 33, 59, 146, 173
Eligible employees, 86

Employee Benefits Security Administration, 42
Employee Plans Compliance Resolution System (EPCRS), 110-111, 214-221
Employee Retirement Income Security Act of 1974 (ERISA), 31, 97, 109, 183, 223
  Section 103(a)(3)(A), 41
  Section 104(a)(2)(A), 198
  Section 204(h), 36
  Section 404(c), 195-197
  Section 407(d)(1), 199
  Section 407(d)(5), 42
  Section 408(b)(1), 42, 199
  Section 412, 41
  Section 501(a), 106
Employee stock ownership plan (ESOP), 12, 51-57
Equal Employment Opportunity Commission, 101
Estate business planning, 165-179

F

Fair market value, 53
Fiduciary
  breach of duty, 54, 189
  definition, 183
  guidelines, 74
  liability, 186
  standards, 184
Form 5330, 192
Form 5500, 42, 192, 205-209
  attachments, 208
401(k) plans, 2
  benefits to employees, 69
  benefits to employers, 69
  catch-up deferral, 32-33, 77, 86
  comparison of types, 87
  hardship distributions, 71
  matching contribution, 74, 76
  negative election, 73
  nondiscrimination testing, 78, 79-83
  plan design features, 72
  plan distributions, 70

M

Minimum funding standards, 29, 33, 57
  waiver, 37
Money purchase pension plans, 2, 6, 60
  contribution flexibility, 65

N

New comparability profit-sharing plans, 3
Nonhighly compensated employee (NHCE), 12, 19, 51, 74, 76, 78, 79, 119, 133, 135, 137, 139, 142, 149, 168, 169
Nonqualified plans, 113
Nonsettlor expenses, 194

P

Paired plans, 20
Party in interest, 189-190
Permitted disparity, 44, 138
  see also Social Security integration
Plan design checklist, 14
Plan design features
  allocations to active and terminated employees, 21
  compensation, 21
  coverage rules, 22
  directed investment accounts, 22
  distributions upon termination, 21
  effective date of participation, 22
  eligibility, 22
  forfeitures, 23
  form of distributions, 23
  hardship distributions, 23
  life insurance, 23
  loans to participants, 24
  plan administrator, 24
  plan number, 24
  plan year, 25
  retirement age, 25
  vesting, 25

Plan document types
  custom plan documents, 17
  master plan, 16
  prototype plan, 16
  volume submitter plan, 17
Plan limitations
  defined benefit plan, 35
  401(k) plans, 32
  money purchase plan, 33
  multiple plans, 35
  profit-sharing plans, 31
Plan requirements, 15
Plan termination, 223
Profit-sharing plans, 2
  deduction limit, 41
  definition, 103
Prohibited transaction, 54, 189, 192
  exemptions, 192-194

Q

Qualified replacement property, 57
Qualifying plan assets, 41, 199

R

Remedial amendment period, 26-27
Retirement plans
  variety of, 1

S

Safe harbor 401(k) plans, 3
Safe harbor target benefit plans, 62
Safe harbor testing, 134
Sarbanes-Oxley Act, 211-212
Securities Exchange Act of 1934, 52
Settlor functions, 194
Shared employees, 162-163
Simplified employee pension (SEP), 66
Small Business Job Protection Act (SBJPA), 82, 190